LIVING WITH LYNCHING

W9-ASU-313

THE NEW BLACK STUDIES SERIES

Edited by Darlene Clark Hine
and Dwight A. McBride

*A list of books in the series
appears at the end of this book.*

LIVING WITH LYNCHING

African American Lynching Plays, Performance, and Citizenship, 1890–1930

KORITHA MITCHELL

UNIVERSITY OF ILLINOIS PRESS

Urbana, Chicago, and Springfield

© 2011 by the Board of Trustees
of the University of Illinois
All rights reserved

∞ This book is printed on acid-free paper.

The Library of Congress cataloged the cloth edition as follows:
Mitchell, Koritha.
Living with lynching : African American lynching plays, performance,
and citizenship, 1890–1930 / Koritha Mitchell.
p.   cm. — (The new black studies series)
Includes bibliographical references and index.
ISBN 978-0-252-03649-1 (cloth)
1. American drama—African American authors—History and criticism.
2. American drama—20th century—History and criticism. 3. American drama—19th
century—History and criticism. 4. One-act plays, American—History and criticism.
5. Lynching in literature. 6. African Americans in literature. 7. Violence in literature.
8. Citizenship in literature.
I. Title.
PS338.N4M455   2011
812'.509896073—dc22   2011014508

Paperback ISBN 978-0-252-07880-4

This book is dedicated to
my mother, Laverne Mitchell,
my aunt, Frances Oliver,
and all the other forebears
who made this possible.

CONTENTS

ACKNOWLEDGMENTS

This project has been with me most of my adult life, so it has required endurance, but I have consistently benefited from the support of institutions that saw the work's potential. As a graduate student, I received encouragement in the form of a fellowship from the David Driskell Center for the Study of the African Diaspora. Its director at that time, Eileen Julien, will never know how powerful her vote of confidence was. The Ford Foundation supported the work with a dissertation completion fellowship and a postdoctoral fellowship a few years later. Most recently, postdoctoral funding from the American Association of University Women allowed me to take my work to the next level. Without question, any quality that readers glean here is largely the result of the support I received from the Driskell Center, the Ford Foundation, and the AAUW. The project also benefited from archival research at the Schomburg Center in New York City, Howard University's Moorland-Spingarn Research Center in Washington, D.C., and Emory University's Manuscripts and Rare Books Library, which funded my visit there. *Crisis* Publishing Company, the official publisher of the NAACP, added value to the project by granting permission to reproduce images that originally appeared in *Crisis* magazine in May 1923 and July 1926. Finally, significant financial support came from the College of Arts and Humanities at Ohio State University.

As much as this project has benefited from institutional votes of confidence, it has required personal support, which I have received from more people than I can name. This journey began when I was a graduate student in the English Department at the University of Maryland, which prepared me for the profession in every conceivable way. Carla Peterson gave me an exceptional master's thesis experience. At the dissertation stage, I benefited from the support of Maryland faculty members Vincent Carretta, Shirley

Logan, Charles Caramello, and Elsa Barkley Brown. The extra something that the project needed to become a book came in many ways from the steadfast support of theater historian Judith Stephens, who served on the committee from Pennsylvania State University and has remained a true mentor and friend while enjoying emeritus status. Kathy Perkins, who co-edited with Stephens the anthology of lynching drama that gave birth to this project, has proved supportive in official and unofficial ways.

John Ernest and Gabrielle Foreman have been extraordinary mentors whose examples inspire me daily. Each gave an invited talk while I was at Maryland, and each was responsive to my attempts to learn more. I admire their research to no end, and they have shown me that even brilliant scholars whose work exceeds the highest standards of theoretical rigor and historical depth can also be good people who care about making the world a better place.

During the transition from graduate student to professor, which could have easily taken a negative turn and altered the trajectory of my career, I found wise counsel and support in Herman Beavers, Houston Baker, Thadious Davis, and Harry Elam—senior scholars who simply did not have to take time to help me, yet they did.

Once I arrived at Ohio State University, the English department provided research pressure and collegiality in equal measure. Americanist colleagues have contributed significantly to my development, reading my work and offering quality feedback as well as helping me to navigate the OSU classroom: Valerie Lee, Debra Moddelmog, Steven Fink, Susan Williams, Chad Allen, Jared Gardner, Beth Hewitt, Elizabeth Renker, Harvey Graff, Beverly Moss, Jacqueline Royster, and John W. Roberts. Although he arrived in Columbus after I did, senior colleague Adéléke Adéeke has offered feedback and encouragement; I see his imprint in this book. I have benefited from the time that scholars in other specialties have given: Brian McHale, James Phelan, Dorry Noyes, Wendy Hesford. Brian has gone above the call of duty, as I have never hesitated to barge into his office for any and every reason. Outside the English department, historian Kenneth Goings has been extraordinarily engaged with my work, offering challenges that stayed with me and led to new insights. Hasan Jeffries, Tanya Erzen, and Leslie Alexander have likewise provided inspiration and support.

In the profession at large, I have been fortunate to encounter similarly sustaining energy. As reviewer for the University of Illinois Press, Daphne Brooks proved incredibly helpful. She saw tremendous potential in the project and offered challenges that pushed me to fulfill it. I will strive to follow her example of intellectual rigor and professional generosity. Daylanne English has also been very generous. She responded graciously to my plea that she read, simply as a favor, even though the request came not only from a stranger but also out of the clear blue sky. I am also grateful to the second reviewer that the Press recruited. There is no question that this book would be less nuanced without such a keen eye and incisive critique. Many, many thanks are also due to Joan Catapano, my editor at the Press, whose expertise made this process very educational. Thank you, Joan, for everything, especially for securing excellent readers for the manuscript.

Without the intellectual communities that have welcomed me, I probably would not be in the academy and certainly not happily so. As a dissertation writer, I gained access to much more than funding when I won a Ford Foundation fellowship. Being welcomed into the family of Ford fellows literally changed my life. I will not attempt to name names, but Ford gives me a space—physical, spiritual, and virtual via the listserv—in which I can never forget that some of the most innovative, rigorous work out there is being done by scholars of color. Later in my journey, I was welcomed into a circle of *Callaloo*-affiliated scholars who have challenged me to grow in surprising ways. Our gatherings in New Orleans, St. Louis, and Addis Ababa, Ethiopia, will remain with me, and I look forward to all that our future interaction will bring. Of course, founding editor of *Callaloo*, Charles H. Rowell, made these experiences possible, and I am grateful. Finally, I hope that this book reflects the influence of the Black Performance Theory working group. This cohort always pushes me to my limits, always makes me wish I were more intellectually limber, always reminds me of everything I do not know, but also gives me the energy to keep working and the courage to challenge boundaries.

Nothing less than true friendship and saving grace have come from Joe Ponce. I can never repay my debt to him, so I am working on becoming a less high-maintenance friend. Alan Farmer and Ryan Friedman have made my life richer; this journey would not have been so educational or enjoyable without them. I have always yearned for a "sister circle" and thank Armelle Hillman, Salamishah Tillett, Ruth Friedman, Kate Masur, Brendesha Tynes, Rebecca Wanzo, Jessica Jones, Aliyyah Abdur-Rahman, and Kimberly Blockett for being some of the reasons that I believe I have one.

Over the years, I have been reminded of a passage from Toni Morrison's *The Bluest Eye*: "Love is never better than the lover. Wicked people love wickedly, violent people love violently, weak people love weakly, stupid people love stupidly." How fortunate that I share my life with a superb human being, Craig E. Jones. He has been a partner in every sense of the word—indeed, the embodiment of God's favor in my life. Craig, thank you for being you. As Marita Bonner might put it, you are the kind of man that

I can look up to without looking down on myself. So, for all that has been, *thank you*. For all that is to come, *yes!*

Finally, I thank my mother, Laverne Mitchell, for giving me a foundation, the stability of which has stood the test of time. Throughout this journey, and long before, she has been my role model, my muse, my motivation, and so much more. And if those gifts were not enough, she is very literally behind and in every word that I have ever written.

LIVING WITH LYNCHING

WHOSE EVIDENCE? WHICH ACCOUNT?

When we hear the word "lynching," most of us think of a hanging body, what Billie Holiday famously called "strange fruit." This image has recently become even more powerful as the pictures produced by mobs have reentered circulation, usually as part of an effort to educate the public about an often-ignored chapter in U.S. history. In these photographs, a crowd typically surrounds the "criminal" it has subdued, and the corpse is often still hanging from a tree, telephone pole, or bridge. Yet during the same decades in which these pictures were originally created and distributed, African Americans wrote plays about mob violence that tell stories strikingly different from those suggested by lynching photography.

Living with Lynching considers the difference between the depictions of racial violence favored by mobs and those valued by targeted communities. These groups were invested in recording and preserving different sorts of evidence about the events that shaped their time. While the mob's efforts centered on black death, African American dramatists helped their communities to live, even while lynching remained a reality that would not magically disappear. In the process, these playwrights created the unique genre of lynching drama.

Lynching plays survive in the archive to enhance our understanding of the United States at the turn into the twentieth century; the genre was developed by African Americans aware of their communities' strategies for living with lynching—strategies that required a keen understanding of U.S. culture. Generally, studies of African Americans who lived during the decades between 1890 and 1930 are overrun with explanations for antiblack violence. Some have found that the more than four thousand African Americans killed by mobs were victims of whites who could not adjust to their own economic hardships. Others have focused on the sexual anxieties that prompted the violence.[1] Studying the period, I have constantly wondered: *How did blacks survive this era? How did they think of themselves at a time when public discourse cast them as brutes who deserved to be butchered? How did they maintain a dignified sense of self when photographs of mutilated lynch victims entered their homes along with the news? When the mob was a palpable threat to their own bodies, families, and communities, how did they manage "to keep on keeping on"? And how did they continue to believe in their status as U.S. citizens?*

I contend that lynching plays served as mechanisms through which African Americans survived the height of mob violence—and its photographic representation—still believing in their right to full citizenship. By definition, lynching plays address mob violence, but as this study reveals, the genre's foundational scripts do not represent, or even describe, the brutalized black body. As theater historians Kathy Perkins and Judith Stephens assert in their anthology of representative scripts, "A lynching drama is *a play in which the threat or occurrence of a lynching, past or present, has major impact on the dramatic action.*" Though American writers had always addressed racial violence, the mode developed, Perkins and Stephens maintain, "when playwrights moved beyond brief references and focused on a specific lynching incident" (4). Four remarkable women laid the foundation for lynching drama: Angelina Weld Grimké, who penned *Rachel* in 1914; Alice Dunbar-Nelson, who wrote *Mine Eyes Have Seen* in 1918; Mary Burrill, who published *Aftermath* in 1919; and Georgia Douglas Johnson, who was the most prolific, with *A Sunday Morning in the South* (1925), *Blue Blood* (1926), *Safe* (1929), and *Blue-Eyed Black Boy* (c. 1930). In this study, I examine these plays, as well as another by a black woman and two by black men: Myrtle Smith Livingston's *For Unborn Children* (1926), G. D. Lipscomb's *Frances* (1925), and Joseph Mitchell's *Son-Boy* (1928).[2]

In contrast to mainstream photographers, dramatists who lived and wrote in the midst of lynching often refused to feature physical violence; their scripts spotlight instead the black home and the impact that the mob's outdoor activities have on the family. Indeed, the dramas most commonly depict exactly what mainstream discourse denied existed: loving black homes. According to dominant assumptions, mobs targeted African Americans because they represented an evil that would destroy society: black men were supposedly rapists who cared nothing for stable domesticity, and black women were said to be whores incapable of creating it anyway. Meanwhile, the dramatists offered their communities scripts that preserve the truth these myths disregarded. They portray black characters leading ordinary lives in domestic interiors where they affectionately sustain each other.

Alice Dunbar-Nelson's 1918 lynching play *Mine Eyes Have Seen* exemplifies the genre's focus on the black home and the effect of racial violence on it. This one-act script appeared in *Crisis* magazine, the official organ of the National Association for the Advancement of Colored People (NAACP). The father of the featured characters was lynched years earlier, and his death frames the current action. The main characters are identified primarily in terms of their familial bonds: Lucy is "The Sister," Chris is "The Younger Brother," and the eldest sibling Dan is announced as "The Cripple." Placing the black family center stage, the play dramatizes the extent to which mobs mutilated black households, not just black bodies. Long after the father's corpse has deteriorated, pain reverberates among those left behind.

By focusing on the survivors of mob violence, Dunbar-Nelson's script offers access to the conversations that African Americans may have had at the turn of the century, and her characters contend that black success *attracts* the mob. Their discussion highlights the fact that whites made a display of their impatience with black prosperity. Dan recalls that there were "notices posted on the fence" for them to leave town "because niggers had no business having such a decent home." Soon, the house was set on fire. In an attempt to stop the vandals, the father went outdoors, where he was "shot down like a dog." Chris later wonders, "And for what? Because we were living like Christians." Dunbar-Nelson's characters articulate an understanding of the mob's practices that has not shaped the historical record to the extent that lynching drama suggests it should. The genre insists that when blacks affirm themselves, obtaining hard-earned success by minding their own business, whites respond.

Dunbar-Nelson's script and the black-authored archive of which it is a part suggest that African Americans interpreted lynching as *master/piece theater.* That is, when real-life lynchings became theatrical, whites literally used *pieces* of black bodies as props to perform their *master* status. In other words, African Americans viewed lynching as a theater of mastery in which whites seeking (not assuming) racial supremacy used the black body as muse, antagonist, and stage prop. The vengeance with which some whites performed their supposedly superior status is quite revealing. As cultural theorists have long contended, hegemony is never complete; it must continually reassert itself.[3] Thus, if white supremacists denied black humanity, black familial ties, and achievement, African Americans must have been convincingly establishing it.

Dunbar-Nelson suggests exactly that, and she does so in a text that is itself a way of establishing the black achievement that whites sought to erase. Her play reminds African American readers that they are not hunted because they are a race of criminals; indeed, the text and the periodical in which it appears, *Crisis* magazine, certify the existence of the kinds of people who belong to these communities: authors, editors, and readers, to name a few. In other words, Dunbar-Nelson produces the kind of cultural self-affirmation that may very well beckon the mob. The drama certainly acknowledges that racial violence is a threat, but it insists that the threat is to those successes that the race has already established and actively continues to augment. If mob violence was a response to already-existent black achievement and black-authored beauty (Lucy remembers the garden they used to have, for instance), then Dunbar-Nelson's text is yet another example of those accomplishments and aesthetic contributions.

Why, then, do so many insist upon placing the label "protest art" on creative works by African Americans that address lynching?[4] Why do scholarly analyses so frequently end with explanations of the extent to which such art responds to white supremacy? Is it possible that black art about lynching is a continuation of African Americans' self-affirmation? Might such art simply be the kind of community-centered success to which white mobs responded?

Recently, additional hindrances have arisen to slow recognition of the insights presented by black-authored texts. Namely, photographs of lynch victims have come to dominate understandings of mob violence. In January 2000, nearly one hundred photographs of mob victims reentered circulation via gallery installations and a book of photography called *Without Sanctuary*. The African American bodies depicted are often bullet-ridden, burned, or both.[5] The images commanded enough interest to take the $60 book of photography into six editions during its first six years of existence. The photographs also helped to sustain academic conferences and journal issues on racial violence as well as major museum exhibitions around the country and a virtual installation on the World Wide Web. Perhaps most remarkably, the pictures led the U.S. Senate to issue in June 2005 a formal apology for having never passed antilynching legislation.[6]

Taken from a privileged position of safety at lynchings, the pictures rarely represent the perspectives of African Americans; still, the message boards on the *Without Sanctuary* website document what seems to be the collection's perspective-changing power. In chorus with site visitors, many of my students have said that the photographs made them realize how often—and how brutally—the United States has contradicted its claim to being a color-blind democracy. They say, for example, that they now appreciate why African Americans seem to be more suspicious of the legal system than whites. Knowing that the police "let such atrocities happen" opened their eyes.

My students and the senators believe that the pictures reveal a deep truth about racial violence, and their confidence arises from much more than the authority that modern society has always granted to photography as a conduit to "the real." After all, few can claim not to have heard these lyrics: "Southern trees bear strange fruit/ Blood on the leaves, blood at the root/ Black bodies swinging in the southern breeze/ Strange fruit hanging from the poplar trees." Billie Holiday made these words famous with her 1939 recording of Lewis Allan's ballad, and since then several generations have heard its haunting message. Versions of the song have come from artists ranging from Nina Simone to Sting, from Dwayne Wiggins to British reggae band UB40.[7] If the "Strange Fruit" lyrics made us imagine the hanging body, the photographs challenged us to face it, and many have risen to this challenge because we were already convinced that the hanging body is the most "natural" and most logical way to represent mob destruction.

The embodied practice of singing that song or reciting those lines has lent credibility to mainstream photographs as an archive to be valued for what it can tell us about mob violence.[8] By *embodied practice*, I mean any bodily act that conveys meaning. The term is deliberately broad, building on Performance Studies, which emphasizes the centrality of performance in how human beings make culture and live their lives.[9] Embodied practices can include speaking or singing, grimacing or gesturing, hugging or hitting, reading a script dramatically or performing in full costume. In emphasizing embodied practice, I acknowledge, following Diana Taylor, that "embodied and performed acts generate, record, and transmit knowledge" (21). However, their importance can be diminished by a tendency to look to documents, including photographs, for establishing "truth." Yet knowledge can reside in the flesh, so to speak, even when one does not seek to reproduce it. As Joseph Roach has suggested, expressive movements can be "mnemonic reserves" whereby patterns are "remembered by bodies" (26). Likewise, cultural memory is "embodied and sensual, . . . conjured through the senses" (Taylor 82). So, the many people who have recited the "Strange Fruit" lines or hummed its tune may not deliberately convey certain messages—such as "corpses best represent mob destruction"—but embodied acts "reconstitute themselves, transmitting communal memories, histories, and values from one group/generation to the next" (Taylor 21). This study therefore understands "embodied practice as an episteme and a praxis, a way of knowing as well as a way of storing and transmitting cultural knowledge and identity" (Taylor 278). As well, knowledges and identities are preserved and generated as much through the mundane practices of everyday life as through formal theater.

Without question, then, embodied practices help account for why lynching photographs have become so influential. Even as historians privilege the supposed objectivity and stability of the archive, knowledge has been shaped by singing (the artists' and our own). Scholars prioritize documents because they seem simply to record facts and remain immune to the corruption and ephemerality of performance, but, in truth, our familiarity with renditions of that famous song has helped to determine the value placed on lynching photographs.

Living with Lynching therefore takes seriously questions of how archives come into existence and why they have been preserved. After all, there are many ways to access lynching history, but only the pictures in *Without Sanctuary* inspired the Senate's apology. When we pause to ask why, we find that the nation has again allowed the archives left by perpetrators to eclipse all others.[10]

Decades of antilynching activism and testimony from victimized black families did not move the nation's leaders at the last turn of the century, and today they are not the inspiration for the Senate's historic gesture or for the majority of lynching scholarship. Instead, white-authored photographs have become the evidence that simply cannot be ignored. Granted, this is partly out of the spirit of letting the murderers condemn themselves. As art historian Dora Apel argues, "the loss to historical understanding incurred by refusing to see [these pictures] would only serve to whitewash the crimes of white supremacy" (6).[11] But this reasoning does not change the fact that when we treat images of mutilated bodies as the ultimate evidence of lynching destruction, we reaffirm the authority of the mob. Ultimately, it is because they come from white perpetrators themselves that we have allowed the images to continue to trump testimony from victimized communities. By treating the pictures as records, we pretend that they offer an objective view, that they are less biased than the testimonies of those targeted by this terror. But the pictures are anything but objective. They represent a particular perspective, and they helped the mob to accomplish its work, during and long after the victim's murder.[12] The photographs did not simply document violence; they very much perform(ed) it.

In fact, the *Without Sanctuary* collection exists because mobs incorporated photography into their rituals. Black success and beauty may have attracted white violence, but whites insisted upon the beauty of their vengeance: there was an art to the mob's deed. Between 1890 and 1930, lynchings were frequently theatrical productions, so newspapers often announced the time and location so that crowds could gather. Spectators knew that they would see familiar characters (so called black "rapists" and white "avengers") and that these characters would perform a predictable script of forced confession and mutilation. Souvenir hunting would complete the drama with audience participation, but because the most coveted keepsakes (such as the victim's bones and burnt flesh)[13] were in limited supply, pictures became souvenirs. Because photographs served as mementos, they survive today to verify lynching's theatrical qualities and the variety of stages that mobs claimed, for bodies dangle not just from trees, but also light posts, telephone poles, and bridges.

When we elevate the photographs above other artifacts, however, we decontextualize them, and our focus on what Billie Holiday called "strange fruit" amounts to an acceptance of a very specific representation of the violence—one that is more limited than we realize. After all, these gruesome images were created and preserved because they fell in line with discourses that supported racial violence. The black corpse is surrounded by a mob of righteous whites—no grieving loved ones in sight. Thus, mainstream lynching photography depicted victims as isolated brutes with no connection to a family or community, or to institutions like marriage. To similar effect, the images today encourage an acknowledgement of black bodies and even black bodily pain, but the interest in them has not naturally led to an appreciation of the community's more enduring losses, including psychological, emotional, and financial suffering.

If we can resist privileging the photographs over other artifacts from the same era, such as the plays of this study, Americans will better reckon with the complexity of the interactions that shaped this historical period. Given whites' power in society, we often assume that they set into motion forces that blacks always found themselves resisting. African American cultural production is therefore viewed through the lens of oppression, with attention to how it protests injustice or counters negative images of the race. Very often, though, turn-of-the-century blacks focused on surviving and on affirming themselves in their new roles as citizens. As they did so, whites confronted them, "resolved to prevent the extension of democracy" (Hunter viii, 3). Given this tendency, African American expressive culture that asserts racial pride and records achievement is not best understood as a response to white oppression but rather as a sign that blacks valued the continuation of their traditions. This is why I am coming to prefer the term "lynching drama" rather than "anti-lynching drama," which I have used in earlier work. These writers were not simply reacting against lynching; they were working to preserve community insights. While offering a cultural and literary history of the genre, I challenge readers to recognize that black art about lynching does not simply respond to violent injustice; it continues affirming discourses in African America—established discourses that *the mob* felt compelled to answer.

Fully appreciating black expressive culture becomes impossible if readers assume that white oppression was so powerful that there could be no psychic or discursive space for anything other than resisting or protesting. It goes without saying that blacks were not magically impervious to the racist messages that bombarded them, but when we insist that their every move was in response to white oppression,[14] then we become blind to the insights that they shared by producing novels and newspapers, poems and plays. To put it bluntly, Alice Dunbar-Nelson's script indicates that blacks understood lynching as a white response to their success.[15] It makes clear that blacks were valuing each other and loving each other, and whites reacted. Granting primacy to white oppression when examining lynching drama would therefore prevent thorough analysis. To assume that blacks were responding to whites when writing these plays would not only diminish the archival evidence that they left, but it might also amount to what John Ernest calls "a ritualized reenactment of the protocols of U.S. racial history" (30). After all, the goal of white oppression was to discount the community perspectives preserved by this unique genre.

Of course, I do not claim that lynching playwrights were completely above reacting to white supremacy. Especially because black-authored lynching drama emerged in the 1910s, the playwrights were indeed engaging the mob's theatrical tactics, which intensified in the 1890s, but they were also building on existing traditions. Plays about lynching joined a long line of other expressions of blacks' conceptions of themselves as dignified individuals and citizens. The continuity of effort becomes apparent when we note that African Americans had long maximized every resource available for self-definition, from written text to spoken word, from photographic image to musical improvisation, from sermon to soulful moan. Accordingly, when turn-of-the-century activist Ida B. Wells launched a campaign to expose the real reasons for lynching, she continued the earlier efforts of Frederick Douglass and others, and she did not rely solely on written texts. Beginning in the 1890s, she represented her community in newspaper features and pamphlets as well as presentations at podiums in the United States and abroad. Similarly, before lynching drama emerged, black photographer J. P. Ball took pictures of lynch victims, but he did so in a way that memorialized, rather than dehumanized, them. Ball's work thereby participates in what Jacqueline Goldsby identifies as "a distinctly black tradition in lynching photography" which involved "paying empathetic visual care to the victims' bodies" and preserving images from the subject's life, not just their death

(246). Lynching plays similarly focus on lives cut short and the effects of those losses, demonstrating that the mob targeted valued community members, not isolated brutes.

Capital Entertainment, Better Representation

Because lynching plays emphasize the lasting damage that mob violence did to households, not just bodies, and to communities, not just individuals, it is significant that the genre emerged in the nation's capital. In the 1910s and 1920s, a number of African American authors turned away from prose and poetry to address racial violence through drama, and nearly all of them lived in or near Washington, D.C.: Angelina Weld Grimké, Alice Dunbar-Nelson, Mary Burrill, Georgia Douglas Johnson, and Myrtle Smith Livingston.[16] Their preoccupation with lynching should remind us that the nation's capital is below the Mason-Dixon line—a fact that shaped its residents' realities before and after Emancipation and into the new century. Washington, D.C., had been a major hub for the slave trade; then, during and after Reconstruction, the city was as segregated as those in the Deep South; and by 1913, President Woodrow Wilson allowed segregation of the facilities in which federal employees worked. As the capital, Washington, D.C., stood for the nation's commitment to protecting American life and liberty, but in the 1920s it was where antilynching bills went to die. As the plays insist that individual mob victims symbolize families and communities under siege, the genre's characters become representatives for a national black population whose concerns are not necessarily shared by their representatives in the Congress and Senate.

As a genre, black-authored lynching drama sheds unique light on the New Negro, the New South, and the New Woman. As African Americans who had never known legal bondage came of age, they laid claim to unprecedented educational opportunities, and like other Americans, they went about the business of defining the contours of their modern identities. As many left the rural South and found opportunity in both southern and northern cities, industrialization shaped their experiences, lending to the belief that their generation was equipped to take the race to new heights. Industrialization also inspired entrepreneurs and politicians to declare that the former Confederate states could fully participate in making the nation a prosperous world power. Women were also gaining economic and social independence, and voting rights appeared to be within reach. In the midst of these national transitions, lynching drama was initiated and dominated by black women writers in Washington, D.C. This fact reflects the uniquely modern quality of the nation's capital city, but it also suggests that these women helped make the city and the nation "modern"—with all of the uncertainty and contradiction that accompanies that term. Considering the archive that these women left reveals the degree to which the District held in perfect tension all of the promises that were presumably inherent in the North and the perils that were supposedly most characteristic of the South.

The genre that these women developed also complicates the notion that New York was the capital of the New Negro Renaissance and the Little Negro Theatre Movement. Black-authored lynching drama emerged when poet and fiction writer Angelina Weld Grimké circulated the play now known as *Rachel*. The script had been written by 1914 because her acquaintances at the NAACP were reading drafts as early as January 1915 (Hull 117–23). Later that year, W. E. B. Du Bois created an NAACP drama committee and, in March 1916, that committee sponsored a semi-professional production of *Rachel*, making it the first black-authored, nonmusical drama to be executed by black actors for a broad audience.[17] Where was it staged? In Washington, D.C.

Rachel shaped the development of black drama by helping to set the agendas adopted by New Negro artists and intellectuals. When the NAACP sponsored the historic production of *Rachel* in the nation's capital, the organization hoped to reach an integrated audience. Grimké's work proved well suited for this purpose. It is a full-length, sentimental play whose emotional appeal largely hinges on the similarity between whites and blacks. In fact, Grimké later explained that she had written the play to convince whites, especially white women, that lynching was wrong, as illustrated by the fact that even upstanding black citizens were vulnerable to it. The script therefore emphasizes the characters' propriety, education, and appreciation for European culture.

The initial production of *Rachel* ran for just two days, but it sparked intense discussion about African American identity, racial violence, and about what black drama should accomplish. *Rachel* had a tremendous impact on writers and thinkers of the time, but Grimké's significance has been underestimated by theater histories that locate the origin of black drama in the mid-1920s.[18] Because Willis Richardson's *Chip Woman's Fortune* became the first black-authored play produced on Broadway in 1923, and Langston Hughes's *The Mulatto* began an unprecedented two-year run on Broadway in 1935,[19] these men are often seen as the fathers of black drama. Yet Richardson admitted that it was Grimké's *Rachel* that prompted him to become a playwright.[20]

"RACHEL"

**The Drama Committee
of the District of Columbia Branch
of the N. A. A. C. P.**

—PRESENTS—

"RACHEL"

A Race Play in Three Acts by
Angelina Grimke

under direction of

NATHANIEL GUY

AT

Myrtilla Miner Normal School

Friday Eve., March 3rd and
Sat. Eve., March 4th, 8 P. M.

Tickets   -   75 and 50 Cts.

Tickets on Sale at Gray and Grays Drug Store 12th & U
Sts. N. W. after February 1st from 6 to 8 o'clock P. M.
All Seats Reserved.

PRINTED BY MURRAY BROS

Figure 1. Playbill for the first production of *Rachel*. Angelina Weld Grimké Papers/Moorland-Spingarn Research Center, Howard University. By permission.

Just as important, Grimké's work inspired conversations that led to an increasing investment in black-authored drama by some of the most influential "New Negro" leaders of the day. Grimké circulated her manuscript before Du Bois formed the drama committee, so her work was not a response to his call for black-authored plays but likely an inspiration for it.[21] Then, once the committee decided to sponsor its debut, Grimké's text helped others to identify their own artistic mission. Alain Locke (often called "the architect of the New Negro Movement") and his Howard University colleague Montgomery Gregory objected to the NAACP's "propagandist platform," which they believed was exemplified by the organization's presentation of *Rachel*. They therefore vowed to create a space in which "purely artistic" concerns reigned. The more Locke and Gregory publicized their approach, the more Du Bois refined his articulation of the need for political art. Without question, then, *Rachel* deeply influenced the founders of both the NAACP drama committee and Howard University's theater department (in Washington, D.C.)—organizations that would encourage and train black playwrights throughout the 1920s. Thus, by 1916 and without reaching Broadway, Grimké's work rejuvenated black drama.

Du Bois, Locke, and Gregory often took their disagreement to the pages of periodicals, and many joined them, including authors who entered the debate by simply executing their own vision of what black drama should accomplish. Some, like Willis Richardson, became playwrights because they were convinced that they could do a better job than Grimké had. Others simply seemed to believe that Grimké's perspective on lynching and black family life was too important to leave unaddressed. When Dunbar-Nelson published *Mine Eyes Have Seen* in *Crisis* in 1918, just two years after Grimké's dramatic debut, she seems to have wanted to address Grimké's investment in appealing to whites, and she did so by using the one-act format. A serious one-act play about African Americans may have been conducive to publication in periodicals, but it would not appeal to theater practitioners who might reach a broad audience. Aside from the fact that the commercial stage did not generally welcome serious depictions of black characters, it was even less receptive to one-act versions of such material. If a writer did not have three complementary one-acts that could serve as an evening of entertainment, the work needed at least to provide comic relief so that it could be inserted between the show's other components.[22] Thus, tailoring one's script for periodical publication also meant writing with amateur performance in mind. It is significant, then, that the other black authors who wrote plays about lynching in the 1910s and 1920s also used the one-act format, for it allowed the genre to perform community-centered cultural work.

Grimké's successors, I argue, were not striving to have their texts come to life before integrated audiences. They did not aim, as Grimké had, to reach whites with the hope of convincing them that lynching was wrong. Instead, they targeted African American readers who might stage these plays in community spaces, such as black churches and schools or even in their own homes. At a time when lynchings were theatrical productions that often attracted large audiences, black artists and intellectuals embraced drama. It is a form that ideally utilizes much more than the written word, even when not formally staged. African Americans could bring these texts to life by performing the action described or by simply reading the scripts aloud. They could involve the neighborhood church or just their family. A participant could animate his entire body or just his voice. Such a range is possible because "every theatrical performance depends on performers' and spectators' collaborative consciousness of the devices in operation and their meanings" (Elam 5). The "unique theatrical negotiation of illusion and reality" can include accepting a prop as a working telephone or accepting that an actor can suddenly address the audience without the other characters hearing what he says. Just as easily, it can mean treating one's living room as a theater or accepting that mother has become a character in a play, even as she simply reads the part while sitting on the other side of the dining room table.

African Americans used all available resources for cultural expression and self-affirmation. Unable to ignore the country's hypocrisy, blacks in the District, as much as anywhere else, understood the necessity of finding ways to sustain their self-images. African Americans saw themselves as modern citizens and behaved accordingly; their doing so prompted reactions from those determined to put them "in their place." When mobs not only killed with impunity but also advertised their activities with photographs that appeared in newspapers and became picture postcards, the intended message was clear: *Blacks are not citizens.* Though not immune to the messages of their society, African Americans nonetheless held on to their conceptions of themselves not only as loving, respectable men and women but also as exemplary citizens. To the extent that lynching drama helped them to do so, it is telling that most of the authors lived in or near the nation's capital when they were writing these plays.

By insisting that lynch victims were isolated brute rapists, mobs destroyed black homes while denying that blacks valued domesticity, and in doing so they sought to erase evidence that African Americans could be modern citizens. After all, an individual supposedly proved ready for the rights and responsibilities of citizenship by becoming domestically successful.[23] It is not surprising then that lynching plays emphasize the degree to which victimized individuals belong to families, which have a rightful place in both black communities and the United States. Certifying that they belonged in both was important, because mobs argued that blacks were a threat to the nation by insisting that they were not meaningful members of their own families.

In this climate, lynching playwrights offered scripts that encouraged African Americans to continue to participate in what I term *embodied practices of black belonging*. As mentioned, this study accounts for the knowledge-producing power of embodied practice—not only theatrical performance but also everyday activities and simple gestures. Blacks had survived slavery, Reconstruction, and post-Reconstruction to enter the new century, and they had done so by acting deliberately. They found lost loved ones; they legalized marriages; they created homes; they engaged each other in serious debate; and in everyday activities, they acknowledged their connection to the race and worked for its welfare. Through the genre of lynching drama, modern readers have access to embodied practices of black belonging that helped African Americans survive the next few violent decades of their American journey—still convinced of their right to full citizenship.

Given the intensity of racial violence at the turn of the century, it is within African Americans' homes that practices of black belonging become most visible, and lynching dramas spotlight this space in two critical ways. First, the scripts utilize the black home as setting. Second, because most are one-acts published in periodicals, the plays encourage amateurs to use the black home as performance space. As the scripts preserve the embodied practices of characters in the play, they register the presence of at least two sorts of embodied practice in the lived world. On the most basic level, the actions of the characters become archival evidence of the fact that blacks existed who behaved in these family-centered ways. At the same time, the scripts' survival points toward the embodied practices undertaken by community members, who performed the plays or simply offered dramatic readings of them.

Lynching scripts would not have proliferated if they did not serve a purpose for communities at the turn of the century. This is no less the case because they were seldom staged formally and did not attract large audiences. Indeed, I contend that the plays survive as imprints of turn-of-the-century examples of what Saidiya Hartman calls "networks of affiliation constructed in practice" (59). Lynching drama reflects self-conscious efforts to build community, and these efforts were motivated by a commonality not reducible to race, nor determined simply by unity against oppression, but based on a desire to see African American individuals and families represented in ways that corroborated their self-conceptions. Given both their content and their form, lynching plays point to "connections forged in the context of disrupted affiliations [and] sociality amid the constant threat of separation . . ." (Hartman 59). Even the nation's capital proved to have Southern sensibilities, so it is not surprising that the playwrights (and the communities served by their work) valued seeing depictions of black family life when mainstream discourse suggested that they had none. It is also no wonder that they soon privileged private performance spaces; public performance could make participants more vulnerable to the violence that the scripts critique. Both the characters in the plays and the readers who accepted them represent turn-of-the-century "networks of affiliation enacted in performance" because both characters and readers engaged in embodied practices of black belonging.

While the Congress and Senate often failed to represent African American interests, lynching drama put forth not only representative individuals and families but also key figures: the black soldier, black lawyer, and black mother/wife. As the genre develops, these figures become its most prominent characters; their presence sparks debate about the quality of black citizenship and calls attention to the process of black identity formation. Taking the soldier as an example, on the one hand, his appearance in lynching scripts allows these texts to stand as accounts of the beliefs and behaviors of real-life black soldiers; the works thus document the pride that they exuded about serving their country as well as the familial concerns that they uttered when reluctant to leave their loved ones. The soldier's dilemma also prompts debate among characters about whether the nation deserves his sacrifice. The scripts are, in this way, archival evidence of community reactions to military service and its effect on black families, shedding light on African Americans' views of the world and themselves. On the other hand, because they are in dramatic form, the scripts point to the embodied practices of community members, for their availability in magazines encouraged black audiences to bring the texts to life formally or informally, through performance or dramatic reading. Thus, African Americans were invited to recreate the soldier's postures, gestures, and tones of voice, and their doing so constituted another embodied practice that marked their connection to those represented in the text as well as to other people reading it.

The playwrights did not simply foreground the black home, then; by using the home to spotlight representative figures, the scripts offer it as an interpretive space, illuminating the era in which blacks were forced to live with lynching. Especially through these figures, the genre both reflected and perpetuated discourses and practices among blacks at the time, and it preserved for posterity evidence of community conversation and conduct. As a result, these texts survive to equip readers to appreciate the dramatists' insights into American culture. To offer an example in the most basic terms: with access to the black mother/wife at home (with her own children and romantic partner, rather than in a white family's home as servant), one discovers aspects of the historical moment in which she lived that cannot be readily gleaned from the archival resources upon which historical understanding is typically constructed.

Because they are showcased in their own homes, the figures offered in lynching drama preserve perspectives that are virtually erased in the dominant archives that have shaped our conceptions of U.S. culture at the turn of the century as the "Progressive Era" or as "the Nadir." The brutality with which blacks were lynched challenges the "progressive" label, especially when many were hung from streetlights, telephone poles, and other symbols of modernization and technological advancement. Also, though mob violence made this a low point for African Americans, the realities that made it a nadir in race relations may have been the very reasons that communities continued to value artistic expression—especially among amateurs. In other words, it is not a low point in African American cultural production, as previously believed.[24] Thus, I view the genre of lynching drama as one example of how blacks used art to sustain their conceptions of themselves as modern citizens, even as they were routinely denied the rights and privileges of that status. Black-authored lynching plays are not simply underappreciated components of the New Negro Renaissance; they are very much a product of the postbellum/pre-Harlem era.

Attentive to the conditions of American modernity, lynching dramatists recognized the home as a space of public privacy, where the impossibility of separating the public sphere from the private becomes clearest.[25] As much as African Americans worked toward citizenship rights in terms of voting and holding political office, there is no question that citizenship was negotiated in private and corporeal ways. Not only did whites successfully resist black political equality by claiming that it was tantamount to encouraging miscegenation, but blacks also understood that the sanctity of their homes and families depended on full citizenship and that full citizenship may not come without creating respectable homes and families.[26] It was a conundrum made more dizzying by the hypocrisy that characterized the nation's actions in comparison to its creed. The nation's hypocrisy did not stop blacks from striving to be true to their own ideals, however, and the representative figures in lynching drama both participate in and fuel community conversations about both the quality of black citizenship and the contours of black identity.

※ ※ ※

Living with Lynching examines lynching drama's emergence and development, identifying insights that the genre offers about turn-of-the-century U.S. culture. The study is divided into two parts. Part I, "Making Lynching Drama and Its Contributions Legible," sets the stage for understanding the genre's ability to shed new light on the history of the so-called "Progressive Era" in the United States. I examine the theatrical tendencies of the mob in modern America as well as the conventions of black theater that led African Americans to begin privileging playwriting over acting by the early 1900s. The majority of the book consists of part II, "Developing a Genre, Asserting Black Citizenship." These chapters detail the culturally affirming tendencies that were reflected and encouraged as lynching scripts proliferated and the genre developed, mostly through one-acts and periodical culture.

Part I, "Making Lynching Drama and Its Contributions Legible," consists of chapters 1 and 2. Chapter 1, "Scenes and Scenarios: Reading Aright," argues that blacks living during lynching's height accurately read the discourses and practices of their historical moment, and their cultural artifacts reflect their insights. Scholars must therefore engage the archive that black dramatists left as well as the embodied practices to which their scripts point. Namely, the plays contain specific characterizations of the nature of lynching, and they inspire black community practices that enable African Americans to continue to interpret their surroundings accurately. For example, the genre helps reveal that real-life lynchings were tolerated because they were read as legitimate scenarios of exorcism. That is, mobs were believed to cast out the evil that blacks supposedly embodied. In an environment where their extermination was said to make the nation safe, African Americans perceived the truth behind the facade—that lynching was really master/piece theater, designed to reinforce racial hierarchy. African American artists therefore offered scripts that encouraged their communities to continue to rehearse an understanding of themselves as full citizens.

Chapter 2, "Redefining 'Black Theater,'" demonstrates that the first black-authored lynching play, *Rachel*, by Angelina Weld Grimké, emerged in 1914 partly because the mainstream stage accepted black actors but limited them to comedy or white-authored material. Grimké and others thus began privileging playwriting over acting in order to control the race's representation. Nevertheless, I demonstrate that African American intellectuals and artists came to value black dramatists because of the success of performers—even minstrels and musical comedians. Black playwrights would not have been called upon to fill a void (and thereby re-define black theater) if their absence had not been highlighted by performers' success. Still, the investment in playwriting yielded Grimké's *Rachel,* which proved influential enough to initiate the genre of lynching drama because other poets and fiction writers also began writing plays. As Grimké's successors offered generic revisions, their efforts helped to redefine black theater again. The chapter therefore identifies the differences and commonalities between their work and Grimké's.

Part II, "Developing a Genre, Asserting Black Citizenship," is made up of chapters 3–6. Chapter 3, "The Black Soldier: Elevating Community Conversation," examines together the first two one-act lynching plays to appear in periodicals. These scripts' presence in the archive offers access to the playwrights' willingness to maximize periodical culture and the diversity of perspectives encouraged by it. Dramatic revisions of Grimké's *Rachel* began with Alice Dunbar-Nelson's *Mine Eyes Have Seen,* a play that compares lynching to black military service in World War I. This 1918 one-act soon inspired Mary Burrill's similarly themed script, *Aftermath,* published in 1919. Heated debate drives the action of both plays, prompting honest, painful conversation in black communities not unlike that among the characters. The plays question to varying degrees black patriotism in a country that tolerates lynching, but they equally underscore the importance of the black soldier. He both represents the race's conception of itself and sparks intense discussion because the nation so often proves unworthy of his sacrifices. These two one-acts offer distinct portraits of the black soldier partly because they appear in periodicals with very different agendas. Indeed, because Dunbar-Nelson published in the NAACP's *Crisis* and Burrill chose *The Liberator,* edited by white leftist intellectual Max Eastman, their texts index community debates about whether socialism is relevant to discussions of black identity and citizenship.

Chapter 4, "The Black Lawyer: Preserving Testimony," traces the shift in the community conversation from an emphasis on black soldiers who return from fighting overseas and must be defended by white attorneys to the increasing visibility of black lawyers. *Crisis* magazine coverage notes this shift, and lynching dramas similarly identify the black attorney as a figure embodying the race's faith in truth and justice. The mob's target in *A Sunday Morning in the South* (of which Georgia Douglas Johnson wrote white-church and black-church versions) aspires to be a lawyer. In *For Unborn Children* by Myrtle Smith Livingston, the mob's victim is already an attorney. Placing a spotlight on these men, the scripts preserve community perspectives that are rejected by courts of law and the court of public opinion.

Chapter 5, "The Black Mother/Wife: Negotiating Trauma," focuses on plays written by Georgia Douglas Johnson in the late 1920s as she hosted a literary salon in her Washington, D.C., home. These texts present the black mother/wife, whose existence is shaped by attempts to delay death. In *Blue Blood,* she prevents the murder of the men in her family by hiding the fact that she has been raped by a powerful white man. In *Safe,* she becomes desperate to avoid what she believes to be the inevitable fate of her newborn son: humiliating death at the hands of a mob. In *Blue-Eyed Black Boy,* she protects her adult son, but ultimately her success in stopping the mob underscores her family's vulnerability. In short, Johnson shows that the black mother/wife must forge romantic and parental bonds in a society that allows white men to rape black women and kill black men with impunity.

Chapter 6, "The Pimp and Coward: Offering Gendered Revisions," demonstrates that, as a genre, lynching drama challenges the assumption that men establish literary traditions and women revise them. Black male authors entered the genre in 1925, and they revised the conventions being developed by women. Women's plays present the home as the lynch victim, portraying its "castration" as the moment when the honorable black man is removed. However, male dramatists depict homes that seem "castrated" even when husbands, fathers, and uncles survive because they become immoral and cowardly to avoid the mob's wrath. I argue that the pimp and coward emerge to mark the community conversation's acknowledgement that their perspectives matter as African Americans grapple with the contradictions of living with lynching.

The conclusion, "Documenting Black Performance: Key Considerations," utilizes archival evidence to further support the book's throughline: scholars must rethink how we identify a powerful theatrical space. Trees, telephone poles, and bridges became stages upon which lynchings occurred, but mobs were not alone in repurposing the spaces over which they had control. African Americans redefined spaces (including their own living rooms) to accomplish identity-sustaining theatrical work.

PART ONE

Making Lynching Drama
and Its Contributions Legible

CHAPTER ONE

Scenes and Scenarios
Reading Aright[1]

The unique genre of lynching drama survives to enhance our understanding of U.S. culture between 1890 and 1930. During these decades, racial violence was often understood as a way of removing evil from society. Mainstream discourses and practices encouraged this interpretation, bombarding all Americans with the message that blacks threatened civilization and progress. In order to survive this era still believing that they were a race of decent people who did not deserve to be butchered, African Americans had to be cultural critics who read their surroundings dynamically. Many also became culture producers, providing art that both reflected and encouraged the community's ability to view national tendencies critically.

Lynching drama is one manifestation of black cultural criticism, and it reflects African Americans' understanding that the most powerful messages of their time were multivalent. Their realities were shaped by communication that involved language but was never limited to it. Because meaning is created and conveyed not only through words but also through gestures, objects, and movement, there are countless resources for creating signs and symbols that represent and reinforce ideas and identities.[2] Emerging from a rigorous interpretation of their surroundings, lynching drama indexes African Americans' recognition that the turbulent decades of the Progressive Era made embodied practice important to all U.S. citizens.

As a result, the genre of lynching drama provides access to what performance theorist Diana Taylor would call *the archive and the repertoire* of turn-of-the-century U.S. culture. As Taylor insists, "the archive" refers to "supposedly enduring materials" such as texts and documents, while "the repertoire" signifies "performances, gestures, orality, movement"—that is, practices that "enact embodied memory" (19–20). Western scholars have consistently privileged the archive, treating it as a resource whose content can be trusted because it is supposedly resistant to change and corruption. On the other hand, the embodied practices of the repertoire have been deemed fleeting and unreliable, having little importance in the production of knowledge. Taylor reminds us, however, that "the archive and the repertoire exist in a constant state of interaction" (21). Therefore, they should be examined together and on equal footing, and black-authored lynching plays present an opportunity to do just that.

In fact, plays written by blacks at the height of mob violence emphasize the degree to which the nation accepted lynching as a valid *scenario of exorcism*.[3] As Taylor explains, a scenario is a well-worn sketch or outline of action. Because it "resuscitates and reactivates old dramas," "the scenario makes visible, yet again, what is already there: the ghosts, the images, the stereotypes" (28). Thus, a *scenario* "structures our understanding," and "because we've seen it all before," it can do so even if there are omissions (28). Racial violence was often interpreted as a legitimate *scenario of exorcism* because it contained what citizens had seen before: supposedly righteous white men casting out the evil forces that might threaten their wives and children.

Though lynching was not always racially motivated, its most culturally significant form was inspired by a white supremacist impulse.[4] After the Civil War, when blacks were no longer property, there was no financial reason not to kill them. This is when lynching took on the characteristics that we now associate with the term; that is, when lynching became ritualized murder. As Trudier Harris and others have established, crowds soon counted on a familiar ceremony. A sort of script developed, which included obligatory accusation and forced confession, followed by mutilation and souvenir hunting.[5] Quite consistently, "white men, women, and children would hang or burn (frequently both), shoot, and castrate the [alleged] offender, then divide the body into trophies" (Harris 6).

These predictable steps, and their standardization across the country, reflected white agreement with mainstream declarations that African Americans were immoral and bestial, that they were not citizens and perhaps not fully human. The torture of black bodies was therefore invested with significance. These rituals were possible and meaningful because, in the sign-system of U.S. society, the black body was consistently presented and interpreted as a sign of evil and immorality, as a symbol of all that would destroy the nation.

Thus, when lynching became racially motivated, it also became theatrical; mobs created and conveyed meaning not only with words but also with props, gestures, sounds, and movement. In essence, they made a spectacle of whites' right to eliminate evil, which they increasingly figured as black and male.[6] Because black men were said to be natural rapists who targeted white women, lynching was hailed as a way of avenging alleged rapes and preventing future ones. This logic was supported by claims that black men were beasts who cared nothing for stable domesticity and black women were immoral whores incapable of creating it anyway. According to this reasoning, mobs performed an unpleasant but necessary exorcism. If blacks were immoral, they must be rooted out for the safety of white women, white families, and the nation.

As this rhetoric circulated through actions as well as words, it helped to restore a sense of superiority for whites whose self-conceptions had been destabilized by the emancipation of slaves and other changes in postbellum life.[7] If dark skin no longer automatically kept individuals from participating in society, blacks' inferiority to whites needed to be marked more deliberately. It is no coincidence, then, that the postbellum era saw blacks cast more frequently as brutes not only in newspapers, magazines, and literary works (the archive), but also via subtle and overt practices of segregation (the repertoire). Messages were created and conveyed through hateful stares, name calling, signs that designated where "colored" people could or could not enter, and through physical violence. African Americans were also literally objectified through toys, games, and housewares featuring Aunt Jemima, Uncle Mose, and pickaninnies, and by the marketing of everyday products such as "Niggerhair Chewing Tobacco."[8]

Because the insistence upon the inferiority of blacks took written, verbal, material, and embodied form, Taylor's *scenario* concept proves invaluable because scenarios must be read dynamically. As Taylor suggests, "instead of privileging *texts* and *narratives,* we could also look to scenarios as meaning-making paradigms that structure social environments, behaviors, and potential outcomes" (28). After all, she writes, "The scenario includes features well theorized in literary analysis, such as narrative and plot, but demands that we also pay attention to milieux and corporeal behaviors such as gestures, attitudes, and tones not reducible to language" (28). Whether they turned their noses up at African Americans or physically attacked them, many whites acted out of some degree of the following logic: white is good, black is evil, and whites are morally entitled to banish as needed. The scenario of exorcism motivated these behaviors and structured their interpretation.

Because lynching was generally understood as exorcism, racial violence went unchecked between 1890 and 1930, but blacks living and writing at this time skillfully read these multivalent scenarios and offered critical analyses of them. As a result of this community process, lynching drama developed as a genre. As the following excerpt illustrates, Alice Dunbar-Nelson's one-act script *Mine Eyes Have Seen* proves representative of the cultural work that lynching drama accomplished at the turn of the century.

> LUCY: (*Coming down front, with a dish cloth in her hand.*) Oh, Dan, wasn't it better in the old days when we were back home—in the little house with the garden, and you and father coming home nights and mother getting supper, and Chris and I studying lessons in the dining-room at the table—we didn't have to eat and live in the kitchen then, and—
>
> DAN: (*Grimly.*)—And the notices posted on the fence for us to leave town because niggers had no business having such a decent home.
>
> LUCY: (*Unheeding* [sic] *the interruption.*)—And Chris and I reading the wonderful books and laying our plans—
>
> DAN:—To see them go up in the smoke of our burned home.
>
> LUCY: (*Continuing, her back to Dan, her eyes lifted, as if seeing a vision of retrospect.*)—And everyone petting me because I had hurt my foot when I was little, and father—
>
> DAN:—Shot down like a dog for daring to defend his home—
>
> LUCY:—Calling me "Little Brown Princess," and telling mother—
>
> DAN:—Dead of pneumonia and heartbreak in this bleak climate.
>
> LUCY:—That when you—
>
> DAN: Maimed for life in a factory of hell! Useless—useless—broken on the wheel. (*His voice breaks in a dry sob.*)
>
> LUCY: (*Coming out of her trance, throws aside the dish-cloth, and running to Dan, lays her cheek against his and strokes his hair.*) Poor Danny, poor Danny, forgive me, I'm selfish.
>
> DAN: Not selfish, Little Sister, merely natural.
>
> (*Enter roughly and unceremoniously Chris. He glances at the two with their arms about each other, shrugs his shoulders, hangs up his rough cap and mackinaw on a nail, then seats himself at the table, his shoulders hunched up; his face dropping on his hand. Lucy approaches him timidly.*)

Publication in the NAACP's *Crisis* magazine gave *Mine Eyes* a place in a recognizable archive, and through both its content and form, the script registers the embodied practices of both blacks and whites. The script is primarily concerned with depicting the conversations and everyday activities of a black family in mourning, and offering that portrait involves acknowledging lynching. In fact, the characters assert that mob violence arises from whites' investment in destroying black households and any trace of the dignified embodied practices that create and sustain them. In this way, the play records blacks' understanding of lynching as one of the ways that whites perform their supposed superiority. At the same time, the play records the embodied practices of African Americans themselves. As Lucy reminisces aloud about their original home, the play describes the life that they enjoyed within it. Having been forced to relocate after their father's death, Lucy and her brothers now live in the North. They made this move under the worst circumstances but have established another home in which they sustain each other. The play records embodied practices of black belonging as the siblings affirm each other with affection and engage each other's concerns in conversation.[9]

The one-act format of the play also points to embodied practice. Published in *Crisis* magazine in 1918, *Mine Eyes* is the earliest example of the form that made lynching drama most conducive to amateur performance, which bolstered African Americans' self-conceptions. While the literary tradition was initiated by Angelina Weld Grimké's three-act play, Dunbar-Nelson utilized the one-act format, which thereafter dominated the genre. As a document, *Mine Eyes* marks the formal shift that enabled lynching drama's development throughout the 1920s, as scripts appeared in periodicals.[10] Dunbar-Nelson not only placed a spotlight on discussions occurring in an intimate setting; by writing a one-act, she also increased the likelihood that her work would be enacted in private spaces. Furthermore, the proliferation of one-act lynching plays suggests that black communities put the scripts to use. At the same time, this formal shift indexes the embodied practices of whites. When mobs not only lynched but also ensured that photographs of their work were created and preserved, there was good reason for blacks to maximize private spaces for racially affirming activities.

When one examines *Mine Eyes* as a product of the critical engagement of turn-of-the-century African Americans, it is clear that the script's domestic setting is not merely convenient to the genre's work but critical to it. Lynching drama suggests that mob violence can be justified only with the erasure of what the genre makes most conspicuous: the scene of black family life. Like *Mine Eyes,* all of the plays of this study are set in the black home, underscoring the dramatists' priorities as they served their besieged communities. As Taylor reminds us, "*scene* denotes intentionality . . . and signals conscious strategies of display" (29). These playwrights understood the significance of showcasing—for themselves, not whites—black family life at a time when mainstream discourses and practices constantly asserted that African Americans had no interest in, or moral capacity for, stable domesticity.

Indeed, *Mine Eyes* uncovers the dialectical relationship between the *scene* of black home life and the mainstream *scenario* that enabled and fueled lynching. It suggests that mob violence and its supporting rhetoric intensified and became increasingly theatrical because blacks were so successfully affirming themselves. Homebuilding among African Americans represented a set of embodied practices of black belonging, and the plays preserve evidence of those practices. If blacks belonged to families and communities, that was more confirmation that they belonged to the nation. The centrality of the black family scene in lynching drama should thus be read as a manifestation of African Americans' understanding that their right to belong to the nation was being erased along with the erasure of their belonging to their own families and communities. As the excerpt suggests, lynching drama as a genre preserves the community conversation that flourished in black homes. Those intimate exchanges declared the beauty and integrity of African Americans while acknowledging mainstream efforts to make blacks' definitions of themselves irrelevant.

African Americans encountered overwhelming and always multivalent discourses that justified killing some and terrorizing the rest with photographs of the fallen. In gruesomely attention-getting ways, the archive and the repertoire operated "in a constant state of interaction," and African Americans understood that. When we read as dynamically as they did, the archive of black-authored lynching drama reveals the degree to which whites and blacks alike invested in performance for identity formation and preservation. However, while whites often attempted to erase blacks' efforts, blacks worked to capture evidence of not only their own embodied practices but also those of oppressive whites. *Mine Eyes Have Seen* and the other plays of this study survive as cultural artifacts documenting African Americans' ability to read their surroundings accurately and their determination to equip each other to continue to do so. Resonating with the nineteenth-century texts examined by Gabrielle Foreman, lynching plays offer "a way to join a collective project of cultural, historical, and intellectual literacy that will teach the new nation to read aright" (77).

Reading Critically and Targeting Black Audiences

Of course, lynching dramatists were not the first African Americans to read against the grain of the nation's rhetoric and encourage others to do the same. In many ways, they followed the path of activist Ida B. Wells, who had extended arguments made by Frederick Douglass to intervene in public discourse. In the pamphlets *Southern Horrors* (1892) and *A Red Record* (1895) Wells traces the excuses that whites gave for targeting African Americans: first, mobs were said to take action because insurrections and riots needed to be prevented, "but this story at last wore itself out" (*Record* 76). The second excuse, Wells asserts, arose under the banner of "No Negro Domination." During the 1870s, mobs killed blacks "whose only crime was the attempt to exercise their right to vote." In those cases, Southerners explained that it was an expression of the "natural resentment of intelligence against government by ignorance" (*Record* 77, *Horrors* 60). Once mob violence and legal disfranchisement had all but reversed black political gains, "the murderers invented a third excuse—that Negroes had to be killed to avenge their assaults upon women" (*Record* 78). The claim that black men rape white women proved to be the most effective, despite the fact that rape was not even alleged in the majority of lynchings.[11]

Given that race-based lynching was most prevalent from the 1890s through 1930,[12] the significance of the black rapist myth cannot be overstated. As Wells put it, " . . . this charge [of rape] upon the Negro at once placed him beyond the pale of human sympathy. With such . . . earnestness and apparent candor was this charge made and reiterated that the world has accepted the story that the Negro is *the monster which the Southern white man has painted him*" (*Record* 78, emphasis added). Wells therefore saw the fight against mob violence as one that must engage how blacks were represented, how one could talk about African Americans. She understood that lynching was about the "politics of representation," defined by cultural theorist Stuart Hall as "the way meaning can be struggled over, and whether a particular regime of representation can be challenged, contested and transformed" (*Representation* 8).

Wells was not alone; many Progressive Era blacks engaged the politics of representation, and they did so in every possible arena. Indeed, representation was at stake when Du Bois edited *Crisis* magazine, beginning in 1910, and prioritized photography. According to cultural historian Daylanne English, *Crisis* became a racial family album that suggested that "the 'Negro family' cohere[ed] enough . . . to permit exhaustive (and wholly positive) representation" (*Unnatural* 49). Du Bois used photography and an ever-expanding catalog of black elites' accomplishments to present "the 'college-bred,' middle-class, urban intellectual man as the authentic representative of an ideal racial family" (English, *Unnatural* 55). In other words, Du Bois's work was not simply a reaction to mainstream images: he offered African Americans a visual archive that accorded with their own ideas about, and hopes for, themselves and their communities.[13]

Yet, Du Bois's work likely gained urgency as he and others read their surroundings and noted that visual representation was being used increasingly, and with increasing effectiveness, to make their very bodies stand as signs of chaos and danger. As historian Grace Hale argues, modernization and industrialization forced U.S. citizens to seek new ways of defining their identities. Between 1890 and 1930, regional networks lost influence. Local money was replaced with federal currency, and neighborhood officials and business owners who had always been independent were suddenly accountable to national authorities and pressures. In response to these and other unsettling changes, Americans reorganized their identities around broader connections, especially skin color. This allowed whites to construct a group identity that was no longer fragmented by differences of class, for example, which had meant so much (Hale 3–30). Increasingly, racial segregation became a "central metaphor" around which U.S. culture was organized, allowing whites to see themselves as part of a coherent group of moral, sophisticated citizens who were all (regardless of lack of education, for instance) superior to blacks.[14] As modern Americans invested skin color with more meaning, photography and visual entertainments became more valuable to those anxious to assert their racial superiority. Photography's role in lynching therefore cannot be overlooked, but like Du Bois, who challenged the message conveyed by the mob's pictures,[15] scholars today must be careful not to reaffirm the perpetrators' assumptions.

Reading against the grain of mainstream lynching photography required recognizing its biases and its strategies for concealing them. Despite the brutality they recorded, these photographs became souvenirs (sometimes even picture postcards) because the country's rhetoric was saturated with assertions about black barbarity and white righteousness. Thus, when the pictures circulated, they contained—and themselves became—visual signs and symbols that corroborated dominant discourse. Their popularity and usefulness depended on ensuring that the black body would be interpreted in ways that connoted anything but humanity and citizenship, and this was achieved by making black bodies appear to be isolated from family, community, and nation. Hence, the "camerawork" that came to define mainstream lynching photography most often presented African Americans as monsters that had been subdued by the calmly triumphant whites who surrounded the black body.[16] Such images unmistakably marked who was a citizen and who was not. In harmony with the nation's rhetoric, the pictures tolerated an acknowledgement of blacks' corporeal existence but required a denial of African American citizenship and familial bonds. It is no accident that the black figure is always surrounded by whites . . . no grieving loved ones in sight.

Lynching drama emerged in the context of not only dehumanizing imagery but also the interventions of activists, such as Wells and Du Bois, whose efforts bolstered the race's positive self-conception while national discourses and practices worked to destroy it. When a number of black writers became playwrights in the early 1910s, they built on and continued the work of countless others[17]; they simply engaged the politics of representation in another arena. As they did so, they often tailored their work for members of their own communities.

Unfortunately, scholars so consistently approach black art as "protest" that most studies focus on identifying whether an artist's work altered whites' perceptions, if not their actions. Especially when lynching is referenced, some scholars implicitly ask, "What good was it if it didn't convince whites to stop the violence?" But African American communities did not just need those who would work to gain whites' empathy; they also needed individuals who could provide tools for surviving. In other words, it is important to consider the strategies used in the fight to end mob violence, but we should also ask, *How did blacks help each other cope while lynching remained a reality?* Yes, they hoped there was a "brighter coming day," but what were they planning to do in the meantime?

Answers begin to emerge when we take seriously the possibility that black artists could serve their communities by addressing them, not just addressing whites on their behalf. As Du Bois edited *Crisis* magazine, he used every available resource for cultural expression and racial self-affirmation. As we have seen, he prioritized images as much as words. In addition, under his editorship, *Crisis* published one-act plays on various topics. Drama was included seamlessly, as simply another contribution to a multifaceted community discourse. Thus, what Susan Harris Smith says about mainstream magazines of the period is true of *Crisis*: "[D]ramatic texts comfortably inhabit both the literary and cultural milieu of periodicals—there are no apologies, no defensive postures, no ambivalences, no anxious rationales for inclusion of the genre. Drama is simply one of the many forms of creative expression . . . that comprise the texture of the magazine" (21). Dramatic scripts contributed to Du Bois's overall goal of using every available resource for racial self-affirmation. After all, drama ideally inspires the use not only of words but also of gestures, objects, bodies—a whole range of tools for creating and conveying meaning.

With its diversity of expressive forms, *Crisis* magazine provides an excellent opportunity for considering the service that black-authored texts could perform for African American audiences.[18] As Anne Carroll has emphasized (following Houston Baker), New Negro artists and activists "went out of their way" to create "multi-media portrayals" of the race (2). Carroll finds that their publications combine visual texts with written ones (4).[19]

Specifically discussing *Crisis,* Carroll asserts that it "demonstrates techniques of representation that were found in a number of periodicals of the time: it includes sharp, vivid, and angry protests of the treatment of African Americans as well as evidence of African Americans' accomplishments and potential" (15). Carroll treats "angry protests" and the listing of accomplishments as separate discursive strategies that often clashed; her analysis does not conceive of them as irrevocably intertwined. Carroll argues in fact that because "protest texts have drawbacks, particularly that they can continue or even reinforce the dehumanization of their subjects," *Crisis* magazine "offsets these drawbacks by *countering* its coverage of lynchings . . . with features that highlight African Americans' achievements in business, education, and politics . . ." (15, emphasis added). Carroll continues: "[A]ffirmations are juxtaposed with coverage of lynchings" and "the cognitive dissonance created by such juxtapositions is crucial to the impact of the magazine" (15).[20]

Carroll is not alone in assuming that images of lynching horror were placed alongside evidence of black achievement solely to highlight a contrast. Russ Castronovo, in a compelling discussion of what he calls Du Bois's "alternative aesthetics," highlights the extent to which "the layout of *Crisis* illustrates that 'Music and Art' is always positioned . . . against death" (111). As such, Castronovo insists upon an opposition between beauty and violence and suggests that these were also in opposition in Du Bois's conception of the challenges before him. As a result, Castronovo's analysis locates beauty only where white audiences would have, even as he admits that whites had made lynching an art and often saw the brutalized black body as an aesthetic object.[21] Beauty and lynching can remain opposed in Castronovo's examination, though, because his goal is to show that blacks understood white standards and tried to use mainstream aesthetics to promote social justice.

Castronovo's methodology is important because some African Americans did indeed hope to create problack propaganda by using beauty that whites would recognize. Castronovo discusses Du Bois's efforts in exactly these terms, but he could have been describing the approach that Angelina Weld Grimké took when working to make her drama *Rachel* appealing to white audiences. When criticism from black communities led her to defend the play, Grimké insisted that she had targeted a white audience in hopes of making white women in particular sympathize with black mothers. Further, she explained that she had been motivated to defend her race to this audience because of the multifaceted attack on African Americans. Grimké

insisted: "Whenever you say 'colored person' to a white man he immediately
. . . conjures up in his mind the picture of what he calls 'the darky.' In other
words, he believes, or says he does, that all colored people are a grinning,
white-toothed, shiftless, carefree set, given to chicken-stealing, watermelon-
eating, always, under all circumstances, properly obsequious to a white
skin and always amusing" ("Reason" 425). Clearly, Grimké was addressing
minstrelsy and the tremendous popularity of stage versions of Uncle Tom,[22]
and she was attuned to the power of multilayered representation. In her
formulation, when one *hears* blacks mentioned, a specific *picture* comes to
mind. Thus, she was concerned not just about the written word but also
about gestures, movements, objects, tones of voice, etc. Surely, Grimké was
pulled away from poetry and fiction to drama by the possibility of having at
her disposal an endless array of meaning-making signs and symbols, which
dramatic texts ideally put into action.

Because she chose to counter images from the mainstream stage and to do
so—in her words—"primarily" for "the whites," Grimké drew her characters
from "the best type of colored people." And she was very specific about how
this group could be identified: "[They live] in homes that are clean, well-kept
with *many evidences of taste and refinement about them*. They are many of
them well educated, cultivated and cultured; they are well-mannered and,
in many instances, more moral than the whites; *they love beauty*; they have
ideals and ambitions, and they do not talk—this educated type—in the Negro
dialect" ("Reason" 425, emphasis added).

In establishing for whites that blacks were not "darkies," Grimké sought
to display black success in a drama whose beauty should be recognizable
to white theatergoers: Grimké's play is sentimental, foregrounds Victorian-
influenced courtship rituals and manners, and emphasizes familiarity with
European culture. It is also peopled with characters who "love beauty" and
live with "many evidences of taste and refinement about them." Namely, the
house is decorated with prints of paintings such as *The Reapers* and *The
Man with the Hoe* by French realist Jean-Francois Millet, and *Golden Stairs*
by Englishman Edward Burne-Jones. Also, Raphael Sanzio's painting *The
Sistine Madonna* from the Italian High Renaissance is highlighted in several
scenes.[23] In Castronovo's terms, Grimké believed that her well-mannered,
beauty-loving characters, and the conventional dramatic structure in which
she presented them, would show whites that lynching was unjust because it
devastates dignified blacks. Ideally, "aesthetics makes propaganda true . . .
in ways that people, including white people, are compelled to recognize"
(Castronovo 108).

Just two years after *Rachel* premiered in Washington, D.C., however, Dunbar-Nelson's *Mine Eyes Have Seen* suggested that it is exactly the sort of success and beauty depicted by Grimké that provokes lynching. Given that Du Bois published this play in *Crisis,* might we reconsider the claims made by Carroll and Castronovo in the same way that Dunbar-Nelson re-thinks Grimké's assumptions? Castronovo speaks, as Carroll does, of "*the repeated juxtaposition* of beauty with lynching in the columns of *The Crisis*" (113). However, it is in the pages of *Crisis* that Lucy, Dan, and Chris indicate that black-authored beauty inspires lynching. Their home was destroyed because they were "living like Christians" and had the nerve to do so in a nice house with a fence and garden.

Was the layout of *Crisis* based on an aesthetic of contrast, or of cause-and-effect? If the latter, then the magazine uses the same strategy that Dun-bar-Nelson had: it tells African Americans that their accomplishments are causing lynching at the same time that it constitutes the very success that it says infuriates the mob. Accordingly, the magazine helps black readers to understand and contend with the ugliness that confronts them in their daily lives—on trees, telephone poles, light posts, and bridges (the repertoire) as well as in newspapers, movie advertisements, and postcards (the archive). The magazine simultaneously confronts and assures African Americans, as if to say: *No, you are not crazy. Yes, your country claims to value fairness and family life, but the evil purportedly exorcised by the mob does not exist: the supposedly isolated brute rapist was actually a family man. Unfortunately, it really is the race's integrity that inspires white rage. Know that . . . and know that it will continue to have that effect. Here, you will find resources to help you weather the inevitable storms that enter African American lives that are marked by the success that we will continue to pursue. Together, we will keep striving, despite the "strange fruit" left by those who insist that it is by mistake that they are no longer our masters.*

Lynching plays were one of the resources that helped African Americans survive this period still believing in their right to full citizenship. These playwrights created characters who often quietly sit, read, converse, and show each other affection, behavior that scripts rarely demanded of black bodies. African American domestic novels had already begun this work of defining black characters through activities that connoted sophistication and familial stability.[24] It was time to create dramas that offered similar portraits, which would be animated by the African American citizens whose real lives served as the black artist's inspiration and the mob's murderous motivation.

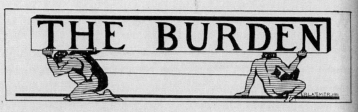

THE BURDEN

ANOTHER SOUTHERN IDYL.

CHAPTER I.

H E received a high-school education and taught school.

CHAPTER II.

He got married and here is the family:

CHAPTER III.

He took the civil-service examination and entered the postal service, being the first colored carrier.

CHAPTER IV.

He received a letter from the "Superior Race," who were his "Best Friends," smeared with blood and reading:

"April 12, 1902.
"To * * *, Negro Postman
"*you had better not* be Seen carrying or delivering mail in * * * after to-day 12th day of April. *Don't forget.*

"If you should your life will pay the penalty. A word to the wise is sufficient.
"We are yours for trouble."

CHAPTER V.

He received a second letter to the "Nigger Mail Carrier":

"Your days are numbered; *leave,* LEAVE, LEAVE. DEATH, DEATH."

CHAPTER VI.

He writes us: "I am still in the service!" Which is what we call pluck.

Figure 2. A black postmaster shares his biography with *Crisis* readers in the March 1913 issue, p. 246. His story, complete with a photograph of his family, illustrates the belief among African Americans that their success beckons the mob. It also corroborates blacks' determination to continue pursuing their goals, despite the danger.

Creating Rehearsal Space[25]

When black artists engage the politics of representation, they must often search for the right form and forum: a form that will enable African Americans to represent themselves and a forum that will advance and preserve the race's self-image. At the turn of the century, drama proved appealing partly because asserting citizenship often requires taking a position in the institutions of one's society, and U.S. theater was establishing itself as an increasingly important entity.[26] As we will see in chapter 2, African Americans had long expressed belief in their citizenship by gaining access to the mainstream stage, beginning with minstrels who donned the burnt cork mask. Later, many insisted that truly empowering the race in this arena required having serious, nonmusical dramas written by black authors. Grimké's *Rachel* fit this description, but for some, it demonstrated that theater was not necessarily an institution that could be easily used to articulate African Americans' perspectives, even if they conformed to its aesthetic standards. By the late 1910s, the one-act drama and the amateur stage became the favored form and forum for many interested in preserving the truths about African American families and communities that the nation's rhetoric worked to erase.

By valuing one-act dramas and amateur venues, turn-of-the-century blacks revealed their belief that theater and lynching were working together to negate their humanity and citizenship. The mob's power arose partly from its use of theatricality, and theater became more relevant to U.S. nationalism as it borrowed characters, themes, and symbols from lynching. Accordingly, both theater and lynching hinged on negative interpretations of African American corporeality. Lynching figured the black body as immorality personified, while minstrelsy and musical comedy used black faces to indicate who was simple and less than a citizen. At this time, it was "good theater" to mutilate a black body and leave it lifeless and on display. This is why newspapers announced the time and location of lynchings, crowds gathered to see them, and then journalists reviewed the performances. Newspaper accounts noted the mob's cheers in addition to describing the victim's howls and contortions and the unmistakable odor of a burning human body.[27] Like good theater reviewers, journalists tried to capture the dramatic moments and sensual pleasures of theatrical production.[28] Meanwhile, and just as consistently, a black (or black-faced) man, woman, or child grinning and shuffling constituted "good theater." These depictions accorded with the idea that African Americans lacked the intelligence and solemnity required of citizens, a message naturalized as mobs and their photographers helped shape how black bodies would be interpreted.

Aware of the partnership between theater and lynching to refute blacks' conceptions of themselves as citizens, the playwrights of this study defined for themselves what was theatrical—blacks comforting each other, not grinning and shuffling—and they decided how the stage itself would be defined—not commercial venues, but communal ones. Likewise, they would not focus on physical violence; they refused to replicate the dramas acted out on the nation's trees. Deliberately out of step with mainstream theatricality and therefore of little interest to large audiences, lynching plays encouraged African Americans to value the affirming theatrical work that could take place in black churches, schools, and homes.

In these intimate venues, amateurs performed their citizenship by duplicating homebuilding practices, by having discussions and debates, and by taking time to mourn. The scripts dramatize the cooking and conversing that helped households to function as well as the affection that comforted inhabitants in times of trouble. Also, because these dramas are rooted in the domestic sphere, readers and viewers are made to focus on not the brutalized body but the household from which it was taken—offering a perspective that mainstream lynching photography does not. While the photographs communicate that the victim was a rapist who deserved his death and should not be mourned, the plays offer characters who have intimate knowledge and testify to his honorable life. Indeed, the scripts provide examples of, and occasions for, community mourning. Reading the dramas allowed for full expression of the pain of having black homes targeted and black humanity and citizenship disregarded.

For instance, like most black-authored lynching plays, *Mine Eyes Have Seen* spotlights a family victimized by the mob, yet it emphasizes mob destruction without depicting physical violence or offering a detailed description of it. While newspapers recounted every dramatic moment of the lynching ritual, this genre focused attention on the mothers and children who "escaped" the violence only to survive as widows and orphans. Refusing to portray the crime perpetrated on trees, telephone poles, and bridges, the plays suggest that the mob's outdoor practices reverberate inside the black home and continue long after the "strange fruit" of the victimized body has disappeared. In these plays, *the home* is the lynched body; it becomes a kind of "strange fruit." The household is mutilated just as a body can be; when an honorable father, son, or brother is taken, the household is "castrated" and its head removed.[29]

While the brutalized black body is absent from these dramatizations of what the mob leaves in its wake, black bodies are central to the genre's mission. As such, it is important to note, for example, that Dunbar-Nelson's stage directions call for Dan, the eldest sibling, to sob as Lucy reminisces about the life that they had in the South. The play also indicates that Lucy "lays her cheek against his and strokes his hair." At this time, scripts rarely called for a black man to weep over familial losses and to be consoled with overt affection. Lynching dramatists therefore operated under a definition of theatricality that did not seem to exist in the mainstream. On the commercial stage, a black body earned its place in the show by being wildly animated, grinning and shuffling. In the mob's theatrical productions, the black body delighted audiences with its pained contortions, followed by its motionlessness. Likewise, black characters most often appeared on the mainstream stage in minstrelsy and musical comedy, and these shows placed them in far-away locales, such as "Dahomey," or in white people's houses as servants—anywhere but their own homes. Given these tendencies, it is important to recall that while blacks were said to be incapable of domesticity, popular culture elevated mammies and uncles. These faithful servants were portrayed as loyal fixtures in white families but seemed incapable of feeling attachment to their own kin.[30] This supposed distance corroborated claims about the race's moral bankruptcy. Thus, as African Americans observed mainstream representational tendencies, they understood that their citizenship within the nation was negated partly by a denial that they were valuable members of their own families and communities.

Quite deliberately, lynching playwrights created opportunities for African Americans to engage in embodied practices of belonging, and when blacks took part in these various practices, they claimed a citizenship that was at least twofold: *they belonged in black communities as well as the nation.* Indeed, the scripts worked on several levels to create and sustain what political philosopher Susan Herbst calls "parallel public space" in harmony with Nancy Fraser's critique of Habermas's conception of the public sphere.[31] Herbst explains that marginalized groups foster alternative spaces because powerful institutions and people work to silence them (10). African Americans at the turn of the century were marginal by this definition because they did not merely *feel* marginalized; they were "systematically excluded" from the benefits of citizenship, such as protection under the law. Indeed, lynching was simply one of the bloodiest tactics in this ongoing process of exclusion. Therefore, if blacks were to express themselves and preserve their self-conceptions, they could not rely on dominant channels of communication; they had to develop alternative public spheres—discursive spaces in which their ideas could be articulated. In doing so, they could not completely escape repression, but they could secure "spaces of withdrawal and regroupment; [which] also function as bases and training grounds for agitational activities directed toward wider publics" (Fraser 124). Alternative discursive space has a dual purpose; it allows socially disadvantaged groups to withdraw, which empowers them to turn outward, if they choose, and demand change.

For African Americans, withdrawing from the public sphere was necessary for survival; working for outward social change would be a bonus. After all, though engaging mainstream society might lead the public to recognize black citizenship, affirming for themselves that they were rightfully a part of the nation was crucial for African Americans, whether others acknowledged it or not. If left only with the nation's discourses and practices, they would not be able to believe in their own decency. Not impervious to the power of representation, blacks deprived of refuge from national rhetoric would be convinced that their community really was an evil that must be exorcised for the greater good. Because denials of their citizenship within the nation often hinged on insisting that blacks were homeless brutes, whores, mammies, and uncles, the first task became affirming for themselves that they were citizens of their own smaller communities; then, blacks could certify for each other that they belonged in the nation.

I want to suggest that lynching dramatists fostered alterative public spheres through their choices about both the form and the content of their scripts. First, they maximized spaces of withdrawal because the playwrights who followed Grimké chose to use the one-act format, which in turn encouraged amateur performance in private venues. Second, the content of the scripts provided a training manual for black communities, encouraging African Americans to rehearse an understanding of lynching that allowed them to mourn because it helped them to maintain a sense of themselves as upstanding citizens unjustly under siege. As Herbst argues, communities facilitate identity formation by serving an "information processing function" (23). That is, belonging to a community helps individuals to filter the many messages with which they are bombarded.

Having an affirming lens through which to view one's surroundings was crucial to African American survival while lynching and lynching photographs were commonplace. For, as Michel Foucault has taught us, power is at work in knowledge production; it is the capacity for controlling what is accepted as *true* and *false*.[32] In Herbst's words, "power is the ability to shape the communication environment" through "persuasion, force, [and] manipulation of symbols" (27). Lynching rituals and photographs were nothing if not ways to manipulate what the black body symbolized, so African Americans needed support filtering that symbolism, and communities that acknowledged their citizenship provided exactly that.

Wisely, lynching playwrights chose drama in order to create and convey meaning in dynamic ways—namely, through the form's intermingling (ideally) of the written word with gestures, objects, bodies, etc. It is significant then that they tailored their scripts so that blacks could do this multifaceted meaning-making work inside community spaces, for their own benefit. The genre brought drama closer to African Americans and ensured that this type of theater, at least, would not be structured around black degradation. They sought to affirm the value of black personhood, and they evidently believed that this could be accomplished on the "margins" of the public sphere.[33] As Daphne Brooks might put it, wedding "political marginalization with cultural innovation, these resourceful cultural workers envisioned a way" toward self-affirmation (3).

In fact, they seem to have been working to make dominant discourse in general, and the mainstream stage in particular, *less important* to black audiences. The post-Grimké scripts offer depictions of black characters who, in some ways, resonate with Grimké's portrait, but they do not aim to put more positive images of the community on formal stages; instead, they declare the value of amateur, private ones. The proliferation of one-act lynching plays therefore points to the dramatists' commitment to what would later be called the Little Negro Theatre movement, which was amateur theater that Du Bois defined in 1926 as that which is "by us," "about us," "for us," and "near us."[34] Lynching playwrights who invested in the one-act format seemed convinced that, because it stood apart from the machinery of the commercial stage, amateur theater could affirm African Americans.

The amateur theater that was encouraged, I contend, also likely took the form of family pastime. Literary historian Elizabeth McHenry demonstrates in *Forgotten Readers* that African Americans have long exercised what she calls "communal literacy" by advocating memorization as a kind of literacy, by reading texts aloud to each other, and by encouraging dramatic readings.[35] Given the legacy that McHenry traces from the 1830s through the 1990s, surely we can imagine families in which each member read or memorized a part in a one-act play. Communal literacy must factor into our assumptions about how lynching scripts were used (and were meant to be used) because African Americans were deeply invested in progressive periodicals.[36] As historian David Levering Lewis asserts, even with remarkable improvements in black literacy rates since the nineteenth century, *Crisis* was published (beginning in 1910) "in an era of rampant illiteracy, when hard labor left Afro-Americans little time or inclination for reading Harvard-accented editorials." Nevertheless, such articles—because they appeared in *Crisis*—drew all strata of the black community. "The magazine found its way into kerosene-lit sharecroppers' cabins and cramped factory workers' tenements. In middle-class families it lay next to the Bible" (*Harlem* 7). Accordingly, literary critic J. Saunders Redding recalled that he and his siblings could "child-handle and mistreat" other magazines, but "*The Crisis* was strictly inviolate until my father himself had unwrapped and read it—often . . . aloud" (qtd. in Wall 46). The established ritual of sharing these valued periodicals now prompted informal performances and dramatic readings about lynching. So, while trees, telephone poles, and bridges became stages upon which lynchings occurred, African Americans claimed equal latitude in redefining spaces (including their own living rooms) to accomplish identity-sustaining theatrical work.

As the 1920s wore on, then, lynching playwrights turned away from the hope underlying Grimké's *Rachel* and its appeal to white audiences. While her work was aimed outward and designed to agitate for social change, her successors did not expect their scripts to convince whites that lynching was wrong. Instead, they worked to bolster blacks' self-conceptions. They wanted African Americans to recognize themselves in the scripts and to take pride in what they saw, even if it was laced with sorrow. If this happened, father or mother might finish reading *Crisis* and suggest that the family gather in the living room and pass the time with a dramatic reading of the play.

Still, the one-act dramatists' motivation for addressing mob violence in specifically family-centered ways, and in scripts that could be easily staged at home, is best exemplified by Ida B. Wells. Now known as the foremost antilynching crusader in American history, Wells admitted in an 1892 diary entry that, until her friends were killed, she thought that lynching might be justified. She confessed:

> Like many another person who had read of lynching in the South, *I had accepted the idea meant to be conveyed*—that although lynching was irregular and contrary to law and order, unreasoning anger over the terrible crime of rape led to the lynching; that perhaps the brute deserved to die anyhow and the mob was justified in taking his life.
> But [my friends] had been lynched . . . *with just as much brutality as other victims of the mob*; and they had committed no crime against white women. This is what opened my eyes to what lynching really was. An excuse to get rid of Negroes who were acquiring wealth and property and thus keep the race terrorized and "keep the nigger down" (qtd. in McMurry 143, emphasis added).

Clearly, if blacks accepted the portrayals offered by the mainstream stage and by those theatrical productions called lynchings, there would be no room for racial pride. If African Americans believed that mobs were responding to rape, they would have no sympathy for lynch victims. Because virtually all public discourse cast black men as brutes, an evil to be exorcised, creating a different portrait required intimate knowledge and intimate settings. Not surprisingly, then, black-authored lynching plays read like domestic plays. They foreground the home as much as they expose the injustice of lynching. More precisely, when the dramatists depicted black homes as they knew them to be, they inherently contradicted excuses for lynching—excuses that were invented to destroy those homes and deny black citizenship. Yet, as Wells's confession demonstrates, blacks needed actively to share with each other their intimate knowledge because, for many African Americans, only unshakable confidence that the death had been an egregious injustice would lead them to rally behind a fallen brother and his family. Lynching playwrights refused to be shamed into accepting the race's slaughter, and they targeted black audiences in order to equip them to do the same.

Lynching dramatists provided African Americans with an invaluable service by offering plays that encouraged the production of self-affirming knowledge through the embodied practices of communal literacy and amateur theater. Rehearsing together the discourses and practices that had created solid black homes fortified their self-images so that they would not be shaken by "the idea meant to be conveyed." They actively reminded each other that theirs was a community of fathers and sons, mothers and daughters, brothers and sisters, not isolated brutes and whores whose existence endangered society. Just as important, rehearsing the proper response to lynching—mourning—reinforced their feeling that lynch victims had belonged to communities and that those pained by their deaths do too. In other words, the plays suggest that African Americans are entitled to express their sadness and anger because they are rightful citizens of the communities that acknowledge them and of the nation that so often fails to do so.

Whether or not individual African Americans touched by these dramas would then participate in public activism, the playwrights wanted them to read aright the discourses and practices of their historical moment, to recognize that the violence was not justified but simply an attempt to suppress the community's truths. However, we know that blacks living during this violent time did in fact risk death to participate in political activism. It is clear, then, that they also engaged in practices privately that allowed them to remain convinced that they were moral and even admirable. Furthermore, they were citizens, despite the messages to the contrary that emanated from the nation's stages and its trees-turned-stages.

CHAPTER TWO

REDEFINING "BLACK THEATER"

The archive of black-authored lynching plays began with Angelina Weld Grimké's turn away from poetry and fiction to drama.[1] By 1914, Grimké was crafting and revising the play now known as *Rachel*. The historical moment in which Grimké labored over her first full-length drama was marked not only by the prevalence of lynching and its photographic representation, but also by debate over the definition of "black theater." On what basis could blacks claim to have created theater? African American performers such as Bert Williams and George Walker had found success on Broadway through musical comedy, and they soon employed all-black creative teams. Was what they were producing on the *Great White Way* of Broadway "black theater"? Or would claiming that black theater existed require that African American performers address African American audiences? If creating black theater required having black viewers, was it enough that they could appreciate the actors' craft from "Nigger Heaven" balcony seats, or did "black theater" require that African Americans have venues that accommodated them with a little more dignity? By the 1910s, all of these issues were under discussion, and African Americans increasingly believed that they could not claim that "black theater" existed unless it was based on the work of a black writer.

However, African Americans came to value black playwriting after 1910 only because of the triumphs secured by stage performers of the late nineteenth and early twentieth centuries. Black performers made space for themselves in minstrelsy and then in musical comedy, and later they invested in performing nonmusical, white-authored dramas on commercial stages in black neighborhoods. By entering each of these arenas, they asserted their citizenship by claiming the right to have access to theater and to represent themselves within it.

Because black performers commanded so much attention, their work fueled conversations in black communities that soon centered on the absence of—and need for—African American playwrights. Angelina Weld Grimké joined this conversation by writing a full-length drama of her own. Through *Rachel,* Grimké agreed with those who asserted that the black-authored, nonmusical script was the strongest foundation for black self-representation in theater. This chapter begins by tracing the stage history that helped inspire Grimké to become a playwright. Next, it offers a gloss of her inaugural text, noting the aesthetic choices that seem to have demanded response from other African American authors. Black writers who turned to drama in the wake of Grimké's theatrical debut offered literary revisions that continued the task of re-defining black theater. Yet, as much as Grimké's successors diverged from her strategies, their works confirmed some of her decisions about how to represent black life and the impact that mob violence has on it. The chapter therefore ends by identifying the features of Grimké's drama that became generic conventions as lynching plays were written in the 1910s and 1920s.

Pitting Playwrights against Performers

A writer-centered conception of black theater emerged after 1910 because decades of success among black performers had created the material conditions that fostered it. Though we often think of them as anything but politically savvy, black minstrels and musical comedians forged a path for playwrights by engaging the "politics of representation," defined as "the way meaning can be struggled over, and whether a particular regime of representation can be challenged, contested and transformed" (Hall, *Representation* 8). Because black theater practitioners struggled for "representational agency," they enabled others to do the same, but their legacy has been unjustly divorced from black drama history.[2] Scholars often seem to assume that minstrels and musical comedians only provided New Negro playwrights with examples of what *not* to do. Yet African Americans working on and behind the nineteenth-century stage preceded playwrights in the struggle to transform U.S. theater so that it did not automatically dehumanize blacks but instead would enable self-representation.

Historians often underestimate the efforts of this early black theater community because it produced virtually no playwrights, apparently accepting the idea that black self-representation in theater was not achieved until after the emergence of dramatists. The tendency to privilege dramatic writing within theater history can largely be attributed to the influence of W. E. B. Du Bois's famous declaration that true black theater must be "about us," "by us," "for us," and "near us." Scholars still treat Du Bois's criteria as timeless and universally applicable, but they arose out of a particular historical moment.

When Du Bois declared that black theater must be "about us," "by us," "for us," and "near us," theater about, by, for, and near African Americans already existed. His preferred theater would be new in that it would rest on nonmusical scripts by black playwrights; only this would make it "by us," in Du Bois's estimation. His statement implied that, although scores of black performers, directors, and composers enjoyed success, it was the emergence of the African American playwright that would finally allow black self-representation in theater. Du Bois's bias toward playwriting was appropriate for his historical moment, but without accounting for the context of his statement, scholars have too often used it as *the* standard against which all black theater efforts should be judged. Blithely applying Du Bois's ideal across space and time, many have overlooked the extent to which black minstrels, musical comedians, and Harlem actors like the Lafayette Players who performed Shakespeare, created "black theater" without having playwrights among them.

In the early twentieth century, Du Bois was not alone in stressing the need for black-authored dramas. Though his 1926 manifesto is the most often cited declaration of the importance of the African American playwright, it represents values that were forming in the 1910s—values articulated in editorials and speeches and with the drafting by 1914 of Grimké's three-act play. Du Bois, Grimké, and others could imagine theater based on black-authored dramas because minstrels, musical comedians, and actors like the Lafayette Players were so successful. Yet early performers did not merely create an audience that supported Du Bois's vision and the dramatists' work; this audience was the very same one *from which* Du Bois and the playwrights emerged as theater critics. That is, early performers drew African Americans to the theater and convinced them of its relevance to their communities. Activists like Du Bois and the soon-to-be playwrights therefore began to trust theater's capacity to enable black self-representation. In short, the playwrights' contributions and Du Bois' manifesto emerged *because* of earlier black performers, not in spite of them.

African Americans first gained access to the professional stage as minstrels in the 1850s. As cultural historian Eric Lott explains, blackface minstrelsy was "the first formal public acknowledgement by whites of black culture" (4). It did not take long for performers to transform disparaging acknowledgement into bill-paying opportunity.[3] Then, to gain an edge over the

white actors who had originated minstrelsy, black entertainers were mar-
keted as "true coons," suggesting that white actors were imposters. Their
successful marketing strategy came at a high price; they seemed like anything but actors. The nation believed that they were simply "being genuine
Negroes" who were not ashamed to "indulge in reality" (Toll 201). There
were moments, however, when black minstrels found ways to subvert their
prescribed roles. Once they gained popularity, they could sometimes deviate
from the material that had made the original white troupes successful. For
example, when presenting plantation scenes that required nostalgia for the
"good ole days" of slavery, black performers presented a special kind of
longing (Toll 245). Whereas white minstrels crooned about how kind master
had been, songs by blacks seldom mentioned master. They may have sung
about plantation dances, possums, and watermelon, but nothing was more
missed than the "loving presence" of "mudder, father, sister, or brudder"
(Toll 245). Even if minstrels found moments of power during their shows,
they also worked to break from the form altogether, because minstrelsy's
entertainment value rested in "oddities" and "peculiarities." The shows
were rigidly stylized, consisting of three parts, each filled with unrelated
scenes, so it was virtually impossible to make a sustained intervention in
how blacks were depicted.

In this climate, formal experimentation became a powerful weapon in
the fight for black self-representation. Black musical comedy emerged when
composer Will Marion Cook became determined to tell a story. Musicals
succeeded by containing songs that became sensations; they did not need
coherent storylines. Therefore, Cook's acclaim as a composer would have
resulted from simply arranging catchy tunes. Nevertheless, he wanted his
musicals to sustain a narrative, thereby creating a new form of entertainment
and black expression. Cook's *Clorindy, the Origin of the Cakewalk* (1898)
is considered the first black musical comedy, although the libretto was not
used because the venue that he secured had such poor acoustics. The next
year, with libretto intact, Cook offered *Jes Lak White Fo'ks*. Soon thereafter,
Cook joined forces with former minstrels Bert Williams and George Walker,
and the black musical became a form through which African Americans
seized more control over how they would represent the race, because it offered more developed storylines.

By the late 1890s, these comedians hired all-black creative teams and controlled the content of their shows to a degree that minstrelsy never allowed.
These professionals became models for what future generations of black
theater practitioners could achieve. Young artists could imagine themselves
writing and directing, not just singing and dancing. If minstrelsy had relied on

blacks being "natural" on stage as "real coons," these musicals foregrounded African American artistic talent because they were completely conceived, developed, and executed by blacks. Emphasizing plot more than "peculiarities," the comedy teams of Williams and Walker as well as Bob Cole and J. Rosamond Johnson supplied Broadway with a major black musical every year from 1898 to 1909. These comedians may have kept white audiences laughing, but they also kept blacks employed.

Though African American viewers sometimes criticized these shows, they often expressed pride that these teams reigned on Broadway. Race men like Du Bois and journalist Lester Walton proclaimed the comedians' brilliance in navigating the theater world. In fact, Du Bois said that "Cole and Johnson and Williams and Walker lifted minstrelsy by sheer force of genius into the beginning of a new drama" (*Crisis*, Aug. 1916). What he says generally should be appreciated more specifically. The honorable black manhood, romantic love, and familial responsibility that was increasingly spotlighted in musical comedies became the most significant themes in black-authored, nonmusical dramas, especially the earliest lynching plays.[4]

It is fortunate that musical comedians cultivated behind-the-scenes talent by employing all-black creative teams, because quite abruptly, mainstream audiences lost interest in black musical comedy, and major theaters denied African American artists employment in practically every other kind of show. As James Weldon Johnson explains in *Black Manhattan*, this was "the term of exile of the Negro from the downtown theatres of New York, which began in 1910 and lasted seven lean years" (170). Theater historians have attributed the exile to everything from industrialization to simple racism.[5] What is most important here, however, is that theaters blossomed in black communities during this time. Ultimately, musical comedies fostered creative confidence among aspiring theater practitioners, and their abrupt exclusion from mainstream opportunities forced them to seek other venues. When this quest led many of them to Harlem, more African Americans could enjoy theater entertainment than ever before.

Beginning in 1909, African Americans who had been touched by the success of black musical comedies energized commercial theaters that catered to black audiences in Harlem and other major cities. For example, theatrical producer Eddie Hunter, theater manager and drama critic Lester Walton, and acting troupe founder Anita Bush all worked to bring black audiences impressive entertainment. Operating on stage and behind the scenes, these trailblazers engaged the politics of representation by building black theater and insisting upon black self-representation. As a young man, Eddie Hunter saw a Williams and Walker musical and knew that he wanted a theater career (L. Mitchell 65). Hunter worked as a hotel elevator operator but always watched for theater opportunities. One day in 1909, he overheard business partners making plans to lease the newly built Crescent Theatre. Partly because Hunter offered to work without a salary, he became Crescent's primary producer from 1909 to 1912, followed by a stint at the newly built Lafayette Theatre from 1912 to 1914.

Hunter's influence at the Lafayette faded when it was sold in 1914, but this house was nonetheless the first Harlem theater to have black management because the new owner chose Lester Walton as his co-manager. Walton was drama critic for the African American newspaper *The New York Age,* but his passion for theater had grown during the musical comedy heyday (L. Mitchell 68). Thus, though he later worked to expose black audiences to drama, musicals helped sustain Walton's investment in stage performance. Walton did not use his authority as co-manager of the Lafayette to offer content that was substantially different from the comedies and musicals that Hunter had provided as producer, but behind the scenes, he was shaping a much different show business reality. He was proud that, during his short term as manager, his performers received "more money than paid in a similar length of time by any other colored theater in America" (*Age,* Feb. 10, 1916). He was also proud that all of the theater's "house help" was black and well paid.

Artistically, Walton used the success of the musical comedy *Darkydom* to underwrite what he felt was most important: drama. Only months after the musical's premiere, he recruited a newly formed troupe led by Anita Bush (Riis 182, 166). He hoped that the group would become a permanent fixture, but he knew that audiences would make that decision. He understood the business well, saying, "Many a play fails, not because it is bad from an artistic standpoint, but due to the failure of the theatregoers to appreciate it" (*Age,* Mar. 25, 1909). Ultimately, "The public has in its hands the fate of all productions. It makes a playwright, a play, an actor, a manager" (*Age,* Mar. 25, 1909). As a manager who recognized the audience's power, Walton influenced public opinion by promoting the acting troupe in the pages of the *New York Age.*[6] He used periodical culture to fuel theater efforts—a natural strategy. After all, periodicals relied on both the written word and the embodied practices of discussion and debate. As Dorothy Chansky has observed about little theater among whites, the early 1900s may have seen the increasing availability and influence of film and other performance media, but there was no diminishing the "politics constructed from books, magazines, and the talk that surrounded them" (22).[7] The power of periodicals was never limited to the printed word.

In his newspaper promotion of Bush's troupe, Walton invested in yet another person whose involvement with musical comedy led to dramatic endeavors. Formerly a member of the Williams and Walker chorus, Anita Bush founded an acting ensemble that made its debut at Harlem's Lincoln Theatre in November 1915. A few weeks later, the troupe moved to the nearby Lafayette, where it enjoyed years of success as the Lafayette Players. Thanks to their stellar reputation, by 1916 the Lafayette Players helped to establish companies in Chicago, Washington, D.C., and Baltimore, and they organized an ensemble known as the Dunbar Players in Philadelphia (Thompson 22; Hatch and Hill 204).

Because Bush formed troupes primarily to give black actors professional stage experience, she did not seek "race drama." With "purely artistic" goals in mind, the actors valued the opportunity to hone their skills much more than the scripts' subject matter. The teams generally performed white-authored plays that were already popular on Broadway, and they often utilized discarded sets and costumes. This strategy kept the main company active from 1916 to 1932, even when Bush was no longer directly associated with it (Thompson 23–24).[8] Bush's troupe would eventually perform more than 250 plays, the most famous of which were *The Octoroon, Madame X, The Count of Monte Cristo,* and *Dr. Jekyll and Mr. Hyde* (Hatch and Hill 204). In *Dr. Jekyll and Mr. Hyde,* the lead actor performed in white-face, suggesting that black actors should not be limited to portraying black characters. Above all, these actors craved dramatic range so that they could perfect their craft. Though many African Americans had developed behind-the-scenes skills, actors were still expected to master only comedy.

Therefore, to Bush's troupe, real "black theater" would encourage a range of theatrical expression from its actors. As former Lafayette Player Clarence Muse remembers: "Our aim was to give vent to our talent and to prove to everybody who was willing to look, to watch, to listen, that we were as good *at drama* as anybody else had been or could be" (qtd. in Thompson 18, emphasis added). Much more than "copy cats," as black theater historian and playwright Loften Mitchell dubs them, these actors expressed African American identity and citizenship by being resourceful and undaunted by their exclusion from Broadway. To use Daphne Brooks's apt phrase, they owned their aesthetic desires,[9] refusing to accept the notion that African American identity was somehow at odds with their love for the most recognized texts of Western drama.

As it showcased Bush's acting troupe, the Lafayette Theatre, which flourished in Harlem in the 1910s, created "black theater" by putting no limit on black talent and by welcoming black audiences. According to James Weldon

Johnson, such houses constituted "a real Negro theatre, something New York had never had before; that is, a theatre in which Negro performers played to audiences made up almost wholly of people of their own race" (170). It is significant that Johnson defines "a real Negro theatre" rather than assume that the term's meaning is clear. As he writes about the 1910s, his definition of black theater emphasizes the black audience, for although black performers had long been successful, black audiences could not enjoy their work without the shame associated with segregated seating. So communities placed importance on having spaces that catered to black audiences. Thus, even if the Harlem troupes brought white-authored plays to life, they were creating black theater because they were black professionals providing quality performances for black theatergoers. Although detractors always existed, African Americans were generally proud to see these actors reach another level of success. When Bush first founded her nonmusical drama troupe, a headline in the African American-run *New York Amsterdam News* read, "New York at Last to Come into Its Own Legitimate Drama" (qtd. in Riis 166).

It was understood that these actors were claiming a wider range of expression for themselves and their communities. By associating black identity with serious acting, they insisted that whiteness was not a prerequisite for dramatic talent. Troupes like the Lafayette Players used the stage to, as Stuart Hall might say, show that the dominant "regime of representation" could indeed be "challenged, contested and transformed" (Hall 8). Not simply bent on assimilating, troupes like Bush's engaged the politics of representation in ways that turned racist ideas, which they could not escape, into resources as they decided how to represent African American identity and assert their citizenship. Knowing that blacks were assumed to be comedians with no real talent or range, the thespians insisted on defining themselves. According to historian Allen Woll, when blacks created theater away from Broadway, "they shed all vestiges of caricature and engaged material that white audiences would not have accepted from them" (54).

These practitioners developed their criteria for "black theater" in ways that addressed the material conditions of their time. Defining black identity—and the theater that best represented it—meant shedding the limitations that skin color was supposed to represent. Hunter's productions, Walton's management, and Bush's acting troupe all illustrated African Americans' commitment to making theater's popularity work for their communities. The venues that they occupied were owned by whites, but Hunter, Walton, and Bush helped ensure that blacks would benefit. These spaces provided professional entertainment in an environment that welcomed African American audiences, and they gave black actors professional experience.[10]

In many ways, however, Harlem success marked the beginning of the end of an era. These professionals cultivated a taste for nonmusical drama within black communities, but the audience that was attracted to the theater by groups like Bush's soon became dissatisfied with what black actors offered them. This growing theatergoing audience began objecting to black renditions of Shakespeare and Broadway hits. Though many factors contributed to the eventual decline of the Lafayette Players' popularity, historian M. F. Thompson acknowledges the role that black criticism played: "Progressive critics who wished Black theatre ventures to succeed complained that, although theatres . . . operated by Blacks and for Blacks existed in New York, Chicago, New Orleans, Jackson, Memphis . . . [and] Atlanta . . ., all of these theatres seemed devoted to imitating the White man's stage and the White man's acting, instead of developing a drama uniquely and distinctly Black" (30).[11] In short, " . . . the time came when the imitation could no longer satisfy Blacks who began more insistently to clamor for a drama of their own" (Thompson 30).

Black critics' abrupt call for a *drama* of their own was exactly that—a call for written texts. Blacks had created a *theater* of their own, so critics demanded what it lacked: African American playwrights. Because the Shakespeare- and Broadway-performing actors had perfected their craft and demonstrated their talent for nonmusical material, theater based on black dramatists' efforts suddenly seemed feasible.

African American theatergoers, like the vocal W. E. B. Du Bois, became invested enough in theater to begin demanding changes. Above all, these early critics wanted to see black-authored plays staged. As one newspaper columnist put it in 1917:

> The theatre-going public desires to see at least occasionally, the work of some Negro playwrights . . . Daily this desire is becoming more intense. And as advice to every Negro in Harlem, I say—demand, kick, agitate until we get the work of our playwrights produced in the Lafayette Theatre; do not cease, for we must see our society reflected upon the American stage even if we have to call a mass meeting of Harlem's theatre-goers and effect a boycott on the Lafayette Theatre. (*Messenger* drama critic Lovett Fort-Whiteman, qtd. in Hatch and Hill 205).

Though aware of the criticism that their performances ignored black culture, Bush's goal had always been "to perform legitimate drama solely for the sake of performing and to prove the capabilities of black performers . . ."[12] (Thompson 30). Seeking black-authored scripts was not a priority for Bush,[13] leading her biographer M. F. Thompson to conclude: "If there occurred a surge toward Black consciousness during this period, the Lafayette Players, as a group, were not a part of it" (30).

I would suggest, however, that their refusal to pursue black-authored material did not mean that the Lafayette Players were not part of a movement toward black consciousness; it is just that this particular surge of energy revolved around writing and *took performance for granted.* Performers had created theater "for" and "near" African Americans and sometimes offered plays "about" them, but audiences now felt that theater of their own must be built on nonmusical scripts written "by" blacks. These new critics inadvertently discounted black actors, not realizing that they would not have been able to envision theater built on the work of black dramatists without the accomplishments of their singing, dancing, and acting predecessors. Black writers could envision a place for themselves in theater, and critics could call on them to fill it because they had already witnessed minstrelsy, musical comedy, and black actors who performed white-authored scripts.

By the 1910s, the "clamor for a drama of their own" emerged in theater reviews as well as magazine and newspaper articles, and it manifested as black-authored plays from writers such as Grimké—who became the change that they wanted to see. These new stakeholders were defining "black theater" as that which is based on the work of an African American author and not dominated by music. As cultural artifacts that offer access to both the archive and the repertoire of the early 1900s, the critics' plays, newspaper columns, and essays bear the mark of the historical moment that produced them. For instance, Grimké's *Rachel* not only negotiated a reality that included lynching and the white supremacist discourses that condoned it, but it also addressed a stage culture that seemed to celebrate black performance while being indifferent to black authorship. Willis Richardson, one of Grimké's playwriting successors, similarly noted these conditions and hoped to recruit new playwrights from other genres. Black theater could be built, he insisted, "if some of our numerous poets will consent to rest from their usual labors for a while and lend a hand towards the writing of Negro plays" (Richardson, "Hope" 437). Alain Locke's assessment of the situation led him to insist that, though the accomplishments of actors fade, training playwrights will create "a granary of art, stocked and stored for season after season" (Locke, "Steps" 440). Both Du Bois's 1926 call for plays about, by, for, and near African Americans, and its precursors from critics such as Grimké, Richardson, and Locke, owed a debt to black performers whose talent called attention to the lack of black-authored dramas.

Yet this new vision of black theater, of which lynching drama was an early manifestation, did not fully accommodate the performers who had made it possible. The drama that early critics demanded was not conducive to commercial theater and would therefore not allow theater professionals to make a living from their craft. Philosophers had to all but ignore commercial viability as they promoted black-authored scripts that contained no rousing musical interludes. In fact, Du Bois and Locke emphasized the writer's role precisely because they wanted black theater to be less vulnerable to the vicissitudes of the market. They did not want it to fade whenever large audiences lost interest. The "exile" from Broadway had already proved that public tastes would not always favor African American productions. Thus, Locke believed that permanent black theater must spring from the efforts of amateurs. In "Steps toward the Negro Theatre," Locke described the progress made at Howard University in Washington, D.C., and posited an academic model as the most viable. He said, "a university foundation will assure a greater continuity of effort and insure accordingly a greater permanence of result" (Locke, "Steps" 441). Du Bois also focused on amateur productions, but he worked to build a community-based theater movement that could flourish without ties to academic institutions.

The actor was of secondary importance to this new black theater, and within it he would not earn enough to sustain himself. Not surprisingly, then, when Broadway ended the exile in 1917 with Ridgeley Torrence's *Three Plays for a Negro Theatre*,[14] performers were easily wooed away from black community stages. Consequently, black theater's fate fell into writers' hands, and as new dramatists developed their skills, many of them chose to write lynching plays.

Rachel and Revision

Grimké's first dramatic effort, *Rachel*, was inspired by a new writer-centered conception of black theater, and as other African American poets and fiction writers embraced drama after Grimké's theatrical debut, their work continued the process of redefining "black theater." Whether impressed or disappointed with Grimké's work, a number of black writers suddenly turned to drama, driven to develop conventions, cultivate themes, and perfect the craft. Grimké's debut therefore played an important role in the process of identity formation that Stuart Hall describes when he insists that "identities are about questions of using the resources of history, language and culture in the process of becoming rather than being: not 'who we are' [. . .] so much as what we might become, how we have been represented and how that bears on how we might represent ourselves" (Hall, *Representation* 4).

On the one hand, Grimké responded to how performers had represented the race; on the other hand, her successors responded to her manner of engaging the politics of representation. All of these efforts helped to define and redefine "black theater."

When Grimké embraced drama, she chose to represent African American life through its connection to mob violence. For her, black self-representation in theater required grappling with the degree to which African Americans were forced to live with lynching. Grimké apparently believed that she could achieve—through writing—what theater practitioners had not in performance: even while racism shaped their lives, musical comedians provided audiences with laughter. While committed to very different content, Grimké sought to approximate black performers' success in terms of claiming a broad audience that included whites. She therefore tailored her work to cross the color line and reach whites with more serious images of African Americans. In part, she aimed to serve her community by addressing whites on its behalf.

Mob violence was a result of how African Americans could be depicted, so Grimké insisted on the injustice of lynching by showcasing well-to-do blacks who might remind whites of themselves. Lynching photography presented victims as isolated brutes who had human bodies but presumably no soul and psyche; Grimké highlighted precisely those aspects of black life and lynching's impact on it. Her drama also depicts lynching survivors in ways that acknowledge that their identities are shaped by mob violence. As Cathy Caruth would assert, Grimké's *Rachel* registers trauma as an identity-shaping phenomenon. Grimké demonstrates that, in permitting lynching, the nation forces upon African Americans both a crisis of death and a crisis of life. Further, she insists on the right to create a text that stands as evidence of the race's unjust predicament.

In *Rachel*, living with lynching requires each African American to negotiate an identity that "is bound up with, or founded in, the death that he [or she] survives" (Caruth 92). The play introduces the audience to eighteen-year-old Rachel Loving, her mother Mrs. Loving, and her younger brother Tom; the father has been dead for ten years. Though the family members love and support each other, their Northern home lacks peace; a disturbing energy is ever present. As the tenth anniversary of her husband's death approaches, Mrs. Loving must face the fact that her silence about lynching has not diminished its impact on her family, so she finally tells her teenaged children what happened to their father in the South.

When Rachel's mother shares her experience, she not only highlights the injustice of the incident by establishing her husband's impeccable character, but she also shows that before dying of lynching, he had lived with it. The mob targeted the father because he had written an editorial denouncing racial violence. He had exposed the fact that a group of "respectable people in the town" had lynched a black man, despite knowing that "a white man was guilty." He was told to retract his words, but the next issue of his newspaper contained an even more searing indictment, and "some dozen masked men came to our house" (40). Mrs. Loving recalls that she and her husband had been in bed when whites "broke down the front door and made their way to our bedroom" (41). When the mob had begun dragging her husband down the hall, her seventeen-year-old son George tried to intervene; "It ended in [the mob] dragging them both out" (41). As his name suggests, Mr. Loving had epitomized love, and his editorial actions confirmed his love for truth and justice. Rachel's mother continues, "Your father was a man among men. He was a fanatic. He was a saint!" (40). Nevertheless, he was killed "by Christian people—in a Christian land. We found out afterwards they were all church members in good standing . . ." (40). Thus, the Loving father is presented as a Christ figure: he is killed by devout congregants who are also lesser men.

The drama highlights the contradiction between whites' actions and their professed Christianity, hoping to inspire sympathy for blacks who suffer because of the nation's hypocrisy. Ten years after Mr. Loving's death, the injustice hovers over the new home that his family was forced to establish in the North, and it continues to challenge the faith of those who avoided the mob's physical attack. Though a religious woman, Mrs. Loving confesses to a lapse in her faith. She explains to her surviving children that when her son and husband had been dragged from the house, "I knelt down by you—and covered my ears with my hands—and waited. I could not pray—I couldn't for a long time—afterwards" (41). No doubt, the incident led Mrs. Loving to question the value of Christian faith because her husband had been so devout. At the same time, by sharing her story, Mrs. Loving preserves truths denied by mainstream society about her husband, the quality of his life, and the tragedy of his death. After all, the scenario of exorcism that empowered the mob sought to erase the extent to which he was targeted for asserting his rights and righteousness. While the town was encouraged to believe that it was free of a black "troublemaker," Mrs. Loving's testimony ensures (albeit belatedly) that a different perspective is recorded. Still, upon hearing her mother's story, Rachel questions the wisdom of investing in marriage and motherhood and doubts God's willingness to protect blacks who do. As a result, though she cares for her suitor, Mr. Strong—and he has already prepared a house for them—she rejects his proposal. She cannot bear the thought of bringing children into a racist society (77).

Grimké's drama aims to show her audience the generational consequences of the nation's hypocrisy by demonstrating not only that Mrs. Loving has lived with a grave injustice but also that learning about her mother's plight leads Rachel to lose faith in marriage, motherhood, and God. Early in the action, Rachel is told in a dream that she is to become a mother (34). The news delights her because she loves children and wonders what could be wrong in the world as long as they are in it (34). However, after realizing that all black males are potential lynch victims, Rachel reasons: "Why—it would be more merciful—to strangle the little things at birth" (42). Later, she agonizes, "And so this nation—this white Christian nation—has deliberately set its curse upon the most beautiful—the most holy thing in life—motherhood!" (42). As the action progresses, Rachel is haunted by the sound of children begging not to be born,[15] and she promises the children that she will not bring them into the world. Feeling forced to abandon her dreams of motherhood, Rachel becomes convinced that she hears God laughing at her pain. As her sanity deteriorates, her anger escalates and she tries to out-laugh God, viewing Him as an enemy (76).

In tracing this spiritual and psychological decline, Grimké's work suggests that mobs did lasting damage to the race's soul and psyche by targeting its homes. When the head of the Loving household is murdered, his wife and surviving children are forced to start over; then his wrongful death haunts their new home in the North, continuing to weaken the already diminished family; finally, it prevents Rachel from creating another home with Mr. Strong. Thus, the black male absence inflicted by the mob does not simply destroy an existing household; it prevents the creation of new ones.

Because Grimké offers this perspective on lynching and its consequences in a drama designed to reach an integrated audience, she represents black experience in hopes of shaping the beliefs and behaviors of whites. Grimké made several aesthetic choices that would increase the chances of drawing a broad audience. The play's adherence to mainstream expectations of dramatic structure, including the fact that it is a full-length play, made it conducive to formal staging. Grimké's text also bears the influence of an Aristotelian conception of dramatic form in that it foregrounds cause-and-effect patterns and emphasizes plot.[16] Also, aiming to make her work resonate with white audiences, Grimké used sentimentality, foregrounded Victorian-influenced courtship rituals and manners, and emphasized familiarity with European culture. Indeed, emphasis is placed on her characters' education and appreciation for European art partly in order to argue that lynching was unjust because it devastated blacks who might remind whites of themselves.

Even the four years separating acts 1 and 2 enhanced Grimké's ability to touch white audience members. Because it depicts Rachel at age eighteen and then at twenty-two, the drama unfolds in ways that resemble a sentimental bildungsroman. For Rachel, coming of age means deteriorating, because a sensitive soul cannot bear the cruelties that U.S. society reserves for African Americans. Tracing Rachel's development as she encounters racial injustices enabled Grimké to explain Rachel's psychological and spiritual decline. Audience members who had not experienced racism firsthand required more "proof" of its power, and Grimké structured her text to bear that burden. Partly because of these aesthetic choices, *Rachel* premiered in March 1916 at the Myrtilla Miner School in Washington, D.C., and received productions in 1917 at New York City's Neighborhood Playhouse and at Brattle Hall in Cambridge, Massachusetts (Hull 119; Hatch and Hill 220).

Because Grimké's aesthetic choices made her work conducive to formal theatrical production, it commanded attention, so it is significant that her successors made decisions that rendered their scripts less suitable for formal staging. Partly because Grimké's work generated substantial interest, her script inspired other black authors to write drama, but as they did so, their aesthetic choices fueled the process of redefining black theater. While Grimké served her community by representing it to an integrated audience, her successors chose to focus on addressing African Americans themselves, not defending them so much as affirming them. Those who followed Grimké by writing lynching plays chose to pen one-acts that lent themselves to periodical publication. The plays' appearance in magazines provided impetus for conversation within families and communities rather than professional or semi-professional production. As periodicals brought these scripts into black churches, community centers, and homes, the practices of what Elizabeth McHenry calls *communal literacy* would have determined their use. As discussed in chapter 1, such traditions encouraged reading aloud, memorization, and dramatic readings. Thus, when engaging a one-act play, one person may have read all of the characters' parts to the rest of the family, or roles may have been assigned. Sometimes, perhaps only a line or two would have been read aloud before a family member interrupted to begin a discussion or to tell a personal story about mob violence. The possibilities are endless, but in each instance, the text becomes a part of a multifaceted conversation in that intimate space.

In writing one-acts that were conducive to periodical publication, authors opened their work to the practices of communal literacy, enabling black readers to engage the material as they pleased—at their own pace, in their own space, and without regard for what whites deemed theatrical or dramatic. It is thus significant that, of the nine lynching one-acts that followed the 1916 production of *Rachel,* six gained an audience through periodicals. *Crisis* magazine published *Mine Eyes Have Seen* (1918) and *For Unborn Children* (1926). Mary Burrill's *Aftermath* (1919) appeared in *The Liberator,* G. D. Lipscomb's *Frances* (1925) was published in *Opportunity,* and Joseph Mitchell's *Son-Boy* (1928) ran in *The Saturday Evening Quill,* an African American magazine based in Boston. Georgia Douglas Johnson was the most prolific lynching playwright, but her lynching plays were generally not published until the 1980s and 1990s. Still, *Blue Blood* was announced in the May 1926 issue of *Opportunity* because it had earned honorable mention in the magazine's playwriting contest.[17] Perhaps more important, as I discuss in chapter 5, Douglas Johnson hosted a literary salon in her home in Washington, D.C., which was attended by a number of the other lynching playwrights as well as Du Bois and Locke. Therefore, her unpublished scripts were likely a record of and inspiration for the conversations and dramatic readings the literary salon encouraged. In other words, lynching drama developed through periodical culture and through the conversations and debates that this culture sustained in literary salons, churches, barbershops, and beauty parlors.[18]

Ultimately, Grimké hoped to effect change by targeting whites and convincing them that lynching was wrong, and when her successors abandoned her full-length, two-hour dramatic structure, they also discarded this strategy and chose a more community-centered one. Rather than represent the race in ways that they thought could influence whites, one-act lynching dramatists targeted African Americans themselves. By doing so, they acted on the belief that blacks mattered enough to be directly addressed; they certified black belonging through the inclusion implied by direct address that was affirming rather than denigrating.[19]

To understand the difference between Grimké's strategy and that of the one-act playwrights who followed, consider Grimké's rationale for her dramatic work. Writing in 1920, Grimké had clearly received enough criticism in the years following *Rachel's* 1916 debut to assert: "Since it has been understood that 'Rachel' preaches race suicide, I would emphasize that that was not my intention. To the contrary, the appeal was not primarily to the colored people, but to the whites" ("Reason" 424). She continued, "The majority of women, everywhere, although they are beginning to awaken, form one of the most conservative elements of society. They are, therefore, opposed to change. For this reason and for sex reasons the white women of this country are about the worst enemies with which the colored race has to contend" (425). Hoping to convert these "enemies," Grimké used the pain that motherhood brings to Mrs. Loving and Rachel to make white women "see, feel, understand just what effect their prejudice and the prejudice of their fathers, brothers, husbands, sons" has on the "souls of the colored mothers everywhere" (425).

Because she strove to convince whites that blacks deserved their sympathy, Grimké did not focus her energies on depicting black life *for* African American audiences, and this helps explain why other lynching playwrights were eager to reject her tactics and her three-act format. In establishing for whites that blacks were decent people, Grimké countered the assumptions underwriting the scenario of exorcism. In contrast, because her successors used the one-act format, deemed (by Du Bois, for example) to be more suitable for engaging black audiences, they moved away from arguing for black humanity and civilization—in fact, they took it as a given—and instead pondered the contours of black identity and citizenship. This was a complex task, given the extent to which national discourses and practices ignored African Americans' status as U.S. citizens—by denying their link not only to the nation but also to their own families and communities. Aware that mainstream rhetoric worked—through words and practices—to erase evidence that blacks belonged, writers of one-acts acknowledged black belonging by addressing African Americans. While Grimké reasoned that whites must be addressed because they perpetrated the violence, her successors considered the impact that their scripts could have on blacks themselves—especially because those scripts reached blacks in the same intimate spaces invaded by newspaper photographs of the mob's theatrical productions.

Dramatic Self-Representation: Lynching Drama's Most Prominent Conventions

Even while speaking "primarily to the whites," Grimké's inaugural drama conveyed a crucial message to African Americans. *Rachel* insists upon the need to speak with pride about fallen community members. Early in act 1, Rachel says that she feels sorry for mothers whose children grow up to be bad. Her mother, Mrs. Loving, asks, "How do you happen to know all this? Mothers whose babies grow up to be bad don't, as a rule, parade their faults before the world" (33). Rachel responds, "That's just it—that's how you know. They don't talk at all" (33). Though Rachel and her brother Tom are nearly adults, neither knows how their father and brother died, but they have noticed their mother's refusal to discuss the past. Mrs. Loving asks, "Did you think—that—perhaps—the reason—I—I—wouldn't talk about them—was—because, because—I was ashamed—of them?" (39). Rachel and

Tom fumble for answers, and Mrs. Loving erupts, "You evade—both—of you. You have been ashamed. And I never dreamed until today you could take it this way. How blind—how almost criminally blind, I have been" (40). If she wants to help her children live with lynching—for they have not escaped it despite her silence—then she must contribute to community efforts to preserve black testimony, just as her husband had through his newspaper.

Like Mrs. Loving, Grimké the author realized that she must tell her people's story, and she must do so in drama. Black writers living at the turn of the century could not be content to use fiction, essays, or poetry; the historical moment demanded a dramatic response. While the community had produced impressive theater practitioners, there was room for more complex representations of African American men, women, and children. Black-authored dramas would constitute an archive that more faithfully reflected the repertoire of embodied practices that matched African Americans' self-conceptions. At a time when the U.S. stage preferred its black men to be buffoons or rapists, silence from black playwrights would be tantamount to their expressing shame and accepting the dominant discourse about the race.

The exchange between Mrs. Loving and her children about embarrassed silence sheds light on not only why Grimké wrote *Rachel* but also, I would argue, why the play inspired other African Americans to become dramatists. Even while offering revisions, Grimké's successors crafted their scripts in ways that suggest how much they agreed with some of her ideas about the nature of black life and lynching's effect on it. The one-acts that complete the genre's foundation[20] repeat the three most striking features of Grimké's drama: 1) physical violence is eschewed because action is set in the black home; 2) definitions of manhood are conspicuously interrogated; and 3) the family's fertile generation is removed or neutralized through *de-generation*, or generation removal and prevention.

These conventions make accessible a theory of black identity formation and citizenship, and it is crucial to interpret their recurrence as a community-centered theoretical statement, especially because Grimké's successors wrote one-acts that targeted black audiences. As Diana Taylor insists, "every performance enacts a theory, and every theory performs" (27). The idea that blacks were not citizens was publicly enacted though the mob's theatrical productions. Meanwhile, when lynching plays were written and performed (whether formally or informally), African Americans enacted their own conceptions of black identity and citizenship. This unique genre would not have survived in the archive if the plays had not served a purpose for turn-of-the-century communities. Because they appeared in periodicals and were part of literary salon conversations, black authors and readers used them to assert their right to represent themselves and their experiences. In this and so many other ways, African Americans certified for each other that they were a race of upstanding individuals unjustly excluded from the rights and privileges of U.S. citizenship.

Here, I examine lynching drama's three major conventions and find that, through them, the plays helped communities as they struggled to safeguard black identity formation so that it continued to include a conception of themselves as citizens. The genre's patterns suggest that African Americans believed their identities to be characterized by virtuous womanhood, honorable manhood, and innocent childhood. In fact, as lynching plays were written in the wake of Grimké's *Rachel,* the genre developed to insist that African American identity is partly shaped by the ability to live through attacks on black womanhood, manhood, and childhood—an unjust situation to be sure, but one that factored into identity formation for those who survived. The conventions also register the trauma to which black communities are subjected and encourage African Americans to affirm for each other that their citizenship (within the community and the nation) gives them license to mourn their losses.

Black Homes[21] and Virtuous Womanhood

By situating their dramas in the black home, lynching playwrights prioritized their own knowledge of black life—undeterred by mainstream images. Rather than depict mob violence in terms of physical brutality, the scripts capture the community's understanding of the spiritual, financial, and psychological damage done. Also, while mainstream discourses and practices emerged from and supported the theory that African Americans did not desire domestic stability, lynching plays demonstrated that successful black households not only existed but also that they were the ones most frequently targeted by mobs. The new genre depicted black bodies inside these intimate spaces, engaged in activities that connoted African Americans' morality and normalcy. Characters sew and cook but they also converse, show affection, and debate the topics of the day. As the form of the lynching play bore witness to community perspectives rejected by mainstream society, it needed a forum that would welcome those insights and found it in the amateur stage—including black homes. Only there, it seemed, was it acceptable to showcase black men, women, and children as the upstanding citizens that the playwrights knew them to be.[22] Only there could they showcase what motivated the mob to respond so violently.

Working from the premise that black identity was marked by virtuous womanhood, the playwrights entered a long tradition of establishing women's virtue with the portrayal of domestic interiors. White writers of nineteenth-century sentimental fiction, black women novelists of the 1890s, and lynching playwrights of the early twentieth century all take their audiences into the homes of women who strive for the highest standards of sexual conduct and domestic order. These literary strategies point to the enduring influence of the cult of true womanhood, and they illuminate the degree to which the domestic was connected to the political, despite the tendency of histories of the period to separate public and private spheres.[23] The ideology of "true womanhood" maintained that women served the nation by staying at home and embodying domesticity, submissiveness, purity, and piety. A true woman created "a cheerful place" that attracted the male members of her family and allowed her to lead them "back to God" (Welter 162). As a result, men would make better choices both within and outside of the home.

Lynching playwrights of the 1910s and 1920s were committed to depicting black domestic role models, but many of them felt free (and perhaps obligated) to create heroines who differed from those typically found in domestic novels, such as *Iola Leroy* and *Contending Forces,* who had white skin and spoke perfect standard English. Because they valued club work, the dramatists spotlighted poor blacks who were not genteel but who were domestically successful. They did not seek to replace elite blacks as role models, for they considered themselves to be teachers of the race,[24] yet they recognized that other women could be examples as well. Especially in the one-act plays, many of the families are poor and uneducated, but their households are filled with love and function as smoothly as middle-class clubwomen's homes presumably did.

Depicting uneducated black women as successful homebuilders constituted a bold statement about black female virtue; as Daphne Brooks might point out, lynching dramatists worked to "rehistoricize [black women's] flesh" (335). After all, anything that suggested proximity to slavery, including lack of education, was often interpreted as moral degradation, so dramatists challenged traditional representational politics by creating uneducated black women who were also moral. White slave owners had insisted on the impossibility of raping black women whom they asserted were promiscuous by nature. In the postbellum era, African American activists often asserted that part of slavery's legacy was that many black women had indeed been degraded and were no longer capable of distinguishing right from wrong in sexual matters. Even those providing aid to black women in the early 1900s established their services based on black women's unquestioned moral corruption. For example, one group of philanthropists argued sympathetically, "The negro women of the South are subject to temptations . . . which come to them from the days of their enslavement. . . . To meet such temptations the negro woman can only offer the resistance of a low moral standard, an inheritance from the system of slavery, made still lower from a lifelong residence in a one-room cabin" (Slater Fund qtd. in Flexner 191).

Understanding the assumptions of their historical moment, the authors of *Iola Leroy* and *Contending Forces* may expose their heroines' slave pasts, but they give these women white skin and perfect command of standard English to establish the injustice of their circumstances. These writers did not trust that the wrongs suffered would be legible if the character were phenotypically black and spoke dialect. In contrast, Georgia Douglas Johnson's *Blue Blood* (1926)—to take one example—depicts a dialect-speaking black woman who has been sexually exploited by a white man but who understands that black women must remain silent about their rapes in order to keep black men from being lynched for trying to protect their honor. Johnson's work spotlights white immorality by giving voice to black women, and it exposes the fact that lynching enables white men to continue dehumanizing practices perfected in slavery. The nation's rhetoric works to erase the truths that Johnson dramatizes, so the many blacks who have achieved domestic stability have often done so despite the worst odds. As Johnson uses drama to engage the politics of representation, she insists that black womanhood continues to be shaped by the need to navigate vulnerability to both physical and representational violence.

Writing in the early 1900s, lynching playwrights depicted black women who had achieved what exemplars of feminine virtue should—even as mainstream society denied their existence. The declaration that helped nationalize the black women's club movement was far from forgotten: "I cannot imagine such a creature as a virtuous Negro woman,"[25] and the plays added to articulations from black communities that this statement was far from valid. Even while inhabiting modest homes, the women in one-act lynching plays answer the high call, as described by black women activists such as Anna Julia Cooper: "Woman, Mother—your responsibility is one that might make angels tremble and fear to take hold! . . . The training of children is a task on which an infinity of weal or woe depends" (22). For even if a man exhibits compassion and a distaste for corruption, "that man has imbibed those impulses from a mother" (Cooper 60). Not only do these uneducated heroines create bastions of moral direction for their children; their homes are also "cheerful places" that black men do not want to leave. Clearly, Mr. and Mrs. Loving shared such a home before his death in *Rachel*. Likewise, the young couple expecting their first child in *Safe* enjoys being at home. Also, *Mine Eyes Have Seen* showcases this sort of atmosphere to the extent that characters reminisce about the household that was destroyed in the South. In other cases, mothers miss their husbands but make the best life possible for their children who remain with them, as in *A Sunday Morning in the South*.

Often, as soon as the drama establishes the family's tranquility, the mob invades. As a result, these works suggest that blacks achieve ideal domesticity but cannot maintain it as long as lynching remains a threat. As the home's destruction is depicted, so is the injustice of its demise because the intimate setting attests to the admirable qualities of all who inhabit it. Lynching dramatists thus honored the accomplishments of black women homebuilders by insisting that they had, against all odds, established havens filled with love, honorable men, and happy children.

Tragically, but just as important, these dramas acknowledge black women's unique insights into mob violence. In these plays, women characters remain in the home before the lynching, during the lynching, and they survive—only to suffer there—after the lynching. Perhaps better than anyone else, they know that the mob may mutilate an individual on a tree, telephone pole, or bridge, but the household continues to be "lynched" long after the body has disappeared.

Black Manhood

In foregrounding the black home, lynching playwrights placed a spotlight on responsible manhood as well. By consistently doing so, the genre puts forth a theory that black manhood is characterized by honor and dignity, but the genre also exposes the consequences of embodying those ideals in a racist society geared toward obliterating black examples of the strength and integrity that are admired in white men. As artifacts of this contradictory historical moment, the plays bear evidence that merely representing dignified black manhood in writing posed unique challenges, requiring the playwrights to engage the repertoire. The authors had to grapple with the same complexities that black men encountered, beginning in slavery, as they navigated the country's treacherous political and cultural terrain.

In order to create literary representations of black men as they knew them to be, the dramatists worked with an awareness that the archive and repertoire constantly interact. Lynching dramatists could not simply portray black family men and trust that these characters would be interpreted as honorable—even by black readers and viewers. They needed to detail the struggles that these men faced and represent the community conversation that critically assessed those obstacles. The plays recorded and encouraged dynamic discussion and embodied practices, so they helped African

Americans to filter mainstream rhetoric, which cast blacks as dangerous and unworthy of civic inclusion. Accordingly, the scripts both served and documented the information-processing function that made black belonging legible and made black citizenship and positive identity formation possible.

The mob's preoccupation with denigrating black manhood helped spur the playwrights to offer dignified male characters, but as they did so, they built on the legacy of African Americans who had previously engaged these complex issues—in writing, speech, and action. In the decades before the Civil War, black men struggled to find nonthreatening but effective expressions of manhood under slavery. For instance, as historian James Oliver Horton has shown, those who refused to be whipped were admired in slave communities, while those who would not defend themselves were less respected (80). Not surprisingly, the relationship of the embodied practices of violence to ideological conceptions of manhood became even clearer when considering strategies for obtaining freedom. Black men worked to resist two contradictory yet equally dehumanizing characterizations of themselves. On the one hand, they were deemed brutes who must be tamed by slavery. To counter that belief, black men needed to refrain from violent expression to increase their chances of emancipation. On the other hand, whites believed that slavery was justified because servitude was supposedly the African's natural and appropriate condition. If black men were to counter that belief and prove themselves men, they, as David Walker proclaimed in 1829, had to "assert themselves to the full" with a willingness to fight for freedom (Horton 83).

The physical assertiveness that Walker encouraged was criticized during the 1830s, however. White abolitionist William Lloyd Garrison insisted that "moral suasion" would end slavery, and he promoted this view in his newspaper, the *Liberator*. Until the 1850s his philosophies dominated because African American leaders like Frederick Douglass remained optimistic that the nation was on the verge of radical change. Though he had proclaimed in his first autobiography that he became a man the day he fought his overseer, Douglass was a staunch Garrison supporter. Thus, when militant abolitionist Henry Highland Garnet argued for the use of force at the 1843 National Negro Convention, Douglass disagreed and the convention voted to reject Garnet's strategies (Horton 89). Through the late 1840s, Douglass remained committed to a nonviolent philosophy of abolition.

Manhood was seen as an assertion of full civil rights, but black men were denied those rights as slaves and as free Northerners. They sought to denounce characterizations of African Americans as savage brutes whose violence must be controlled, but at the same time they worried that not *literally* fighting for freedom would prove that they were a race of wretches who deserved slavery. Thus, black men—free and enslaved—reached an impasse, as individuals and as a group, as they contemplated the best ways to represent and express themselves.

By the 1850s, however, violence seemed a more reasonable strategy. The optimism about moral suasion faded when the Fugitive Slave Act of 1850 empowered white masters to hunt for slaves in the North and even to kidnap and enslave free blacks. Seven years later, the Dred Scott decision upheld the Fugitive Slave Law, essentially declaring that blacks could not be citizens. At this point, new advocates for physical force emerged to demand military training for African Americans. By 1861, more than 8,500 men had joined black militia groups, and they were more than willing to fight when the Civil War presented the opportunity. As Horton notes, "Black men marched off to win freedom for slaves and respect and equality for those already free" (93).

By 1865, the violence of the war gained blacks their freedom, but they had come to this violence reluctantly. Even while in the throes of battle, many surely did not see themselves as violent but simply pragmatic. With the war behind them, they looked forward to peaceful, prosperous lives as free citizens. Accordingly, community conversations emphasized economic and social responsibility. Now that they were no longer slaves, black men insisted on competing in the marketplace to provide for their families.[26] In response, white men became more interested in asserting themselves through violence. Also, because they were now unable to "tame" blacks through legal slavery, whites began more fervently to claim that black men were unworthy of "manhood rights" because they were not men at all. The logic, according to U. S. cultural historian Gail Bederman, ran thusly: men must be civilized, and only whites are capable of civilization; as the antithesis of whiteness, blacks are also anything but civilized, so they cannot be men (Bederman 50). Mainstream denial of black manhood often took the form of lynching violence because these "uncivilized brutes" were purported to be rapists.

Once again, black men individually and collectively struggled with how best to express their manhood. If struck by a white man, should they turn the other cheek or strike back? If they retaliated, they not only faced lynching but also potentially gave whites more ammunition for characterizing all blacks as uncivilized. Of course, blacks recognized whites' barbarity, but they were not in a position to punish or control it. They therefore concentrated on their own behavior, evaluating and adjusting it with an awareness of the dangers and insults that they would face.

Lynching playwrights recognized black men's complex predicament. Their work therefore continued that of Ida B. Wells, who, beginning in the 1890s, addressed the ways in which dominant models of manhood were being reworked within a racialized discourse of civilization that excluded black men. The women writers who laid the foundation for lynching drama portrayed the race's fathers, brothers, sons, and husbands with great care. Like Wells, they "depicted black men as manliness personified," suggesting that, in contrast, the mob "embodied white men's lust running amok, destroying true black manliness" (Bederman 58, 59).

As lynching gained momentum from the 1890s through the early 1900s, manhood could be proven first by "manliness" and later by "masculinity." Understanding the difference between these two terms sheds light on how national discourse evolved to encourage and excuse mob activity and why Wells and the playwrights addressed the nation's discourses and practices as they did. "Manliness" emerged from Victorian values that were widely held by middle-class white men before and during the 1890s; to be "manly" meant to be morally upright, show good judgment, and control one's passions (Bederman 11–12). Especially in the era of the self-made man, "manly" applied to middle-class whites whose integrity and good judgment brought them prosperity.[27] As Bederman explains, though, white men began to lose interest in "manly" characteristics once they no longer guaranteed business success. The number of self-employed men fell from 67 percent to 37 percent between 1870 and 1910 (12). "Manly" men could now fail, so qualities like frugality and hard work became less appealing and admirable (12).

While "manly" connoted morality, "masculine" was neutral and referred to anything male (Bederman 18). When Victorian manliness began to fail middle-class white men, they turned to masculine activities for new ways to feel powerful. As Bederman chronicles, some men joined male-only organizations, celebrated all things male, and avoided activities associated with women or femininity (16). Most striking, though, is that they coined the term "masculinity" to shape a new conception of manhood (17). Whereas a morally upright, emotionally restrained man exemplified "manliness," a primitive, physically strong and instinct-driven man exemplified "masculinity." Though white middle-class men preferred the former *before* the 1890s, the latter became more admirable *during* the 1890s. "Masculinity" did not overtake "manliness" with white middle-class men, however; each could be effective, depending on the situation.

Still, both conceptions were understood within the framework of "civilization." The civilized supposedly radiated "manliness," while masculinity came from one's uncivilized side, what contemporaries called the "Natural Man" (Bederman 71). It is important to note that the link between manliness and civilization was a racialized one, wherein "the White Man" was the epitome of civilized manhood, and "the Negro" was the ultimate primitive (22). As the taboo fell from behaviors associated with the Natural Man, however, it became acceptable for a white man to shed the constraints of his civilization and embody masculinity with aggressiveness, physical force, and instinctive reactions. Not surprisingly, as white men began to admire aggressiveness in themselves, they more often insisted that, being their opposites, black men were cowards.

With the introduction of "masculinity" as a positive trait, racial violence could gain momentum without disturbing white men's self-conceptions. Lynching was barbaric, not civilized, and Ida B. Wells identified it as such. Nevertheless, as they convinced themselves and others that black men were rapists, many white men took pride in being masculine enough to react to accusations of rape with savage intensity. Accordingly, white journalists often referred to "'the white man' of the lynch mob as the epitome of manhood, in contrast to the 'shivering Negro'" (Bederman 71). In this scenario, the black man becomes a frightened animal facing a mighty hunter. Black men were already deemed unmanly because they were assumed to be uncivilized, but rhetoric like this also cast them as cowards who were not even masculine. "Masculinity" also encouraged lynching because it made manhood more corporeal. The term emerged alongside the idea that the ideal male body was one of mass and muscle. As a result, one could confirm manhood through brute strength rather than economic success and moral integrity (15). In this climate, black men became a more pronounced threat to white supremacy. If manhood could be proven with the body, a black man could threaten a white man's self-conception with the mere possibility of over-powering him physically. The simple existence of a black male body thus became a menace, and destroying that body seemed tantamount to destroying (feared and therefore denied) black manhood.

This body-based conception of manhood also explains the mob's impulse to mutilate its victims and to do so in theatrical fashion; the visual and corporeal gained significance. Masculinity also encouraged an obsession with the sexual, and black men could not be disregarded, no matter how much mainstream discourse cast them as subhuman. As a result, some white men felt emasculated and looked to comfort themselves by castrating lynch victims (17). Where morality-based Victorian manliness would not have been so easily threatened, corporeal masculinity was, and lynching became a way of reinforcing white manhood.

Although Bederman demonstrates that manhood existed in two very different forms at the turn of the century and addresses how those forms related to race and civilization, her analysis does not take the next step of examining the ways in which a man's race virtually determined how he could express himself. Yet doing so is important for understanding community conversations about how blacks perceived and expressed identity and citizenship. Just as black men found themselves in a quandary in the antebellum period, the discourse of manliness and civilization kept them there at the turn of the century. As Marlon Ross observes of this era, black men faced consequences whether they accepted gender norms or rejected them (395).

Black women playwrights sympathized with black men's predicament by engaging in the discussion and offering opportunities to continue it through the embodied practices of communal literacy and amateur theater. Their dramatic representations stand as evidence of the belief that blackness was not antithetical to civilized manhood. Though lynching playwrights were not always explicit about the physical and sexual nature of the war between white and black men, awareness of it clearly fueled their insistence on theorizing the meaning of manhood, which they saw as inextricably linked to black womanhood, childhood, and citizenship.[28] They did not simply counter stereotypes, declaring that black men were not brutes; they depicted their partners, fathers, sons, brothers, and neighbors as they saw them: as civilized, moral, Christ-like men who loved their homes and families. Taking the same approach to portraying black men as clubwomen had to representing themselves, the playwrights defined black men "not by noisy protestations of what [they] are not, but by a dignified showing of what [they] are" (Josephine St. Pierre Ruffin qtd. in Lerner 443).

Once again, Grimké led the way. When Rachel's brother Tom realizes that a white friend no longer visits because she has been criticized for associating with blacks, he vows never to speak to her again. His mother says she understands how he feels, but "I wish my son to always be a gentleman." Tom quickly responds, "If being a gentleman means not being a man—I don't wish to be one." Tom questions the standards by which his behavior should be judged. His mother implies that a "gentleman" would be courteous in spite of the slight against him. However, for Tom, accepting the insult would make him a coward and a disgrace to his courageous father's memory. In this debate, the issue is whether the code of conduct for a "gentleman" applies to situations involving the kind of disrespect that black men encounter. To fulfill his mother's expectations, Tom would argue, is to deny his specific experience. With the disagreement between Tom and his mother, Grimké

acknowledges the difficulties a black man faces in fulfilling gender expectations. He cannot apply either of society's conceptions without pause. The
manliness that would bring honor to white men only brings him shame.
Meanwhile, masculinity—his instinct to defend himself and his loved ones—
will get him lynched, like his father. Though she is proud of her late husband,
Mrs. Loving says that she "used to plead with him to be more careful. I was
always afraid for him" (40).

In interrogating definitions of manhood, the genre's foundational scripts
put forth the playwrights' theory that race influenced all expressions of
it. Depending on the situation, middle-class white men could adopt either
manliness or masculinity. Because they were assumed to be civilized, their
civilization was not negated by occasional acts of savagery, including lynching. Black men did not have that privilege because they were so frequently
cast as savages, whether cowards or brutes. They therefore could never
cease being moral and civilized. Blacks recognized white hypocrisy, but they
focused on what they could control—their own behavior. African Americans
felt pressure to personify morality, and this often led them to see parallels
between their lives and that of Jesus Christ.[29] Since a black man was likely
to be targeted and tortured by lesser men who refused to believe that he
was who he said he was, lynching dramatists did not shy away from saying
as much, and often cast lynch victims as Christ figures.

By presenting black men as righteous, home-loving individuals, black
women playwrights affirmed their communities' belief in the civilization
and morality of their men and their race, questioning the mainstream theory
that they were brutes. These writers were determined to keep blacks from
accepting the lies that society told them about themselves. Insisting on self-
representation, they put forth what blacks of the time could refer to as drama
"about us," "by us," "for us," and "near us"—bolstering African American
identity and citizenship by providing refuge from the violence inherent in
how the race was otherwise represented.

De-generation

As lynching plays proliferated after *Rachel,* the genre continued to foreground the attack on the race's soul and psyche through its households. The
genre also kept a spotlight on the resulting generational damage. Thus, the
playwrights used their scripts to honor the dead and encourage the living
to mourn collectively, thereby putting forth the theory that mob victims
were citizens who deserve to be mourned and that those left behind are
citizens whose grief is justified. While lynching photographs exclude the
family and community that experienced the loss, the plays assert their pres-

ence and certify their belonging. They encourage blacks to come together and to express and enact their view of themselves and their communities. When engaging these scripts, African Americans could support each other through their mourning process because they certified for each other that their pain was valid, given that they were upstanding citizens—and therefore *unjustly* under siege.

Besides affirming black womanhood and manhood, lynching drama insists that mob violence alters the very structure of the black home, placing a spotlight on the devastation that was not represented when newspapers printed pictures of the mob's victims. In fact, the genre's foundational texts expose a phenomenon that I have termed *de-generation, meaning generation removal and prevention.* The plays demonstrate that, with a particular animosity toward black men, the mob alters the structure of the family by eliminating, or neutralizing, the generation whose romantic unions and resulting offspring would normally guarantee the healthy survival of black communities. The plays usually feature a grandmother and grandchildren, but in the middle generation, the father (and sometimes the mother) is missing, or lynching keeps the husband-wife unit from functioning.[30] In four of the seven early plays—*Mine Eyes Have Seen, Aftermath, A Sunday Morning in the South,* and *For Unborn Children*—there is no middle generation at all.[31] In these texts, grandmothers replace mothers to ensure that the household can function. But the grandmothers are themselves widows, so there is no substitute for the ejected father, making his absence more detrimental. Furthermore, the absence of the grandmother's partner is never explained, implying that he too could have been a victim of the mob. By making degeneration a literary convention, the playwrights point to the genius of the mob's craft: removing black men from homes while destroying all evidence that they were ever a part of them.

There are plays in which a middle generation is depicted, but the mother is often its only representative. In *Rachel* and *Blue Blood,* black women survive—but only to bear witness to marriages that have been destroyed. For instance, in *Rachel,* Mrs. Loving shares the truth about her husband's life and death. The story convinces her daughter that danger surrounds all black males, so Rachel rejects her suitor's proposal because she refuses to have children when the nation allows lynching. With her widowed mother testifying to the mob's power, Rachel would rather remain childless than produce prey for barbaric whites. In *Blue Blood,* John and May's wedding ceremony is only moments away, and the future seems full of promise. But as their mothers work in the kitchen, Mrs. Temple reveals the name of John's father, and the women realize that, years earlier, they were raped by the same white man. Having exchanged stories, the mothers must stop the wedding because John and May are actually brother and sister. John and May's is not the only union affected, however. Their mothers had kept their rapes a secret because they did not want the men in their lives to defend their honor; they knew that a protective black man would be a dead black man. Although the plots of *Blue Blood* and *Rachel* are quite different, their similarity lies in the moment when middle-generation mothers share their experiences. Johnson and Grimké depict mothers who survive, but their presence demonstrates how lynching alters not only their individual past and present but also their family's future.

Most interesting, we see de-generation at work even when both the husband and wife live, though only one of the foundational scripts—*Safe*, by Georgia Douglas Johnson—depicts such a family. This drama features a loving marriage but shows how lynch-law prevents ideal domesticity. When his spouse needs him most, John is hiding. He leaves to check on a friend whose life has been threatened, but while he is away, the lynch mob drags that friend past the house. Liza, John's happily pregnant wife, hears the victim call out for his mother. Johnson suggests that if black women are not haunted by the sound of children begging not to be born, as Grimké's Rachel is, they may have to contend with their tortured screams later. Shocked and distraught, Liza goes into labor before John returns. Having killed one man and restrained another, the mob takes male leaders from both families, but Liza soon confirms that racial violence jeopardizes future generations. When her child is born a boy, she strangles him to death. Johnson thus enacts in 1929 what Grimké only suggested in 1916. After learning how her father and brother were killed, Rachel declares, "Why, it would be more merciful to strangle the little things at birth" (42). Because she is traumatized by her neighbor's murder, Liza asks, "What's little nigger boys born for anyhow?" At the end of the play, she is in a daze and insists that her baby is "safe—safe from the lynchers—safe . . ." (112).

Liza's disturbing declaration in *Safe* illustrates the most important distinction between de-generation and degeneration. While the latter would indicate pathology within the black family, the de-generation in lynching drama points to the degeneracy of the mob. Blacks had already proven their ability to build successful homes. So if African American characters do not reproduce or if they resist by terminating young lives, it is not because they do not value family.[32] They simply give voice to the despair that African Americans must have felt as they lived in a nation that left white barbarism unchecked. The genre's women create homes in which children can be produced and nurtured, but they are forced to realize that a household whose head is vulnerable to attack is a deathbed for future generations, not a safe haven.

Grimké defended her play by asserting that it could not have been preaching race suicide because its message was not aimed primarily at blacks. By targeting African American audiences, then, her successors believed that their texts could serve their communities in ways that *Rachel* did not. Nevertheless, their scripts corroborate the despair over reproduction that Grimké portrayed. Clearly, there was agreement about the challenges that black communities face, and Grimké's successors were as concerned as she was about identifying whose pathology threatens American democracy. As cultural historian Daylanne English has shown, mob violence arose alongside an American interest in eugenics—but tellingly, lynching selected *against* the "fittest" African Americans. Most often, victims were the community's "best and brightest," those who according to the nation's rhetoric should have been considered productive, upstanding citizens. As de-generation becomes a literary convention, it produces repetition within lynching drama. However, as English insists, this repetition "is not an individual [author's] psychological response or symptom and certainly not writerly error; it is a shared representation of the social symptoms of a modern lynching culture that perversely selects against the 'fittest,'" and does so "generation after generation" (*Unnatural* 121).

Liza's actions are not offered as a solution to the injustice that blacks face, but rather as an expression of black parents' despair. Likewise, the genre does not offer characters who respond this way in order to suggest that black parents should feel guilty. The critique is of the society that makes life dangerous for black children,[33] not of the parents whose romantic love brings them into the world. As English points out, "The abnormal symptoms here are not Liza's . . . but the modern lynching culture's" (*Unnatural* 129). Indeed, by spotlighting the joy with which Liza and John expect their firstborn, the play exemplifies lynching drama's investment in representing the happy families that make up black communities. These are the black family scenes that the mob seeks to destroy. Yet while committed to highlighting domestic success, the genre does not downplay the devastation that the mob accomplishes; it does not suggest that these solid homes are able to withstand the blow.

While lynching photographs featured disfigured bodies, the playwrights presented their communities' losses in terms of mutilated households. If a body can be identified because it coheres and has integrity, the home is recognizable for the same reasons. Therefore, it must be shown intact so that the nature of its mutilation comes into stark relief.

Admittedly, while preserving evidence of intact homes, lynching drama spotlights heteronormative examples. To the extent that playwrights constructed family scenes with an awareness of what master/piece theater sought to erase, they were less interested in showcasing the fact that blacks had created successful familial structures that differed from the nuclear family. For similar reasons, authors were not invested in highlighting complex conceptions of sexuality.[34] No matter how stable and loving the writers knew nontraditional households to be, it was the existence of black homes that fit the nuclear family model that was being erased by the scenario of exorcism. As they worked to record community insights, lynching dramatists—not unlike their predecessors who wrote domestic novels such as *Iola Leroy* and *Contending Forces*—put on display the familial structure that they knew was deliberately left out of mainstream portrayals of the race. As they did so in one-act plays, they often put forth characters that are not middle class but have nonetheless succeeded in realizing the moral ideal associated with the well-to-do family. These characters may have been servants in social status, but when portrayed by black dramatists in their own homes, they are anything but mammies and uncles.

Yet at the same time, the recurrence of de-generation makes room for valuing the alternative family structures found in real-life black communities because the convention acknowledges the hypocrisy of the nation's nuclear family rhetoric. In a society determined to cast ordinary black citizens as rapists, whores, mammies, and uncles who are not meaningful members of their own families, adhering to strict codes of propriety could not save African Americans from white barbarism. As the genre highlights the vulnerability of even the most traditionally successful domestic spaces, it suggests that, regardless of the configuration of black homes, any semblance of dignity within them could inspire racial violence.

In other words, *all* black homebuilders infuriate the mob because they call into question whites' exclusive claim to morality. With this perspective represented, the plays become outlets for the despair of those targeted by murderers whose actions are unjustly excused. While highlighting the nation's hypocrisy, the plays acknowledge the reverberating pain with which so many were forced to live. The scripts affirmed for turn-of-the-century African Americans their right to mourn their spiritual losses, and they encouraged difficult discussions about racism's effect on black coupling and reproduction. In this genre, long after the physical attack, the intensity of the loss leads some characters to regret having children, realizing that familial bonds make them more vulnerable.

Taking seriously the implications of de-generation, we must call for new sociological studies of the black family. American views of black domestic life have been substantially shaped by Daniel Moynihan's 1965 report *The Negro Family: The Case for National Action* and E. Franklin Frazier's *The Negro Family in the United States* (1939). Moynihan insisted that the "deterioration of the Negro family" began with the "deep-seated structural distortions" that accompanied slavery. Because the institution denied black men the right to act as heads of households, it crippled blacks' ability to function successfully in a society based on patriarchy (29). Decades earlier, Frazier had argued that Emancipation and the freedmen's poor preparation for it wrought havoc on African American familial ties; black women were forced to become matriarchs because black men were increasingly unreliable (102).[35] Frazier further asserted, "Promiscuous sexual relations and constant changing of spouses became the rule with the demoralized elements in the freed Negro population" (79–80).

Herbert Gutman's 1976 study *The Negro Family in Slavery and Freedom* set out to test Frazier's claims and Moynihan's conclusions, and it found that contrary to common assumptions about African American communities, "the double-headed household did not decline in importance over time" (xx). Though Gutman challenged sociological models based on black pathology, older ideas have remained remarkably resonant. It is still not uncommon to hear policymakers blame teenage pregnancy in African American communities on absentee fathers who have left their daughters with a void and sons with no decent role models. Often, folk historians (on porches and in pulpits, for example) explain that these irresponsible fathers are continuing unhealthy patterns established in slavery and after Emancipation. They would apparently agree with Frazier's characterization of "demoralized" freedmen who preferred promiscuity to stable domesticity.

Yet when we consider the record that lynching drama presents, we must question these popular assumptions. Early studies rightly emphasize the negative impact that collapsing marital bonds had on black communities after Emancipation, but they underestimate the role that mob violence played. As activists like Frederick Douglass, Ida B. Wells, and Walter White established long ago, race-based lynching emerged only after Emancipation![36] It is unfortunate, then, that prominent scholars have not investigated the effects that racial terrorism had on the black family. They have not considered the "structural distortions" sustained by the household when a husband/father is lynched. Too many have assumed that all absences were voluntary.[37] Similarly, scholars do not consider how unattractive marriage must have been to those who knew that—at any time and without penalty—whites could make their wives widows and their children orphans.[38] Lynching plays of the 1910s and 1920s provide us with new ways of viewing black family life at the turn of the century. They preserve a perspective that survived despite negative stereotypes of black men that were prevalent at that time and that are perpetuated into the twenty-first century.

In writing lynching dramas, the playwrights preserved evidence of embodied practices of black belonging, including traditional homebuilding, which helped African Americans to survive this era. Even as African Americans recognize the injustice of their situation, lynching violence can give blacks heartbreaking motivation for reducing the number of their offspring. The older generation had produced children under slavery; after Emancipation, these children were no longer sold at auctions, but they entered adulthood amidst mob violence. As progeny of missing fathers and sometimes missing mothers, this generation sometimes regards bringing more children into the world as an unnecessary cruelty. Thus, the genre insists that the mob's unchecked power makes it dangerous for blacks to wed and reproduce. The plays preserve evidence that loving black homes abound, but they also depict the extent of the damage inflicted on African American souls and psyches. In doing so, they tell a story about our racist society that the hanging body cannot.

※ ※ ※

Today, artists and intellectuals continue to redefine "black theater," but the transitions of the late nineteenth and early twentieth centuries laid a remarkable foundation. The U.S. stage refused to accommodate African Americans until they made a place for themselves by becoming minstrels. However, it did not take long for blacks to create the less restrictive form of musical comedy. By the 1890s, musical comedy commanded significant audiences, and by the early 1900s, the celebrated teams of Williams and Walker and Cole and Johnson reigned on Broadway and were welcomed abroad.

Violence was always a backdrop to their success, however. For example, when a race riot broke out in New York City in 1900, the mob was invigorated by cries of "get Ernest Hogan and Williams and Walker and Cole and Johnson" (Johnson, *Black Manhattan* 126–27). The humor and music of the most celebrated black performers did not match their off-stage realities. In this climate, Grimké entered drama hoping to reach an integrated audience with material that acknowledged the injustices that African Americans, including stars, faced.

Grimké therefore worked to redefine "black theater" so that it did not simply entertain whites or give dramatic actors opportunities to showcase their skills. By reaching across the color line with more favorable depictions of African Americans that also revealed the injustice of the violence that shaped their lives, Grimké's drama represented those forsaken by the law and legislature. The revisions that Grimké's contribution inspired from other black writers suggest that she made an impact, but rather than address whites on blacks' behalf, they worked to address African Americans themselves. In writing one-acts, they redefined "black theater" as that which not only represented blacks but also directly addressed them and called on them to participate in the identity-sustaining work of performance.

As lynching drama developed as a genre, both its content and the one-act format that came to dominate it gestured toward blacks' belief that African American citizenship entitled them to hash out within their own communities how to express identity and belonging. Indeed, the texts register a tendency to operate under the assumption that black communities are marked by democracy that the nation would do well to model. As such, the plays (because they spring from and perpetuate those communities) prioritize conversation and debate more than action and closure. Extensive exchange is key because black identity and citizenship are so complex. Encouraged to partake in the embodied practices of communal literacy and amateur theater, black communities supported an intimate "black theater" that included lynching drama and bolstered their belief in their right to full citizenship.

PART TWO

Developing a Genre,
Asserting Black Citizenship

CHAPTER THREE

The Black Soldier
Elevating Community Conversation

Lynching drama proliferated because playwrights maximized periodical culture to contribute to a community conversation that accommodated diverse perspectives. Long before appearing in print, Angelina Weld Grimké's *Rachel* inspired debate when it was produced in Washington, D.C., in 1916. Much of the evidence of the debate survives in periodicals,[1] including the responses of those who entered the discussion by becoming lynching dramatists themselves. *Rachel* first appeared in print in 1920, making Alice Dunbar-Nelson's *Mine Eyes Have Seen* (1918) and Mary Burrill's *Aftermath* (1919) the first two published lynching plays by black authors, with both appearing in progressive magazines. These scripts therefore exemplify why the genre could help African Americans to survive the height of mob violence and its photographic representation. These texts emerged in periodicals that empowered marginalized groups by fostering alternative public spaces, and they invited these communities to utilize the knowledge-producing power of embodied practices.

Writing one-acts and making them available in periodicals demonstrated an investment in black audiences and in intensifying the conversation among them. That is, these scripts serve as a declaration that African Americans are worth targeting and their opinions are worth representing, discussing, and shaping. It simply was not enough to attempt to subvert mainstream discourses and practices, and because these scripts enter the archive through progressive periodicals, their authors suggest precisely that. Earlier, Grimké had sought to intervene in mainstream politics by showing the larger public admirable black characters and insisting that lynch mobs target them, not just criminals. Dunbar-Nelson revised Grimké by tailoring her script for black audiences and by creating characters who are honest and hard working but not middle class. Dunbar-Nelson also altered the portrait of black life in the midst of lynching by marking the connection between the mob and the military. As a result, her text represented an existing community conversation about the degree to which African American identity included patriotism, and it encouraged further discussion and debate. Mary Burrill seems to have entered the debate hoping to take it in directions not represented by Dunbar-Nelson's work. Burrill's script emerged within a year of the appearance of Dunbar-Nelson's, and it more aggressively questions the wisdom of black military sacrifice in the midst of mob violence.

Mine Eyes Have Seen and *Aftermath* are examples of how blacks living in the midst of dehumanizing discourses and practices reinforced their self-conceptions through representative figures. Both reflecting and perpetuating community perspectives on African American identity and citizenship, the black soldier became an affirming figure, and women lynching dramatists participated in making him so. During and after World War I, whether he resisted the draft or went willingly, whether he died valiantly in battle or returned home demanding the rights for which he had fought, the black soldier personified African Americans' admirable character and valid claim to full citizenship.[2] Thus, whether blacks discussing his experiences were loyal to the war effort or not, their representations of him facilitated racial self-affirmation. Accordingly, periodicals brimmed with discussion of black soldiers; *Mine Eyes* and *Aftermath* became dramatic contributions to this conversation.

By publishing one-acts in progressive periodicals, both Dunbar-Nelson and Burrill ensured that their scripts were available to communities to a degree that Grimké's had not been. While many had been privy to the debate about what Grimké's three-act play did or did not accomplish, the script itself was not readily available, but *Mine Eyes* appeared in *Crisis,* and a year later, *Aftermath* was published in *The Liberator,* so they were in community members' hands to be discussed and performed. The plays therefore remind us of the different types of expression that groups encouraged within alternative public spheres. Blacks had created parallel public space since the 1820s by editing their own newspapers, but other periodicals added new dimensions to an already multifaceted community conversation: magazines more often featured literature. Short stories, serialized novels, and dramas joined poetry and became increasingly common. Not unlike mainstream periodicals at the turn of the century, those considered in this study incorporated dramatic texts as simply another contribution to "the texture of the magazine" (Smith, *Plays* 21). Of the literary forms available, drama was particularly poised to encourage embodied practices that could affirm African Americans while they refined collective identity and delineated the contours of their citizenship.

Figure 3. May 1919 cover of *Crisis* magazine summarizes all that black soldiers represented within the community conversation.

Because *Mine Eyes* and *Aftermath* mark lynching drama's transition to the one-act format, they exemplify the genre's role in helping marginalized communities to filter mainstream rhetoric that would otherwise obliterate their self-conceptions. As discussed in chapter 1, lynching plays are products of and prompts for African American cultural criticism; they engage the politics of representation by both recording and shaping community members' views of themselves and each other. Indeed, the scripts survive to gesture toward a repertoire of embodied practices of black belonging, not the least of which is debate. As they continue a conversation sparked by Grimké's *Rachel*, both Dunbar-Nelson's *Mine Eyes Have Seen* and Burrill's *Aftermath* are dominated by intense debate, so the content of these plays foregrounds the fact that blacks do not agree, especially on key, complex issues such as lynching and patriotism. At the same time, the format of these scripts promotes honest, painful conversation in black homes, conversations not unlike those among the characters. With a tradition of communal literacy, blacks likely read these one-acts aloud, often pausing to offer their own views about the attitudes depicted. The plays also point to disagreements among the authors and to their belief in the value of continuing difficult conversations in the flesh-and-blood community. After all, when Burrill answers Dunbar-Nelson's script, she chooses to publish in an outlet that could accommodate a more radical militancy in the black soldier than *Crisis* had been ready to offer.

Mine Eyes and *Aftermath* were both published in progressive periodicals, so they each offer access to the black soldier via alternative discursive space, but these spaces prove to be quite different. *The Crisis* was founded by Du Bois for black self-affirmation (although under the auspices of an interracial organization), and *The Liberator* was edited by Max Eastman, a white activist determined to challenge mainstream values. Using *Mine Eyes* and *Aftermath* to access both the archive and the repertoire of U. S. culture in the World War I era, one finds that the black soldier's characteristics in *Mine Eyes* help illuminate the form that racial self-affirmation took among those who embraced patriotism. Meanwhile, his very different demeanor in *Aftermath* suggests that publications committed to questioning patriotic rhetoric enabled another articulation of black self-affirmation.

Mine Eyes Have Seen

Scholars have consistently read *Mine Eyes* as a prowar text that articulates, in dramatic form, the stance that Dunbar-Nelson took by doing war work herself and encouraging other African Americans to do the same.[3] However, a close reading of the script troubles that interpretation and reveals a deep anxiety on Dunbar-Nelson's part that she could not consciously articulate while remaining committed to the war effort. Ultimately, this anxiety springs from and sustains black self-worth. It acknowledges, even if unconsciously, that blacks are being asked to make unreasonable wartime sacrifices, given the nation's treatment of them.

As a schoolteacher living approximately one hundred miles from the nation's capital, Dunbar-Nelson was no stranger to American contradictions. Because she was biracial and light enough to pass, Dunbar-Nelson was keenly aware of the lunacy of the color line, and her political activism exposed her to the duplicity with which both the Democratic and Republican parties dealt with African American voters. Also, in 1901, after attending the funeral of President William McKinley, Dunbar-Nelson was beaten by a police officer in Washington, D.C., and her social standing did little to yield the justice she felt she deserved (Gaines 217). Despite her light skin, education, and impressive political and social network, Dunbar-Nelson knew that blacks in the United States could live as exemplars of American ideals and still not enjoy basic rights and privileges. As she writes a play about lynching and black military service in the midst of her own war work and other activism, Dunbar-Nelson corroborates the findings of *A Spectacular Secret,* Jacqueline Goldsby's study of lynching in literature. "Precisely because the work of literature is to imagine what we otherwise cannot know and say about our lives," Goldsby asserts, "genres and their representational conventions leave rich and surprising evidence of authors' perceptions of lynching's violence" (42, 33).

Dunbar-Nelson's protagonist Chris names all of the reasons that blacks should not fight willingly in the Great War, so when he seems to acquiesce by play's end, he epitomizes the quandary of patriotic black citizens—those whose faith in the country's ideals somehow overpower their awareness of the nation's betrayals. As Chris puts it, African Americans served in the Revolutionary War "as slaves [who were] promised a freedom they never got" (273). Then, they served in the War of 1812 and in the Civil War, but only "when the Nation was afraid not to call them. Didn't want 'em at first" (273). And they fought in 1898 in the Spanish-American War, "only to have their valor disputed" (273).

The United States entered the latest world conflict on April 6, 1917, and this military challenge also carried insults for blacks. Accordingly, the April 1917 issue of *Crisis* included "The Perpetual Dilemma," an editorial by W. E. B. Du Bois addressing the fact that blacks could not be officers in the military. African Americans were at the time being offered a segregated officer training camp, and because they would not receive training if they rejected it, Du Bois concluded that they should make this compromise with Jim Crow. Black newspapers continued to debate the issues, but hundreds of African American college men applied for admission and recruited their peers. Meanwhile, the fourteen officer training camps from which the War Department would pull for upcoming battles had been established by Congress for white men only (Williams, *Torchbearers* 42). Undaunted, young college men organized themselves to continue recruitment efforts to secure the twelve hundred applicants required to persuade the War Department to open a black camp.

The men thereby agitated for the opportunity to put their lives on the line for the nation, and they succeeded; the segregated camp opened in July 1917, and from the beginning, the recruits were plagued with racial hostility. The white residents in their host city were often violent, and black soldiers were explicitly forbidden to defend themselves. As black officers-in-training tolerated these indignities in Des Moines, Iowa, a race riot erupted in another northern city: East St. Louis, Illinois.

At the end of July 1917, the NAACP sponsored a Silent Protest Parade in New York City, an example of black embodied practices designed to call attention to the oppressive behavior of whites. In September 1917, Du Bois ran "The Massacre of East St. Louis," an article that, like the parade, helped to identify the exploitive practices that had caused the violence in East St. Louis. In writing and in action, blacks worked to raise awareness of racial violence, understanding that even if spectacle lynchings were on the decline, antiblack violence was not.

In August 1917, the injustices suffered in Houston, Texas, by blacks training for military service came to light and received attention in the pages of Du Bois's *Crisis*. More than one hundred soldiers had armed themselves against whites who had been harassing them for months. The clash left fifteen dead, including four police officers (Williams, *Torchbearers* 35). *Crisis* investigated and found that black trainees had long tolerated abuse from residents but especially from officers of the law, and the magazine reported in November 1917 that the habitual cruelty of the Houston police force was to blame. Sixty-three black soldiers were charged with mutiny, murder, and assault, and a military jury sentenced thirteen of them to death. On December 11, 1917, they were executed and buried in undistinguished graves. The January 1918 issue of *Crisis* carried Du Bois's editorial "Thirteen," which characterized the unjustly killed men as martyrs.

Such investigations and editorials no doubt explain why the army wanted to keep *Crisis* magazine out of its camps (Kornweibel, *"Seeing Red"* 54) and why the federal government began monitoring the periodical, despite the fact that its pages had helped inspire black men to lobby for a Jim Crow officer training camp. In June 1918, less than a year after that camp opened, Du Bois published "The Black Soldier," which criticized the conditions under which all black troops served. As someone who had encouraged many to enter the military, he felt attached to the results, including their mistreatment. Nevertheless, that same month, federal authorities were assured that Du Bois "had promised to 'change the tone of *Crisis*' and make it 'an organ of patriotic propaganda hereafter'" (Ellis 107). In fact, Du Bois's white confidante Joel Spingarn had informed the government that "all the material for each issue was being submitted before publication to [the NAACP's attorney], who would ensure that it was innocuous" (Ellis 107). Despite Spingarn's comforting words to federal authorities, Du Bois's actions ultimately fell in line with the sentiments of the *Baltimore Afro-American* newspaper, which held that "quiescent but not acquiescent should be the attitude of everybody in war times" (April 14, 1917).

While black men grappled with contradictions in real life about military service and civic duty, about enduring or resisting discrimination, and about how much they should say publicly about all of these issues, Dunbar-Nelson created Chris, a character who receives a draft notice but articulates why he should not enlist. In his own home, Chris is surrounded by characters who insist that it is his duty to serve. In fact, some of their arguments anticipate the advice that would appear in *Crisis* just two months later: Du Bois's famous July 1918 "Close Ranks" editorial encouraged African Americans to "forget our special grievances and close ranks shoulder to shoulder with our own white fellow citizens . . . fighting for democracy." Though outnumbered, Chris insists that his real duty is to his family (272). Further, he is not interested in becoming the "Deuce of Spades" in the card game that politicians play with other men's souls (272). Finally, Chris objects not simply because he has no complaint against other nations, but also because he has a justified quarrel, as a black man, with his home country.

Why, then, do scholars routinely conclude that the play's "blatant intent is to persuade black people to support the war"?[4] Certainly, it is not because Chris capitulates. Nor does he suggest that those who encourage him to serve have made good points. Chris never articulates agreement, but his eventual silence allows one to believe that he is persuaded by patriotic rhetoric.[5] Though Chris defends his position for most of the play, Dunbar-Nelson withholds his sentiments at the end, and this proves to be the best approach for a script published in a magazine that is on the verge of promising the U.S. government that it will work even harder to encourage blacks to support the war.

Du Bois will print his "Close Ranks" editorial in *Crisis* just two months after *Mine Eyes* appears; perhaps it was the script's seeming retreat from its main character's resistance to patriotic rhetoric that made it safe for a publication under federal scrutiny. Thus, it is worth examining how the text creates distance from its main character's stance. Above all, the black family scene portrayed in *Mine Eyes* proves unique among lynching plays in that it incorporates several outsiders, and those outsiders create dissension. The play is set in a Northern tenement apartment because Dan, Chris, and Lucy's father was lynched in the South. When the mob removes the successful head of household, his progeny relocate, and their new home is soon filled with painful memories: their mother dies after arriving in the North because she is not accustomed to the bleak climate,[6] and Dan is maimed because the Northern economy forces him into factory work. With the wage earner lynched and his successor crippled, they must "eat and live in the kitchen." Surely, the family's descent will be complete when the war claims Chris, its newest breadwinner. It is significant, then, that the script equates the mob and the military by giving them similar weapons. When local whites had grown tired of watching a black man own a nice house and educate his children, they posted notices that the family should leave town. Next, a mob set the house on fire, and when the father had tried to save it, they shot him. When Chris is drafted, Lucy proclaims, "Oh, it can't be! They won't take you from us! *And shoot you down, too?*" Just as Lucy predicts her younger brother's fate, the reader can predict the family's. The black man's absence means sorrow and poverty for his loved ones, whether he is victimized by a mob or drafted by the army.

The father's original prosperity had enraged his white neighbors, so his survivors' financial problems in the North represent a victory for the mob. Their new home is "sordid," "dark," and even "damp"—in stark contrast to where they lived when their father was alive. Yet the family's devastation is best demonstrated not by the shabby space that they occupy, but by the dissension that flourishes within it. The home accommodates a number of visitors who advise Chris to obey the draft, dismissing his reasons for resisting, including, most notably: "Must I go and fight for the nation that let my father's murder go unpunished?" The resulting debates make up the majority of the script, and it is clear that these characters are not concerned about Chris or his family, only about an abstract definition of patriotism that ignores how the nation has treated African Americans. Essentially, the guests create conflict, and their ability to do so proves how damaged the household is. The deceased father would have been much less tolerant of visitors who questioned his lived experience, so this scene is possible because he was lynched for being a strong head of household.

Especially because Lucy begins the action by reminiscing aloud about their former lifestyle, the play records the characteristics of the enviable black household in the South while dramatizing the instability and further deterioration of their home in the North. First, the family's Irish neighbor Mrs. O'Neill stops by to be helpful. She does not want Lucy to miss the opportunity to buy provisions, and because Lucy hurt herself when she was young, Mrs. O'Neill says that she can protect Lucy's "game foot" from the crowd (273). However, when a distressed Lucy shares that her brother has been drafted, Mrs. O'Neill callously answers, "An' ef he has, what of it? [. . .] they took me man from me . . . an' it's a widder I am wid me five kiddies, an' I've never a word [of complaint] to say . . ." (272). She seems to feel that, if her husband has been sacrificed, why should her neighbor be spared? Next, Jake (described as a "Jewish boy") says that Chris should fight because "there's a future, Chris—a big one. We younger ones must be in that future—ready for it" (273). To Jake, the nation's record for mistreating blacks is of no real consequence. In fact, he insists, "There isn't a wrong you can name that your race has endured that mine has not suffered, too" (273). With this, Jake overlooks the specific experience of African Americans in the United States and Chris's personal lynching-inspired reasons for not feeling obligated to Uncle Sam. Jake's sympathies do not lie with Chris or African Americans; he believes that the race should stop "grieving because you're colored" (274). As it depicts the visitors' ability to cause tension by giving "advice," the play suggests that there are reverberating consequences when a head of household is forcibly removed.

A successful generation is missing from this new home, and those who remain struggle to reclaim their dignity—even as they are surrounded by reminders of everything they have lost. The missing father may have been killed by the mob, but the family that is left behind certainly did not escape the violence. Their deteriorating household is just a different kind of "strange fruit."

In order to treat *Mine Eyes* as a prowar text, one must assume that it privileges the views expressed by this influx of visitors over Chris's arguments—and doing so seems reasonable because their beliefs are ultimately echoed by Chris's brother, sister, and fiancée—but the family's agreement with the visitors only underscores troubling contradictions. Chris's brother Dan is the most adamant and most vocal, and through the debate between Dan and Chris, Dunbar-Nelson foregrounds the sorts of challenges that black men face. As United States citizens, African Americans' conceptions of themselves were shaped by patriotism. Yet they could not avoid dealing with the many ways the nation denied their citizenship. Did a country that begrudgingly accepted blacks into military service deserve their loyalty? Even for black men resolved to be patriotic, expressing that devotion was complicated by the fact that problems accompanied a black man's adoption of either standard of manhood. Did one best demonstrate one's readiness for citizenship through manliness or masculinity? In *Mine Eyes,* Chris associates manhood with education (manliness), and Dan links it to physical power (masculinity), but it is not at all clear that either would improve their lives. After all, their father had adhered to the manly tenets of hard work, integrity, and constraint—only to become a target for white hatred. On the other hand, although Chris is told to "be a man" and become a soldier, embodying masculinity will separate him from his family and bring the household more pain and poverty.

Dan argues that black manhood is best demonstrated through military service, but his predicament highlights the futility of his philosophy. Dan declares that black soldiers are *real* men who brought honor to the race in 1776, 1812, 1861, and in 1898 in the Spanish-American War (273). He is ashamed that Chris does not want to continue that legacy, and he wishes that he could go in his place. Dan declares, "Oh God! If I were but whole and strong! If I could only prove to a doubting world of what stuff my people are made!" As Dan speaks, he "half tears himself from the chair, the upper part of his body writhing, while the lower part is inert, dead" (274). He cannot embody the type of manhood that he admires because he is crippled, but his condition does not kill his patriotism—despite the fact that his father's lynching precipitated it. In this and other ways, Dunbar-Nelson uses Dan's desire to serve in order to mark contradictions in prowar rhetoric. For instance, Dan wants to prove to the world that black men are honorable and brave. Yet, he has just explained that blacks fought in four wars "and saved the day, too, many a time" (273). Given this history, why does the world still question black manhood? Furthermore, will dying in one more war convince this doubting world? Because these and other questions hover (like the father's spirit) over these scenes, *Mine Eyes* contributes to and advances important conversations about the contours of black identity and citizenship.

Blacks discussed whether their racial identity included patriotism, but it was a debate, not a foregone conclusion. The script's dialogue therefore highlights disagreement, and the gestures and postures encouraged by stage directions add complexity. As a result, *Mine Eyes* is ambiguous, and its ambiguity is intensified by the patriotic didacticism that it depicts but does not ultimately replicate or endorse. Prowar readings of this script do not engage its nonlinguistic meaning-making elements. Such interpretations also overlook the fact that it is not the accusation that he is unpatriotic and disloyal that most upsets Chris. Instead, it is the suggestion that he is less than a man for prioritizing his family over the country that has never proudly claimed him or guaranteed him justice:

> CHRIS: (*clenching his fist.*) Brother, you've called me two names today that no man ought to have to take—a slacker and a weakling!
> DAN: True. Aren't you both? (*Leans back and looks at Chris speculatively.*)
> CHRIS: (*Makes an angry lunge towards the chair, then flings his hands above his head in an impatient gesture.*) Oh, God! (*Turns back to window.*)
> JULIA: Chris, it's wicked for them to taunt you so—but Chris—it IS our country—our race—
>
> (*Outside, the strains of music from a passing band are heard. The music comes faintly, gradually growing louder and louder until it reaches a crescendo. The tune is "The Battle Hymn of the Republic" played in stirring march time.*)
>
> DAN: (*singing softly.*) "Mine eyes have seen the glory of the coming of the Lord!"
> CHRIS: (*Turns from the window and straightens his shoulders.*) And mine!

Chris has been explaining his position throughout the play, fending off accusations of selfishness and disloyalty, but he does not respond with anger until he is called a *slacker* and a *weakling*. Chris clenches his fist when saying that no man should have to tolerate those labels. Dan is pleased to have riled his brother in this way; he leans back in his chair and "looks speculatively" at Chris, as if sizing him up. Chris seems to interpret the posture as further judgment and lunges in anger, but Dunbar-Nelson is careful to say that he lunges "towards the chair," emphasizing his awareness of his brother's disability. Determined not to hurt his brother but needing to vent somehow, Chris "flings his hands above his head" and then "turns back to the window" where the band is approaching.

Soon, when Dan sings "Mine eyes have seen the glory of the coming of the Lord," Chris declares "and mine!"—but this response is left ingeniously ambiguous. We do not know what *seeing the glory of the coming of the Lord* means for Chris. Perhaps the song is a reminder that the nation's military victories have not brought blacks true freedom and equality. That is, when others have seen the glory of God's coming to ensure U.S. victory, it has never meant victory for blacks. Though he does not verbally elaborate, Chris says "and mine" as he turns *away* from the window and straightens his shoulders. He moves in the opposite direction of those who have made prowar arguments. Given everything that he has said throughout the play, it is likely that he imagines a God who would avenge his father's death, not sacrifice another member of the family to the country's agenda. His body language suggests that he has made a decision (his shoulders stiffen), but not one that accords with the patriotic sentiment of the song. Interpretations centered on the written word risk missing the meanings conveyed by movement, gestures, and postures.

These defiant movements are followed by a lack of movement in the remainder of the action, confirming that Chris is not at all overcome by the patriotic sentiment that he has so eloquently and explicitly resisted. He need not say more because he has made every argument necessary to stand his ground. Thus, when the play concludes, Chris is the only able-bodied character who has not gone to the window to admire the band that is passing by while playing "The Battle Hymn of the Republic." Again, the tension between words uttered and Chris's movement (or lack thereof) should not be overlooked:

> CORRELIA LEWIS [the settlement worker]: As he died to make men holy, let us die to make them free!
>
> MRS. O'NEILL: An' ye'll make the sacrifice, me boy, an' ye'll be the happier.
>
> JAKE: Sacrifice! No sacrifice for him, it's those who stay behind. Ah, if they would only call me, and call me soon!
>
> LUCY: We'll get on, never fear. I'm proud! PROUD! (*Her voice breaks a little, but her head is thrown back.*)
>
> (*As the music draws nearer, the group breaks up, and the whole roomful rushes to the window and looks out. Chris remains in the center of the floor, rigidly at attention, a rapt look on his face. Dan strains at his chair, as if he would rise, then sinks back, his hand feebly beating time to the music, which swells to a martial crash.*)
>
> CURTAIN.

Because Dunbar-Nelson places these comments at the end of the play and because they follow the trajectory of the patriotic sentiments voiced throughout the text, they gain significance despite lacking heft. That is, these final lines gain authority partly because of the momentum built into the structure of the play and the audience's reasonable expectation that matters are being resolved. However, because the comments are weak, if one is attentive, they cannot stand against Chris's arguments. Cornelia simply quotes the song, implying that Chris should be proud to sacrifice his life, as Jesus Christ did. Is the United States to be viewed as God—whose will is always righteous and should be fulfilled, no matter how bitter the cup? Next, Mrs. O'Neill makes a comment that does not really make sense: why would Chris be the happier if he makes the sacrifice? Then, Jake seems masochistic in his hope to be drafted. Finally, Lucy tells Chris not to worry, but Dunbar-Nelson has used her to express fear throughout the play. As we learn early on, her soul has been "shriveled with fear since [they] were

driven like dogs from [their] home." Thus, she is the last person to believe
when she tells Chris "never fear," and this is underscored by the fact that
her voice breaks as she says it. She throws her head back as she declares
her pride, trying to embody the bravery and sincerity that would suit her
words, but her cracking voice betrays her.

Throughout the play, prowar arguments had been less forceful than Chris's
logic, but in these final moments, one realizes why weak slogans nevertheless carry power. The patriotic tune and all of the emotion that it conjures
become substitutes for logic as the music becomes louder. When the band
marches through the streets, all are encouraged to let the song not only
speak *to* them but also to let it speak *for* them, as it drowns out individual
voices. Only in this context can these hollow statements go unchallenged.

In the midst of these weak and faltering pronouncements, Chris embodies
a clarity of purpose that Dunbar-Nelson crafts perfectly to maintain a tension
in the text between the written and spoken word and the main characters'
postures and gestures. When the characters who have made these final patriotic declarations rush to the window to admire the band, Chris remains
at the center of the room. He stands alone physically as he stands alone
ideologically.[7] His appearance emits resolve, for he is "rigidly at attention, a
rapt look on his face" (275). Especially for readers and viewers who identify
with the spoken words, it is easy to interpret this as confirmation that he has
been persuaded to enlist, but his actions do not corroborate that reading. The
"rapt" look on his face may have more to do with his considering how he
will avoid the draft, or perhaps how he is honoring his father's memory by
refusing to fight for the country that let his death go unpunished. There are
several readings of Chris's "rapt" expression, but Dunbar-Nelson's careful
silencing of his voice at this point, together with his defiant body language,
make untenable the suggestion that this militant character has undergone
a patriotic conversion. Indeed, as the band plays "The Battle Hymn of the
Republic," those who approach the window singing along encourage themselves by saying, "Oh, be swift, my soul, to answer . . . Be jubilant my feet!"
Meanwhile, Chris stands stock-still. Of course, Dan also stays put, but for
very different reasons. Dunbar-Nelson leaves her audience with a portrait
of Dan that emphasizes his inability to embody the patriotic manhood that
he values above all else—certainly above his brother and their relationship.
He wants to be at the window admiring the band, but he is confined to his
chair. He must therefore be content to tap his hand to the music.

The play's concluding moments suggest that blindly patriotic blacks must
accept conceptions of justice and righteousness that are grounded in white
supremacy. In order to continue his unequivocal support of U.S. involvement

in the war and his outrage about German atrocities, Dan must disregard much history—or at least disregard the worth of black life within that history. Literary historian Claire Tylee insists that Dan is "the character in the play who carries the most moral authority" (158). For her, he represents the play's message that "those against whom discrimination has been practiced should be the first to adopt the policy of no discrimination" (160). Tylee believes Dan's to be the most righteous voice because he suggests that "black men should be prepared to die on behalf of white French babies" (Tylee 160). Yet as Chris argues, while there is outrage about the deaths of innocent women and children at the hands of Germans, there is little anger about the fact that "our fellow-countrymen throw our little black babies in the flames" (273–74). In other words, the notion that African Americans should be willing to risk their lives for whites is tied to an ethical obligation that never seems to flow in both directions. In fact, the idea that whites should sacrifice *anything*—not necessarily their lives—to end lynching and other racial injustices never even emerges. In our history, blacks are routinely asked to make these sorts of sacrifices, but scholars seem slow to emphasize the fact that these consistent requests keep black morality in question, something to be tested, while white morality remains largely unchallenged. Tylee is not alone in suggesting that blacks best demonstrate their decency with a willingness to overlook personal and collective injustices and do the "right" thing.

There is no question that blacks were sincerely patriotic, but being so required an intellectual negotiation far more complicated than wholesale acceptance of mainstream rhetoric. African Americans recognized that antiblack violence undergirded the nation's most basic practices. As James Weldon Johnson asserted, a black American would perform his civic duty, but "not stupidly, not led by any silly sentiment, not blindly, but with his eyes wide open . . ." (qtd. in Williams, *Torchbearers* 27). African Americans read American culture accurately enough to see that its definitions of justice and democracy never prevented the denial of blacks' basic rights or the mutilation of their bodies.

With Dan, Dunbar-Nelson created a character who completely accepts U.S. rhetoric and does not question the sacrifices it asks African Americans to make, but the text that Dan inhabits reflects a much more complicated understanding than he can espouse, suggesting that despite her commitment to war work, Dunbar-Nelson is not as certain about investing in the nation as her character is. In fact, I contend that it is only because blacks found ways to vent their doubts and anxieties about being loyal to the nation that they could muster any verbal loyalty at all. They were too familiar with the racism upon which the nation was built to be totally convinced that their country would do right by them. Nevertheless, blacks wanted to believe, and being able to do so meant finding ways to express their fears and anxieties. Reading their surroundings accurately, they saw that the nation's most basic tendencies were undergirded by antiblack discourses and practices that would likely perpetuate the denial of black citizenship. This is precisely what Dan cannot admit.

To the extent that doubt about the nation's integrity seeps through this seemingly patriotic script, Dunbar-Nelson acknowledges (even if unconsciously) the country's hypocrisy. When African American patriots did so, they could see themselves as more devoted to American ideals than those who set them forth in the Declaration of Independence, the Constitution, and most recently in the determinations to make the world "safe for democracy." As historian Chad Williams has found, even black soldiers who had never been able to vote "embraced and affirmed their relationship to the state" despite having "every reason to denounce the government on the basis of its lack of reciprocity in fulfilling the social contract of American citizenship" (Williams, *Torchbearers* 59). Indeed, he notes, "As indicated by the frequent appearance of 'my' in their responses, [countless African Americans] internalized a strongly possessive conception of American citizenship . . . that held valuable personal meaning" (Williams, *Torchbearers* 59). In other words, even as the nation refused to acknowledge them, blacks claimed their rightful place. This was possible only because they did not rely on the nation's acceptance of them as citizens to see themselves as such. Thus, real-world black patriots are a testament to the information-processing power of communities. As they affirm for each other that they belong, members of marginalized groups generate discourses and practices that shield them from the social forces designed to destroy their self-conceptions.

Mine Eyes and the periodical in which it appeared remain artifacts of this process among African Americans at the turn of the century. Even as the tenor of Du Bois's *Crisis* editorials on soldiers changed, blacks' right to citizenship was never in question. Though the NAACP worked to reach white readers with *Crisis* magazine, the publication and the parallel public sphere that it fostered reminds us that alternative publics may sometimes try to influence the mainstream, but reaching out to intervene is often secondary to enabling cultural expression and self-affirmation (Herbst 16, 24, 25). If their self-conceptions had depended on how the country treated them, African Americans could not have believed in their status as citizens or even believed in their right to full citizenship. In other words, black patriotism may be best understood as loyalty to oneself and to the belief that African Americans are the true exemplars of democratic ideals; it is not necessarily a self-deprecating loyalty to a nation whose flaws blacks cannot see or whose integrity they implicitly trust.

If blacks were not blindly patriotic, then they were watching for a return on their investment, and Mary Burrill's creative work in the months immediately following the war epitomizes this attitude of expectation. Sacrifices in previous wars had not yielded equality, but blacks wanted to believe that this time would be different. November 1918 brought an end to the military conflict and, the next month, Burrill was publicly considering the price paid by African Americans. The December 1918 issue of *The Liberator* included her poem "To a Black Soldier Fallen in the War." It reads:

> O Earth, lie light upon him
> Deep pillowed on thy breast;
> O Winds, blow soft above him
> And gently lull to rest.
>
> O questioning Heart, be silent,
> Allay the bitter cry—
> "Why should *he* thus perish?
> Why, for freedom, die?"

This poem gives voice to the anxiety that many must have felt, knowing that the community had once again placed faith in U.S. citizenship. Blacks were proud of those who fought but worried that their sacrifices would not bring what they had hoped. If blacks were driven to fight because they felt loyalty to the country, the United States may again prove less than grateful to them; it may even ignore their contributions, only celebrating and memorializing white soldiers.[8] Or, if the men had fought hoping to win greater freedom and equality for their race, their loved ones may still be plagued with discrimination and denials of citizenship. These were valid fears, and only time would tell.

Yet as Burrill's poetic persona focuses on the men who had paid the ultimate price—those who would not be able to return and see if the nation would make good on its democratic promises—the speaker can only hope that the Earth and Wind will be gentle. The poem seems to suggest that the black soldier could expect more comfort from nature in death than he had received from his country in life. The black soldier had probably not felt "pillowed" in the United States nor encouraged to "rest" in his native land. More likely, he had been hounded by a lack of economic opportunity and terrorized by mobs. Even as the speaker in the poem prays that the soldier will rest in peace, he or she cannot find peace for his or her own heart, which persists in questioning the circumstances. The heart's cry will not be allayed. The dash after the word *cry* suggests a long pause, during which the persona attempts to set the questions aside, but they nevertheless emerge. In order to fight for the nation that had so consistently disappointed him, the soldier had, as Du Bois once encouraged, set aside his "special grievances." In this poem, the loved ones and community that outlived him cannot continue to do so.

Just months after Burrill's poetic tribute to fallen soldiers appeared in *The Liberator,* the magazine published her lynching play *Aftermath,* wherein the main character returns from fighting overseas and seems more militant than ever. African Americans who lived to see the end of the war faced challenges to their beliefs about their rightful place in the nation, and Burrill's lynching play reflects their willingness to engage the questions and feelings sparked by those challenges. Appearing in April 1919, it emerged in the midst of postwar tensions that would soon produce the famous "Red Summer," during which race riots erupted in several U.S. cities.[9] Indeed, I would suggest that Burrill's play embodies the black self-determination that made the Red Summer possible, not because that spirit sparked a surge in white violence—white violence had been ever present—but because blacks were less often simply massacred; they fought back as Burrill's protagonist does. Turn-of-the-century periodicals bear evidence that black militancy intensified in response to the leadership of those who fought in the Great War. Burrill's script is another dramatic example of the role that magazines played in making the black soldier central to this militancy, both reflecting its existence and fueling its growth.

Aftermath

Burrill's *Aftermath* reflects the spirit of expectation bred by the community's knowledge—largely through periodicals—of the injustices that black soldiers had faced at training camps and at war overseas. Given all that soldiers endured and given the grief of black families mourning fallen heroes, communities' reasons for expecting real reciprocity were multiplying. Nevertheless, black dignity, pride, and expectation continued to be met with opposition, as reflected in both the archive and the repertoire of the early 1900s. Even before black soldiers returned home from the Great War, whites were preparing to obliterate any confidence that they may have gained from serving overseas. For instance, Southern employers who were used to paying blacks low wages expected that "insolence to the whites . . . will probably be worse when the troops come home, flushed with the praises that they have received for their work in France" (Williams, *Torchbearers* 227–28). Thus, as black soldiers looked forward to the better lives for which they had risked life and limb, whites prepared themselves to crush any signs of self-worth. The same proved to be true when black troops returned to Chicago and New York City in February 1919. There was much fanfare in both cities, but when New York's own 369th Infantry landed, one million people watched as they marched up Fifth Avenue to Harlem (Franklin 383). These public displays of self-affirmation were answered by a revived Ku Klux Klan. According to John Hope Franklin, "Within ten months, shortly after the close of the war, the Klan made more than 200 public appearances in twenty-seven states" (384). The organization now had a presence in areas that had not previously been known for overt racial hatred, and many candidates for public office believed that they would not be competitive if they were not on good terms with the Klan (Franklin 384).

For decades, blacks had defended their reputations, and they had again defended their nation.[10] Now, "all over the country the black press was asking how the race would be rewarded for helping win the war. Several organizations had picked delegates to attend the Paris peace talks and present the world leadership with Black America's grievances" (Kornweibel, *"Seeing Red"* 79). Also, many individuals no doubt decided to pursue their own interests with the same vigor and in the same ways that the country had compelled them to work for its interests—which rarely took them into account. During this time, the returning soldier increasingly "symbolized the development of a masculinist spirit that characterized the New Negro,"[11] and thirty-five-year-old schoolteacher Mary Burrill reminds us that black women helped make him a representative figure. Seemingly concerned that Dunbar-Nelson's protagonist Chris could be read as a sacrificial Christ figure, she created John, a returning soldier who makes it clear that the War Cross is the only cross that he will bear.

When Mary Burrill used drama to answer Dunbar-Nelson's contribution to the conversation on patriotism and lynching, she placed in the archive additional evidence of the intellectual diversity found in African American communities. Like Dunbar-Nelson, Burrill maximized drama's nonlinguistic resources, but she chose to make her protagonist's body language match his self-affirming words, eradicating uncertainty about his feelings and intentions. She also emphasized props and symbols, especially the Bible, the gun, and the War Cross. In the final analysis, Burrill's play is also about what "mine eyes have seen," but in this case, the author proves willing to admit explicitly that she has observed the nation's hypocrisy and can predict its (justified) "aftermath."

Aftermath begins six months after the father of the family has been lynched, and it continues the genre's tradition of spotlighting de-generation. The middle generation is missing; the father has been murdered and the mother is never mentioned. The household is now made up of Mam Sue, who is eighty years old, and her grandchildren, sixteen-year-old Millie and eighteen-year-old Lonnie. Their older brother John is overseas fighting in World War I. Millie and John correspond by mail, but Millie has refused to tell him about their father's death. However, the family has received word that the war is over and that John will be heading home, so Mam Sue expects Millie to mail a letter containing the truth. Millie continues to resist, but they are interrupted by a visit from Reverend Moseby. Shortly thereafter, Lonnie comes home with news that John will soon arrive because his company has landed at Charleston, and he has some free time before they board the train that will take them to Camp Mead for official discharge. Lonnie and Reverend Moseby leave with plans to return to see John; when they are alone again, Millie and Mam Sue continue their discussion about the need to tell John about his father's death. Millie maintains, "Don' let's tell him now! He's got only a li'l hour to spend with us . . . Let 'im be happy jes a li'l longer" (86).

Against Mam Sue's wishes, Millie becomes a set designer, arranging the room to suggest that the beloved patriarch is still alive. The audience never learns his name, but his presence is felt through a prominent prop, the Bible. Because they know that John will be eager to see his father, Millie decides to "fix the Bible jes like dad's been in an' been a-readin' in it" (86). Indeed, as the stage directions dictate, "*Millie takes the Bible from the mantel and opening it at random lays it on the table; she draws the old armchair close to the table as her father had been wont to do every evening. . . .*" Thus, in spotlighting this home, the play preserves evidence of the father's reverent life but also shows that the blow dealt by the mob leads Millie to use remnants of his Christian lifestyle to conceal his death. Mam Sue shakes her head at Millie and then begins singing a spiritual. Soon thereafter, John is heard whistling as he approaches the house (86). Millie fields a few questions, but her set design works.

John responds enthusiastically to the evidence of his father's presence: "Let's see whut he's been readin'—" (88). Picking up the open Bible, John finds the passages that he believes his father has been studying: "love your enemies" and "do good to them that hate you." John angrily lets the Bible fall to the table, protesting, "That ain't the dope they been feedin' us soljers on!" (88). At this point, lynching has motivated Millie to use the Bible as a prop in a deceitful performance, and John has handled it with less respect than his father would have. This household is experiencing a changing of the guard, and Burrill would have her readers and viewers remember that an unjust lynching precipitates it; her text therefore registers the embodied practices of both blacks and whites. This Christian nation has tolerated the murder of a devout Christian, giving those who survive him less and less reason to believe in the morality of their countrymen. Like Rachel and Mrs. Loving, the family in *Aftermath* must live with lynching, and doing so involves grappling with their wavering faith.

Millie's facade crumbles when a neighbor stops by, admires John's medals, and laments that his father did not live to see his success. John soon shakes Millie for answers, declaring that he is man enough to handle the news. He demands, "[D]id he suffer much? Wuz he sick long?" (90). Millie finally exclaims, "They burnt him down by the big gum tree!" (90). As Millie recounts the circumstances of the father's death, gruesome details are few, but a more violent truth comes into focus: the death brings consequences for his family but not for his murderers.

Because the spotlight remains on the family, not the victimized man himself, the script preserves debates about Christianity's value to African Americans. As I have suggested, debate is one of the embodied practices of black belonging made accessible by lynching drama. When the action of *Aftermath* begins, Mam Sue is singing a hymn. Then, by "reading" the fire in the hearth, she predicts that something "big" will happen that night. The last time that Mam Sue prophesied, Millie's father was lynched, so she asks Mam Sue to stop. However, her grandmother insists that young people should value her prophesies because God sends her messages in the fire just as he did with Moses (83). She also clarifies: the night Millie's father died, she had not seen "big doin's" in the fire but "evil doin's." She had therefore warned him to stay away from town with his cotton, "but he wou'd'n lis'n tuh his ole mammy" (83). Here, Mam Sue suggests that God sends her warnings, and the family would have avoided sorrow if her son had listened. Millie is not comforted, however. She says that the prophesies only scare her. Mam Sue insists that her granddaughter's fear stems from her lack of trust in the Lord; instead, she should believe that "He kin tek keer o' yuh no matter whut com'!" (83).

Millie challenges Mam Sue's claim because she trusts her own ability to read her surroundings and experiences accurately. Millie maintains, "Sometimes I thinks that Gawd's done fu'got us po' cullud people. Gawd didn' tek no keer o' po' dad and *he* put *his* trus' in Him!" (83). Millie continues to vent, "He uster set evah night by dis fire at dis here table and read his

Bible an' pray—but jes look whut happen' to dad!" (83). Mam Sue inter-
rupts Millie, scolding her for "dat sinnertalk." Mam Sue reminds Millie that
she had prayed for her brother John to return safely from the war and the
letter that they received yesterday said that the fighting had stopped and
John has survived "all dem battuls" (83). Millie relents, "I reckon youse
right, Mam Sue. But ef anything had a-happen' to John I wuz' nevah goin'
to pray no mo'!" (83).[12]

Once John enters, the script features debates about whether full citizenship for African Americans will more likely result from the gun or the Bible.
Because both tools were used by the "founding" fathers, these discussions
represent an awareness that identifying the contours of African American
citizenship requires considering blacks' relationship to both violence and
faith. After giving Millie and his grandmother the gifts that he has brought
them, John takes two army service pistols from his bag, saying "An' these
las' are fu' youahs truly" (87). At one point, Mam Sue says that John sounds
like he has forgotten God. Without hesitation, John explains that he has
not, "but I've quit thinkin' that prayers kin do ever'thing" (88). After all,
he had watched some men go into battle with a curse on their lips and live,
while those who had "read their Bible befo' battle, an' prayed to live" died
on the field (88).

Just as John questions the idea that prayer is sufficient, he questions the
Bible itself. He likens the Bible to a drug, insisting that the commandment
to "do good to them that hate you" is "dope." While those clinging to the
Bible are intoxicated, allowing alterations to their ability to reason and make
decisions, John suggests that he is the picture of sobriety and discipline when
he handles a gun. When Millie is frightened by the sight of the two pistols
and reproaches John for bragging about the accuracy of his aim, he assures
her, "Nevah you worry, li'l Sis, John's nevah goin' to use 'em less it's right
fu' him to" (88). This makes the moment when guns fill the space that the
Bible had occupied even more significant, and Burrill emphasizes it. The stage
directions are explicit: "(He places the pistols on the mantel—on the very
spot where the Bible has lain)" (88). Convinced that guns are sometimes
more relevant than Bibles, John insists that judgment is key; one must be
able to discern when it is "right for him to use it."

As intense as these textual conversations about Bibles and guns are, the
script itself enters larger debates about manhood and the implications of
black men's decisions about how to express it. Aftermath registers an awareness of lynching as master/piece theater, embodied practices among white
men who want to assert their superiority. The father had led a manly life,
working hard to provide for his family. A white man had insisted upon

challenging the father's price for cotton, calling him a liar, and hitting him (90). The father's reaction had been natural: to hit back. Thus, the father had exhibited manliness in his daily life—working hard, providing for his family, and reading his Bible every night (86). White manhood assaulted his manliness. Then, when the father acted out of masculinity by physically defending himself, white manhood was equally intolerant and lynched him. The father's manhood had been problematic for whites whether expressed through restrained manliness or by reactionary masculinity. Thus, while he does not offer himself as a sacrificial lamb, as many expect Chris to do in *Mine Eyes Have Seen*, the father becomes a Christ figure in that he was killed by lesser men determined to contradict his view of himself.

In the dramatic present, eighteen-year-old Lonnie is entering manhood, and Burrill highlights his active and critical assessment of his choices. The family asks Lonnie why it took him so long to get home with the news that John's company had landed in Charleston. Lonnie explains that he saw some white hoodlums, so he took the long way home. Millie laments, "Po' Lonnie! He allus dodgin' po' w'ite trash!" Lonnie responds, "Well, yuh see whut dad got by not dodgin' 'em" (85). Clearly, Lonnie believes that a black man's decisions will largely determine his experiences.[13] He does not simply trust in God, but neither does he believe that he is capable of defending himself. Lonnie understands that the gun and the Bible represent traditional lenses through which to consider his life choices, but he refuses to invest in either. He trusts neither symbol of American self-determination because he recognizes white men's commitment to keeping black men subordinate. Lonnie is therefore uncomfortable when he notices John's pistols on the mantel. According to the stage directions, upon seeing the guns, he draws back in fear and warns, "You'd bettah hide them things! No cullud man bettah be seen wid dem things down heah!" (85). For Lonnie, the only wise choice is to avoid embodying manliness or masculinity. His reading of dominant discourses and practices leads him to avoid the props and postures of manhood that white men claim as their exclusive province. His choices place him in opposition to both John and his deceased father. Through Lonnie, Burrill not only represents a different way of being a black man; she also emphasizes how much racist violence keeps them negotiating a treacherous terrain—even at home where they are supposedly not at war.

John does not approve of Lonnie's approach. John says that he will never hide his guns, because when he was wounded in battle, he lost "all the rabbit-blood 'at wuz in me!" (85). Even before he knows about his father's death, John says that military service would have benefited his brother by taking "some of the skeeriness out" of him (88). When he learns of his father's murder, John "strides over to Lonnie and seizes him by the collar" and demands, "An' whut wuz you doin' when them hounds come in here after dad?" (90). Lonnie responds pitifully, "They wuz so many of 'em come an' git 'im—whut could Ah do?" John does not relent: "Do? You could 'ave fought 'em like a man!" (90). Mam Sue interjects on Lonnie's behalf, reminding John that they do not have guns, but John insists, "Then, he should 'ave burnt their damn kennels ovah their heads!" (90). For John, a violent attack warrants physical retaliation of some sort. Even if Lonnie could only burn down the perpetrator's houses, he would have inflicted some loss on them rather than simply accept the great loss that they imposed on him and his family.

Retaliation will not neutralize the injustice or bring their father back, but in John's eyes, an attempt at preserving dignity must be made, so he grabs his gun and leaves to find his father's killers. Right before exiting, he reasons, "I've been helpin' the w'ite man git his freedom, I reckon I'd bettah try now to get my own" (90). This sentiment is preserved in both the archive and the repertoire through creative works like this play as well as written and oral accounts of real-life riots and other instances when blacks defended themselves against racist violence. Thus, John is an example of how the black soldier served as a representative figure who embodied existing perspectives on black identity and citizenship and encouraged more discussion and debate.[14]

Though the characters in *Aftermath* approach dilemmas in vastly different ways, they all speak dialect, and Burrill creates this commonality to highlight the intellectual diversity in black communities.[15] The text assumes that even those without formal education are interested in debating the complex issues surrounding African Americans' racial identity and national citizenship. These are not the concern only of those who speak so-called standard English; speaking dialect does not mean that one has a particular stance on an issue, and it certainly does not mean that one has *no* opinion.

This point is vividly made when Burrill has John foreground his awareness of his own logic. The script thus encourages its audience to value intellectual exploration and to recognize the validity of black experiences. That is, the black soldier, as representative figure, models weighing mainstream rhetoric and conventional wisdom against personal and community knowledge, so African Americans' ability to critically assess their surroundings is both represented as an existing asset and encouraged to continue. John shares, "I've seen a heap an' I've done a tall lot o' thinkin' since I've been erway from here. An' I b'lieve it's jes like this—beyon' a certain point prayers ain't no good! The Lawd does jes so much for you, then it's up to you to do the res' fu' yourse'f. The Lord's done His part when He's done give me strength an' courage; I got tuh do the res' fu' myse'f!" (88). With this, John suggests that his God-given strength and courage are resources that he should use to improve his life, and he says that he reached this conclusion after pondering his beliefs and his circumstances. He did not rely on the religious aphorisms that he had been taught in a household headed by a man who read his Bible daily. John saw the need to test those beliefs against his experiences, trusting his capacity to interpret his surroundings.

Ultimately, all of Burrill's characters speak dialect but they do not agree on anything, so as the script was read or performed formally or informally, it encouraged audiences to consider, discuss, and debate the many perspectives represented. At the same time, the text itself seems to have come into being because its author wanted to put forth a perspective on lynching and patriotism that had not been forcefully explored by her predecessor. In fact, Burrill entered a larger debate with this play by publishing it in a white-run periodical committed to socialist critique. By choosing *The Liberator* magazine, Burrill made clear that socialism offered valid ideas and concepts to those considering the contours of African American identity and citizenship. *Aftermath* survives as an imprint of blacks' engagement with leftist politics as they continued to assert their "New Negro" status.

Just as important, because Burrill chose to publish in *The Liberator*, her script reminds us that African Americans recognized that some of the alternative spaces that would accommodate black perspectives had been created by whites who were willing to operate on the political margin. One-act lynching dramas more readily targeted black audiences because they were conducive to publication in magazines, but mainstream periodicals would not have welcomed them,[16] so the publications that proved receptive to lynching plays catered to and helped create alternative discursive spaces. African Americans read their surroundings accurately enough to recognize when mainstream discourses and practices were being challenged, whether the groups doing it were led by blacks or not. Because it entered the archive via *The Liberator* magazine, *Aftermath* stands as an example of the role that interracial networks could play in black self-affirmation.

The Liberator was a white-run magazine edited by Max Eastman, who prioritized leftist beliefs over the comfort of the political mainstream; the magazine therefore created a space for black self-affirmation, partly because acknowledging black worth was always outside of the mainstream. Still, it is important that artists and editors such as Eastman chose their position on the margin; they were not forced there by exclusion. Thus, the space that they fostered for black self-affirmation was qualitatively different from that created by magazines like *The Crisis*, which was founded to advance African American civil liberties.

At a time when federal authorities were suspicious of anyone who was less than enthusiastic about the war effort, blacks felt especially vulnerable to having their civil rights revoked, and history has shown that they attracted disproportionate suspicion, even when not involved in particularly subversive activities.[17] On the other hand, whites needed to be quite radical to attract federal ire. Of course, some did, such as Eastman, who was placed on trial for his work on *The Masses* magazine in 1918, but the fact that he soon began editing of *The Liberator* with the same political convictions may suggest how safe he ultimately felt.[18]

One way to gauge the difference between *Crisis* magazine and publications edited by whites in the era of federal surveillance is to consider one of Claude McKay's most famous poems. McKay's "The White Fiends" was rejected by *Crisis*, so McKay submitted it to *Pearson's* (Hutchinson 130). *Pearson's* published the poem, which unabashedly highlights white barbarism and American hypocrisy. Soon, *The Liberator* featured "The White Fiends" on the very page on which Burrill's *Aftermath* ends. Given that the poem critiques white hypocrisy as fearlessly as *Crisis* reported on lynchings, what does the magazine's rejection of the poem indicate? There are many possibilities, but we must consider the fact that *Crisis* and other black publications fell under tremendous federal pressure designed to preempt radicalism, not simply respond to it. Blacks found to be disloyal could expect poor treatment. Even the most loyal were lynched, so black editors were cautious with very good reason. The appearance of radical black literature in magazines edited by whites may therefore reflect the latitude that whites safely enjoyed but that black editors did not take for granted. Of course, I am not suggesting that whites did not have their rights violated and/or revoked for holding subversive political views, but given our nation's history, if they were stripped of their rights and dignity, it often came as an appalling surprise. Meanwhile, blacks would more likely be surprised if their worth was acknowledged. It makes sense that people who have routinely seen their rights violated—indeed been assured constantly that they have no rights—will more strategically express their antiestablishment views than those accustomed to having their rights respected.

I would suggest, in fact, that publishing the harsh critiques that characterize "The White Fiends" and *Aftermath* in a white-run magazine proved attractive partly because radical publications under white leadership were subjected to less harassment than those with blacks at the helm. Those magazines may have represented a sort of shield for black authors. The alternative space that they provided seemed to be less severely suppressed.

Another way to understand the relative latitude enjoyed by leftist magazines edited by whites is to consider the difference between choosing to operate at the margin and being forced there by exclusion and denigration. Those whose work appeared in *The Masses,* for example, could and did publish in mainstream magazines, but they were "more excited" about "distributing their experimental drawings, radical stories, and challenging editorials" (Herbst 99). Furthermore, when these editors and artists were indicted under the Espionage Act, newspaper coverage of the trial highlighted "the social status and talents of the men" (131). In stark contrast, when editors of the black leftist magazine *The Messenger* were detained for their views, the judge released them from jail, convinced that "these two fresh-faced bombastic Negroes . . . could never produce such a sophisticated paper" (Williams, *Torchbearers* 25–26). In this instance, blacks were marginalized to the point that editors A. Philip Randolph and Chandler Owen avoided a lengthy trial; their competence was so fundamentally questioned that they were not deemed to be a political threat. This unspeakably insulting outcome was fortunate to the extent that the slightest acknowledgment that blacks may present a political threat can lead to unpunished black death. Just as certain, though, the incident exemplifies routine denial of black citizenship; they could not expect due process and equal treatment under the law. While Owen and Randolph's intelligence seemed unimaginable, Eastman and his colleagues were admired for their intellect. Also, there was friendly exchange between Max Eastman and President Woodrow Wilson as the president explained resistance to Eastman's work. Wilson essentially asked that Eastman try to understand that war times called for extraordinary measures, requiring strategies that would not normally be considered, especially regarding free speech and privacy (Herbst 131). Though Eastman worked at the political margin, he seemed to have freedom of movement toward the center that was unavailable to Randolph and Owen.

Because Eastman used his position as editor to critique the status quo and challenge conventional political wisdom, *The Liberator* offered an alterative space that would welcome black expression. As George Hutchinson has found, "*The Masses* and *The Liberator,* often citing John Brown, consistently argued for the necessity of racial self-defense, by violence if necessary, and repeatedly published works emphasizing the irony of (white) American freedom being bought with black lives" (250). However, it is equally true that these magazines were ambivalent toward blacks, moving "back and forth between two positions—righteous indignation about the treatment of African Americans (especially in the South), and the worst sort of racist stereotyping" (Herbst 116). In fact, the staff and artists were "far more sophisticated and humane" when addressing "[white] women's rights" (Herbst 116).

In other words, ~~white leftists created outlets that could become a unique space of freedom for African Americans, but not because they sought to enable black self-affirmation.~~ For instance, though *The Liberator* exposed U.S. hypocrisy, it did so to encourage African Americans to support a world-wide workers' movement that diminished the role racism played in creating inequality.[19] Nevertheless, *The Liberator* was part of an infrastructure that enabled expression of ideas that otherwise would not be tolerated, so blacks could use this alternative discursive space for their own purposes. White editors' goals did not necessarily limit what blacks could do with the spaces that they provided. As Susan Herbst explains, it is impossible to act without alliances and constituencies,[20] and African Americans recognized the potential power of the connections fostered by *The Liberator.*

The Liberator was an important venue that Burrill could maximize as she answered Dunbar-Nelson, whose play *Mine Eyes Have Seen* evokes socialism but refuses to articulate whether African Americans have anything to gain by considering its tenets. When Chris is defending his decision to avoid the draft, his neighbor Jake says with derision, "Bravo! You've learned the patter well. Talk like the fellows at the Socialist meetings!" (272). Chris's brother and sister shout, "Socialist meetings!" Their tone is not specified by the stage directions, but when Chris asks "Well?" he is "defiant." His defiance seems to have been both appropriate and unnecessary. That is, he seems to have read correctly a certain amount of judgment from his siblings, but they are not prepared to press the point. The only verbal response to his "Well?" is from Dan: "Oh, nothing; it explains. All right, go on—any more?" (272). Thus, ~~Dunbar-Nelson crafts her text to leave completely unclear where socialism should stand in the community conversation.~~ The political orientation is important enough to include, and its influence on African Americans is acknowledged, yet there is a refusal to condone it—even as the condemnation issued by the text is noncommittal.

Burrill seems to have found this treatment less than sufficient because she publishes her similarly themed play in an outlet that explicitly aligns itself with socialism. Her doing so suggests that socialism is relevant to private discussions of black identity and citizenship that might be fueled by periodical reading. In this way, the work reflects attitudes in the community that gave rise to the many groups and individual activists that wedded class consciousness with racial solidarity.[21] For many, black nationalism was not at all at odds with a class-based analysis of the race's problems, and Burrill's play became evidence of that position when it entered the archive via *The Liberator.*

Of course, Burrill could have taken this stance by publishing in the black-run socialist magazine *The Messenger*; however, its African American editors were so often under attack that its schedule proved erratic. The debut issue appeared in November 1917, the second emerged in January 1918, and the third issue corresponded with the editors' speaking tour six months later in the summer of 1918, which commanded the government's aggressive attention. The spoken word of editors A. Philip Randolph and Chandler Owen at podiums around the country led to their detainment in Cleveland in early August and later to the government's revoking of their second-class mailing permit. The fourth issue of the magazine therefore did not appear until March 1919, another six months later (Kornweibel, *"Seeing Red"* 78). Also during this time, Owen was called to military service, so the magazine's unpredictable schedule points to the suppressive practices undertaken by the local draft board, which was likely following federal guidance (Kornweibel, *"Seeing Red"* 78). Clearly, during and immediately after the war, African Americans were under intense scrutiny, making the appearance of militant literature in white publications even more practical.

Whether they used outlets created by progressive whites or worked to strengthen all-black organizations, African Americans found ways to express perspectives that mainstream discourses and practices sought to erase. Because they maximized several kinds of publications and different sorts of spaces, evidence remains of a range of embodied practice in black communities that suggests anything but homogeneity. For example, when Washington, D.C., officials made it difficult for black activists to host Owen and Randolph at Dunbar High School, they moved the lecture to a church (Kornweibel, *"Seeing Red"* 96). Similarly, a tailor shop in Harlem was a hub for black socialist and communist factions at the height of government surveillance (Kornweibel, *"Seeing Red"* 94). In all instances, blacks were invested in affirming each other, often by debating. It was common knowledge that black leaders and activists had very different ideas about how to proceed politically and otherwise. Also, some were overtly activist while others hoped to effect change via art and literature. These differences and disagreements indicate that many blacks believed that addressing themselves to their own communities was important. They assumed that the members of their communities were intellectually engaged and held views that were worth hearing and influencing.

As an access point for both the archive and repertoire of U.S. culture in the World War I era, Burrill's *Aftermath* marks the extent to which the community conversation was characterized by debate. Burrill lived in Washington, D.C., when the city was abuzz with controversy regarding Grimké's *Rachel*—controversy that helped to inspire Dunbar-Nelson's *Mine Eyes Have Seen* and its explicit engagement with lynching and patriotism. Like

Dunbar-Nelson, Burrill linked the mob and the military, and she seems to have valued periodical culture, writing and publishing a one-act script. Yet, it is clear that Dunbar-Nelson's work left Burrill convinced that an important contribution remained to be made. Burrill's one-act adds to a community conversation in which the black soldier serves as a representative figure for black citizenship, but as we have seen, her portrait of him differs from Dunbar-Nelson's.

Different Beyond Words

Because both Burrill and Dunbar-Nelson invested in periodical culture—and, by extension, in the embodied practices of communal literacy[22]—it is worth comparing the meanings that their scripts create with resources other than words. Both dramas were available for amateurs to bring to life and both offer much in the way of black self-affirmation, but *Mine Eyes* contains

Figure 4. The image of "Lucy" that immediately precedes the text of the play *Mine Eyes Have Seen,* by Alice Dunbar-Nelson. *Crisis,* April 1919, p. 271.

elements that diminish the power of the protagonist's self-affirming words while *Aftermath* corroborates the black soldier's bold declarations. Burrill's play represents divergent opinions, but as it does so, it enacts certainty that blacks' experiences should influence their decisions as much as biblical teaching and patriotic rhetoric. Burrill animates this certainty by making her protagonist's embodied practices match the spirit of his words. In this way, she revises Dunbar-Nelson's handling of the resources of drama, including gestures and objects, as well as its emphasis on the corporeal and visual.

Figure 5. The sketch that ends *Mine Eyes Have Seen*. Most characters are at the window admiring a marching band while Dan is confined to his chair and Chris stands alone. *Crisis*, April 1919, p. 275.

Aftermath allows no ambivalence about the validity of its soldier's perspective, but in publication *Mine Eyes* is accompanied by two black-and-white sketches that corroborate—not the militancy voiced by Chris—but the impotence of Lucy and Dan. For instance, just as Lucy has been associated with fear and limited possibilities in the words of the play, her picture evokes vulnerability. She looks frail and her big eyes are doe-like in their beauty, which seems in need of protection. One cannot help but notice too that the design of her clothing seems haunted by lynching—victimization, not the armed resistance of race riots. She is wearing a top reminiscent of a sailor outfit, and the decorative collar and tie resemble a noose. The design is just suggestive enough to be eerie. Also, her facial expression is only mildly sad, certainly not one of horror or terror, and she seems to be looking out, perhaps pondering the future. Thus, the tie seems both appropriate and out of place; it seems to belong to the outfit but also to evoke another register. One cannot be sure whether this is intentional or not, a coincidence with no meaning or a deliberate evocation designed to create just the slightest discomfort in the reader.[23] As a result, the tie parallels the father in that he is not represented in the script but haunts it.

Likewise, the image that appears on the last page of *Mine Eyes* punctuates the play's final moment by emphasizing passivity, not self-determination. Everyone except Chris and Dan is at the window admiring the band marching down the street. Dan is in the foreground of this image. The patchwork quilt that covers his maimed lower half is closest to the viewer. Following the line of the quilt up toward Dan's torso, one sees that Dan is facing away from the window where everyone has gathered to admire the parade. Though he does not look directly at his quilt-covered lower half, the final image is one of unfulfilled longing and palpable limitation.

While Dunbar-Nelson's play is accompanied by sketches that underscore the limitation her characters feel, Burrill's script emphasizes embodied practices that corroborate the self-worth that her main character articulates as he tests religious sayings against his lived experiences and assumes the right to defend himself and to feel and express personal pride and dignity. In fact, even though it is clear that whites will attack either expression of black manhood (manliness or masculinity), Burrill uses John to showcase the dignified militancy that has won black men honor abroad and that they deserve to exemplify at home. Furthermore, this soldier's militancy represents the grief and indignation that he is entitled to express about the injustice that greets him at home. John rages: "I'm sick o' these w'ite folks doin's—we're 'fine, trus'worthy feller citizuns' when they're handin' us out guns . . . an' chuckin' us off to die; but we ain't a damn thing when it comes to handin' us the rights we done fought an' bled fu'!" (90). After a few more bitter words, he picks up his service pistol and heads for the door, demanding that his younger brother come with him to avenge his father's death. The play ends with their departure, and the reader knows that John's rage will likely bring more violence to this home. John assures his grandmother and sister that he is not scared of the whites who might kill him, but his bravery does not erase the fact that the family has already lost the father and will likely lose two sons. Thus, John's justified militant grief also predicts the additional mourning that his family will do in its wake. It is important to note, however, that if the mob retaliates more forcefully after John's attempt at retribution, it will be responding to explicit black self-affirmation. John insists on his right to define for himself how to express his manhood and citizenship, not allowing biblical "wisdom" and white definitions of patriotism to convince him to accept less than his white counterparts enjoy.

Because the play makes clear that manliness offers no more guarantee of safety than masculinity, it suggests that community debates must continue because no clear answer exists for the questions that blacks face in the postwar era. At issue was not simply whether black men would be killed but whether a life of dodging whites was worth living at all. It was not merely a question of whether black families would find sorrow but of *how*—with the loved one murdered for maintaining dignity or killed even as he bartered it? These were weighty questions, and black women encouraged discussion of them.

Indeed, the gravity of these questions makes the performance history of both *Mine Eyes* and *Aftermath* more suggestive, because that history demonstrates the importance the dramatists placed on inspiring difficult community conversation. It seems that *Mine Eyes* was produced only because Dunbar-Nelson herself brought it to life at the high school where she worked (Perkins and Stephens, *Strange Fruit* 411). While many black theater histories discount work staged under such circumstances in order to boast about the few scripts that made it to Broadway, such biases hinder our understanding of the cultural work that early black-authored dramas accomplished. Dunbar-Nelson clearly recognized the potential of the amateur stage to represent, interrogate, and mold blacks' perceptions of themselves. She ultimately declared drama to be the "best medium" for depicting black life (qtd. in Hull 73).

Given the tension that characterizes *Mine Eyes,* Dunbar-Nelson would have her audience feel conflicted as the plays ends, and she surely accomplished this in the production at Howard High School in Wilmington, Delaware (Perkins and Stephens, *Strange Fruit* 411).[24] Though pictures of the production are not available, the stage was likely modest and the audience would likely have known the actors as members of the community. The intimacy of an amateur production like this would have allowed the audience to feel Dan's disappointment and his straining against his chair. Moreover, many of the students and teachers in attendance would have known blacks who were serving overseas at that very moment. Surely, their pride in their acquaintances' military service did not obliterate their conflicted feelings about their risking their lives. Dunbar-Nelson presents African Americans' vexed relationship to the country of their birth, insisting that it is worth writing about and talking about. After all, the damage caused by the War is equal to that caused by lynching. Her work suggests that in either case, the black household loses its men to a nation that never acknowledged their manhood. No number of optimistic *Crisis* editorials could have eliminated their misgivings, and Dunbar-Nelson tapped into exactly those feelings—helping her audience to insist that the black community's anxiety become a part of the conversation.

Mary Burrill was also a teacher who prioritized drama, the amateur stage, and the dynamic discussion they fostered. Private performances of *Aftermath* likely took place, but the archive most explicitly preserves a performance that very much upset Burrill because her ending was modified. In 1928, the Krigwa Players brought the script to life at the Frolic Theatre in New York as part of David Belasco's Little Theatre Tournament. Rather than closing with John and Lonnie's departure, the Krigwa performance concluded thusly: "Shots are heard off stage, the soldier staggers in . . . and dies melodramatically" (*Billboard*, May 19, 1928, 7). Burrill complained in a letter to Du Bois that "the ending tacked on by the players changed what might otherwise have been an effective dramatic close into cheap melo-dramatic claptrap" (Du Bois Papers). Thus, it is clear that Burrill deliberately ended her play in a way that merely pointed to future tragedy. Doing so was important to her, I believe, because it avoided simplifying the issues to be considered, thereby allowing the play to provoke further discussion. It seems that, to Burrill, "an effective dramatic close" would have inspired difficult conversations about how best to respond to lynching, especially in light of black military service—as well as discussions about how difficult a question that is to answer.

Because the 1928 Krigwa performance was for the David Belasco Sixth Annual Little Theatre Tournament, the audience was predominantly white, and scholars have speculated that this fact led to the change in the ending.[25] This may be the case, but Burrill was not disappointed because her work was reaching whites; after all, she published this piece in *The Liberator*. Her dissatisfaction more likely stemmed from the idea that content should be changed for whites, for *The Liberator* had welcomed her play as an important contribution to the conversations that it hoped to generate. When they began publication on February 12, 1918, the editors vowed to "conduct a remorseless campaign against lynch law" (*Liberator* inaugural issue). Clearly, Burrill never assumed that militant black self-affirmation could only take place in all-black discursive spaces, but she was not interested in placing her work where acceptance was predicated on changing her message.

In working with *The Liberator*, Burrill contributed to her community's conversation about how black identity should develop. Should socialist ideas influence blacks' sense of themselves? Should Christianity? Will they adhere to mainstream definitions of patriotism? Of manhood? Should black men swallow indignities to stay alive for their families? Like Grimké and Dunbar-Nelson, Burrill raised painful questions and encouraged relentless discussion of them, understanding that—as long as they were living with lynching—closure would remain elusive.

CHAPTER FOUR

THE BLACK LAWYER
PRESERVING TESTIMONY

As they continued to write lynching plays, black women authors preserved African Americans' perspectives on themselves and their communities. One-act revisions within the genre initially depicted the upstanding character of the race by showcasing the black soldier, but it was not long before the black lawyer became the centerpiece of conversations about identity and citizenship. In fact, the black soldier helped set the stage for the increasing visibility of black attorneys. First, some of the most prominent court cases after World War I involved black soldiers. Second, African Americans inspired by the soldiers' heroism defended themselves in the race riots of 1919, and years later many remained in jail and on trial.

The conditions under which the black soldier and lawyer became pivotal figures remain legible in the issues of *Crisis* published between 1919 and 1925. The magazine demonstrates that blacks' experiences with courts of law came to epitomize their sense of themselves and their citizenship—according to the extent to which they were respected as witnesses, included on juries, taken seriously as plaintiffs, and encouraged to become lawyers.[1] In the years immediately following World War I, a shift occurs in *Crisis* coverage: its spotlight on black soldiers represented by white attorneys moves to draw attention to black attorneys defending African Americans from every walk of life. Out of this moment of transition in black legal activity and written accounts of it, the next two one-act lynching plays emerge. Georgia Douglas Johnson writes *A Sunday Morning in the South* (1925) and Myrtle Smith Livingston publishes *For Unborn Children* (1926), and both gesture toward the black attorney as a figure who embodies the race's faith in truth and justice and its commitment to preserving community testimony.

One of the most prominent legal cases after the war involved Sergeant Edgar Caldwell, and *Crisis* coverage revolved around his soldier status, the discipline, integrity, and loyalty it represented, and the citizenship rights that it should have guaranteed. In December 1918, about a month after the Armistice, Caldwell boarded a streetcar in Alabama while on a brief recreational leave from his labor battalion. The conductor attempted to put Caldwell in his "proper" place.[2] Using considerable force to remove Caldwell from the streetcar, the conductor and his motorman initiated an altercation that ended with Caldwell's gunfire and the conductor's death. Ultimately, Alabama courts handed the soldier a death sentence, and NAACP attorneys intervened, arguing that Caldwell's case should have been handled by court-martial, not civilians. Applying pressure to the attorney general, the War Department, and the president, Caldwell's supporters insisted that "because [he] 'was an honored sergeant in the U.S. Army when he was tried,' . . . the federal government had a 'duty' to 'see to it that he got a fair trial'" (Lentz-Smith 190). Through a multifaceted legal struggle, NAACP lawyers insisted that Caldwell's national citizenship, especially as a soldier, gave him federal rights and protections that the state of Alabama could not disregard. Because state law "codif[ied] the degradation of African Americans, it reified the cultural practices of white supremacy," so if Caldwell had *not* defended himself, "he would have ended up just another black man beat down on a Southern streetcar, and the law would have provided little recourse" (Lentz-Smith 189–90). The NAACP therefore pressed for legal practices that would acknowledge Caldwell and all African Americans as citizens guaranteed the right to protect their person, property, and liberty—whether traveling in Alabama or not.[3]

In January 1920, *Crisis* reported, "This case is also remarkable for the whole-hearted and able defense of Caldwell's rights by the white Alabama lawyers . . . who have contested every point in his behalf . . ." (130–31). Nevertheless, in April 1920, more than a year after the streetcar altercation and despite the intervention of NAACP legal teams, the Supreme Court ruled against Caldwell, and he was sentenced to hang on July 30, 1920. Before hanging, he spoke briefly to his wife and son. He was also allowed to address the crowd of twenty-five hundred gathered in front of the jail. Among other things, he declared himself to be just "one of the many victims among my people who are paying the price of America's mockery of law . . ." (*Crisis*, October 1920, 282). The fight to save Caldwell's life had ended, giving black communities reason to despair. After all, African American support for Caldwell had indexed "a grander story of community vision . . . as black people in cities across the country used the circumstances created by the war to push the federal government to protect one of their, and its, own" (Lentz-Smith 171). Individuals of all classes had responded

A SOLDIER

DO you want this boy to be hanged?

This is the picture of Edgar Caldwell, who is under sentence of death, for defending himself against the crew of a street car in Anniston, Ala., and killing one of them.

His case will be argued before the Supreme Court of the United States, about March 1.

We want 500 Negroes who believe in Negro manhood, to send *immediately* one dollar each to J. E. Spingarn, Treasurer of the N. A. A. C. P., 70 Fifth Avenue, New York City, for Caldwell's defense.

Figure 6. Column about Sergeant Edgar Caldwell, including a plea for donations. *Crisis*, March 1920, p. 233

to notices in *Crisis* to donate money for Caldwell's legal defense because many believed that the black soldier symbolized the race's contributions to the nation's causes and its expectation for "concrete protections to their rights as citizens" (Lentz-Smith 190). If an actual black soldier could not find such protection, who among them could?

As much as the Caldwell case occupied NAACP attorneys throughout 1919 and early 1920, the organization's official publication, *Crisis* magazine, more often contained accounts of their work with African Americans who had been jailed during the Red Summer. Very often, the articles include the names and credentials of the defendants' attorneys. White lawyers took center stage for their service to the race, but over time black attorneys were featured more often and received equally reverent treatment.[4]

Because blacks had asserted their right to defend themselves in race riots, legal battles became necessary; these battles received increasing attention in the black press, which depicted African American attorneys as the soldiers of a new era. Accordingly, when a black lawyer in South Carolina died, *Crisis* remarked: "William Pickens once said that it took greater courage for a colored man to *just live* in Mississippi than to be a hero in France. Butler Nance was the living exemplification of that race of courageous black men who chose to remain in the South and fight there against the evils which burden men of color" (*Crisis*, April 1923, 23). This sentiment had evolved during the years immediately after the war, when reports of cases involving African Americans of all backgrounds remained in the pages of periodicals. For example, when a group of Arkansas sharecroppers had organized to secure improved working conditions, white opposition led to a riot; the majority of those arrested were black. They had been imprisoned since October 1919, but as the case continued in the 1920s, state officials pressed for more extreme punishment by arguing that blacks had instigated the violence, intent upon slaughtering helpless whites. By May 1923, NAACP legal efforts had secured a victory for several sharecroppers, so *Crisis* included an impressive photograph and declared, "The N.A.A.C.P. is gratified that a colored lawyer, Scipio A. Jones of Little Rock, stood at the forefront of the four-year legal battle which culminated in this important decision of the United States Supreme Court" (23).

As the *Crisis* spotlight on black soldiers morphs into increasing coverage of black lawyers, the magazine preserves evidence of a shift in the community conversation that correlates to the lived experience of Charles Hamilton Houston, a black Washingtonian who helped shape the American justice system for generations to come. Houston had been born and reared in the District, and his father was an attorney, but he did not necessarily want to follow in his father's footsteps. In 1917, a few months before his twenty-second birthday, Houston was one of the young men who entered the segregated officer training camp in Des Moines, Iowa, that Du Bois had encouraged blacks to accept. Houston served honorably in World War I while experiencing indignities every step of the way.[5] Military combat was dangerous enough, but the prejudice of white American peers and commanders placed black soldiers in even more mortal danger, and this sparked Houston's interest

SCIPIO A. JONES

LAWYERS HAIL ARKANSAS DECISION

THE Supreme Court's decision reversing the conviction of five colored Arkansas riot victims, has been widely discussed among lawyers and in the press. *The New Republic* devotes two editorials to the legal points involved. Mr. Louis Marshall, noted lawyer, who was counsel for Leo Frank, has written to the N. A. A. C. P. calling the decision "a great achievement in constitutional law" and saying that in this decision the Supreme Court adopted the viewpoint that was rejected in the Leo Frank trial. "Due process of law now means," says Mr. Marshall, "not merely a right to be heard before a court, but that it must be before a court that is not paralyzed by mob domination." Walter Nelles, of counsel for the American Civil Liberties Union, states that the Supreme Court not only reversed a lower court in the Arkansas case but hails its decision as one of the most far reaching on *habeas corpus* that the Supreme Court has ever made. The N. A. A. C. P. is gratified that a colored lawyer, Scipio A. Jones of Little Rock, stood at the forefront of the four year legal battle which culminated in this important decision of the United States Supreme Court.

Figure 7. Photograph of attorney Scipio Jones and notice about his leadership in a key legal battle. *Crisis*, May 1923, p. 24. Used by permission from Crisis Publishing Co., Inc., publisher of the National Association for the Advancement of Colored People.

in practicing law (McNeil 123–24). The legal profession no doubt became more appealing to Houston when black soldiers were welcomed home by the Red Summer of 1919. Houston himself returned from fighting overseas only to be greeted by a race riot in his hometown, the nation's capital. In the fall after the Red Summer, Houston entered Harvard Law School, where he distinguished himself.[6] He began practicing law in Washington, D.C., in 1924 and began teaching at Howard Law School that same year (McNeil 124). Houston's mistreatment as a soldier seems to have inspired his tireless efforts in making the nation's laws reflect its claim to love justice and equality. In the 1930s, he led NAACP legal teams as they brought desegregation suits that laid the foundation for the 1954 *Brown v. Board of Education* decision.[7] Along the way, he trained an army of civil rights attorneys who continued his work long after his death in 1950—the most famous of whom was Thurgood Marshall.

Black Washingtonians like Houston were particularly poised to view the black lawyer as the soldier needed for the next phase of the struggle to assert modern citizenship. The riot that had rocked their city in 1919 continued to fuel community conversation, and *Crisis* coverage of the resulting legal cases never failed to include African Americans' perspectives on how the violence started on July 19, 1919. Washington's four major newspapers had been "sowing the seeds of a race riot" by printing headlines suggesting that black men were on a raping spree (*Crisis*, Sept. 1919, 241–44). As early as July 9, the NAACP's Washington branch had written to the newspaper editors, encouraging them to be more responsible and accurate. In other words, African Americans had critically read the actions and the rhetoric of their white neighbors and worked to intervene. When blacks were ignored and violence resulted, they made sure that their insights remained relevant to the community conversation, as black lawyers took on the responsibility of correcting wrongs that could have been prevented.

In a few short years, black soldiers had fought overseas, black civilians had fought in American streets, and a generation of African American lawyers emerged to fight in the nation's courts; meanwhile, lynching drama developed to reflect these transitions. Like Charles Hamilton Houston, the playwrights responsible for the genre's spotlight on the black lawyer lived in Washington, D.C. Myrtle Smith Livingston was a student at Howard University when Houston was working to bring national recognition to its law school,[8] and Georgia Douglas Johnson was a long-time District resident with strong ties not only to artists but also to black educators and federal employees.[9] Like Houston, these women were sensitive to the contradictory lived experience of black Washingtonians, and they had a front-row seat to the government's disregard for black citizenship.[10] Surely, these injustices were especially difficult to witness in the nation's capital. Not only should democratic ideals have reigned supreme there, but the District had also been home to generations of "aristocrats of color"—men and women who had met and exceeded every standard the nation claimed to use for gauging one's readiness for full citizenship[11]

Washington, D.C., was the hub of American law and order, but it was also where headlines about mythical black rapists led to days of whites' attacking every black person they saw. African Americans could not miss the link between the city's 1919 riot and the defeat of the Dyer Anti-lynching Bill in 1922.[12] Once again, assertions that mobs protected white women from black sexual predators overpowered the government's obligation to ensure that African Americans could not be killed for sport. United States law again proved to be shaped by lynchers' claims, which were made not only through actual mob murders but also through lynching photographs.[13] Recognizing that arguments made by mobs and their photographers became the foundation for mainstream newspaper stories and legislation, the progressive press was diligent in correcting the public record, and it highlighted the attorneys (black and white) whose belief in African Americans' testimonies motivated their commitment to them.

Lynching drama worked in concert with the alternative press's efforts to address the distorted images that Americans accepted when exposed only to dominant discourse. Georgia Douglas Johnson, the most prolific lynching playwright, wrote two versions of a script that dramatizes the moment when white authorities willfully disregard African American voices. One version of Johnson's *A Sunday Morning in the South* uses hymns from a black church as background to the action; the other features a white church, but both show that police officers abruptly reject black testimony. To similar effect, Myrtle Smith Livingston's *For Unborn Children* challenges the black rapist myth by exposing the mob's insistence on treating an interracial relationship as rape. The accused man in both versions of *Sunday Morning* aspires to be an attorney, and the mob's target in *For Unborn Children* already is one.

Using the figure of the black lawyer, these scripts affirm African Americans' belief in their right to full citizenship, demonstrating that black identity is characterized by a commitment to abiding by the law, even when white countrymen do not. While lynching photographs circulate to justify violence that was said to keep black criminals in check, the dramas discussed in this chapter capture the very moment when community testimony is rejected in order to create a criminal almost out of thin air. African Americans' honesty and integrity are dramatized, becoming most evident when whites use those very traits to deny black citizenship. Like earlier scripts, these survive as testimonies to black male innocence, but they alter the genre's tendencies by allowing the accused to stand briefly in the presence of the white woman whose virtue his death will supposedly serve.

Just as black soldiers of earlier plays devoted themselves to a nation that would not protect them, Johnson and Livingston depict black men who invest in the law as a source of justice, only to have it fail them and their families in the most painful way. Lynching violence is therefore shown to confirm not black criminality but the extent of the nation's willingness to reject black testimony and deny black citizenship. In putting forth the black lawyer, lynching drama, in harmony with *Crisis* magazine coverage, offers access to the archive and repertoire of postwar community efforts to preserve the testimonies typically rejected by the nation's courts.

A Sunday Morning in the South: It Takes Two

As Martin Luther King Jr. would later famously assert, "The most segregated hour of Christian America is eleven o'clock on Sunday morning." Recognizing this truth decades earlier, in 1925, Georgia Douglas Johnson wrote two versions of *A Sunday Morning in the South*—one featuring a black church and one with a white church. Both versions of the play affirm African American identity by featuring a black man whose character is defined by his honesty, sense of civic responsibility, and faith in law and order. Tom wants to study law to equip himself to help blacks targeted by the mob. This protagonist therefore comes to represent black identity under siege when both versions of the play spotlight police officers' eagerness to disregard African American testimony. In fact, Tom's arrest—based on the rejection of black witnesses—proves so central to both texts that one wonders why two versions were necessary. Affirming African American identity with a portrayal of honest black citizens, Johnson exposes the hypocrisy of this Christian nation. Even on Sunday, and even with the church's singing dominating the environment, mob violence (bolstered by a biased justice system) goes unchecked.

Is Johnson's point that black and white churches fail equally to inspire the nation to fulfill its creed, or does she have another goal for penning two scripts whose major differences emerge only in the final moments? To work toward an answer, I consider the action that the versions share, their different endings, and what Johnson accomplishes with each. Ultimately, I find that Johnson's work highlights the importance of having a community that recognizes one's place within it. The lynch victim's grieving loved ones do not enter the church in either version, but the melodies from the black congregation suggest that the family is not alone in its struggle, while the white church's music only underscores the fact that their white brethren do not recognize African American humanity and citizenship on a Sunday morning—any more than they will on Monday.

I.

Johnson seems to have had a single goal in mind when crafting the first three-quarters of both versions of *Sunday Morning*. Like most lynching one-acts, dialogue dominates the action, and both versions are set in 1924 in "a town in the South." Sue Jones is preparing breakfast for her grandsons, Tom and Bossie, ages nineteen and seven. She calls them to the table and sings until they enter. She jokes about how hard it is to get them out of bed on a Sunday morning. Tom says that he had planned to rise in time to attend church, but his back still hurts from lifting boxes the previous day. Sue says that he works too hard and that he should have rubbed oil on himself last night. Tom agrees but admits that he had been so tired that he just fell into bed; he assumes that he must have been asleep by nine o'clock. Sue teases him, "Nine er clock! You is crazy! T'want no moren eight" (140). Bossie adds that Tom had been snoring so loudly that he thought he might choke. When Bossie asks for more food, Sue refuses him, saying "When you get big and work like Tom you kin stuff all you wants to" (141). Bossie answers, "I aint never gointer break my back like Tom working hard" (141).

Just then, Sue notices her friend Liza passing by the window and tells Bossie to let her in. She prepares a plate for Liza, who is on her way to church. Liza asks how Sue's leg is doing, and Sue reports that she does not walk on it anymore, which is why she enjoys living next door to the church. Soon, they hear "Amazing Grace." Liza is ready to join the congregation, so Sue asks her to share town news before leaving. Liza admits that she has no good news to report, only that the police are looking for "some po Nigger they say that's 'tacked a white woman last night right up here near the Pine Street market" (142). Liza also reports that "short work" will be made of the alleged attacker whenever he is caught. Sue shares that she is in favor of punishing the guilty, but too often, whites mete out punishment without even establishing guilt. Tom agrees and adds that he is determined to "git a little book learning so as I can do something to help—help change the laws . . . make em strong" (142). He continues, "I sometimes get right upset and wonder whut would I do if they ever tried to put something on me . . ." (142). The women insist that that would never happen because everyone knows that he is a good man, but they commend him for wanting to help those who will be targeted. Another hymn is heard as Tom begins, "It takes a sight of learning to understand the law and I'm gointer . . ." (143).

Just when Tom is about to share his plans, "*a quick rap is heard at the door and it is almost immediately pushed open . . .*" (143). Two police officers barge into the house, demanding to know where Tom had been at ten o'clock the previous night. He tells them that he had been asleep, and Sue and Bossie corroborate this fact, but the officers declare their word to be worthless. After insisting that Sue and Bossie's testimony cannot be trusted because they would lie for Tom, the officers bring a white woman forward, tell her that Tom fits their description, and encourage her to identify him as her attacker. She does so, but with much hesitation and uncertainty. They have the handcuffs on Tom in no time, and his grandmother begins protesting. She insists that the girl is too upset to know what she is saying. She explains further: "That white chile ain't never seed my granson before—all Niggers looks alike to her" (144). The officers continue to disregard Sue, and she is growing hysterical, so Tom tries to comfort her. He says that he will go with the officers and explain to the sheriff "how I could't a done it when I was here sleep all the time" (144).

In both versions of *Sunday Morning*, ~~Johnson sets the scene by highlighting the depicted family's domestic tranquility.~~ Because the audience is privy to family jokes and hearty laughter, the terror inspired by the police officers' intrusion is especially palpable, and the elements that had marked domestic success now spotlight the family's pain. Appreciated food is forgotten, laughter turns into tears, and the knowledge that Tom had been in bed at eight o'clock changes from a family joke to a cruel one, for it proves that he is arrested without cause. Also, the fact that there is no mention of a father or grandfather gains significance. The missing men could have been unjustly removed from the home; being a black man is clearly Tom's only "crime."

Impeccable character does not protect black men from rape charges, and Johnson underscores the injustice of this fact by allowing her audience to encounter Tom before he knows that he is a suspect. Exemplifying manliness, Tom does not rage about society's wrongs or feel defeated by them; he resolves to "git a little book learning to [. . .] help change the laws . . . make em strong" (142). Because the laws and their enforcement are currently weak, the family knows that many mob victims are innocent, and Tom wonders what he would do if he were ever targeted. Grandmother Sue agrees that whites often frame black men, but she insists that Tom's reputation would prevent accusations. Sue says, "No sonnie, you won't never hafter worry bout sich like that but you kin hep to save them po devels that they do git after" (142). When Tom is accused of a crime that he did not commit, he remains manly, refusing to act out of emotion. He comforts his grandmother, saying "Granma, don't take on so. I'll go long with him to the sheriff. I'll splain to him how I couldn't a done it when I was here sleep all the time—I never laid eyes on that white lady before in my life" (144).

As Johnson shows Tom clinging to his belief in the justice system while being arrested, it is clear that his desire to become a lawyer emerges from his belief in the values that his nation espouses, fair play and equality, for example.[14] Tom acknowledges that racial injustices take place, but he seems convinced that they stem from the "weakness" of current laws. That is, when African Americans' rights are disregarded, it is only because the legal system has not managed to tame unruly mobs. Tom is sure that the nation is committed to justice, so he is determined to help strengthen the system. Tom's conception of citizenship revolves around what political theorist Melissa Harris-Lacewell would identify as responsibility-based demands on the state. Rather than focus on his basic right to be protected by the nation, Tom focuses on gaining tools to improve society.[15] For an honest young man like Tom, being handcuffed is shocking and terrifying, so as he tries to keep his wits about him, he has no choice but to believe the policeman's advice: "[T]he quieter you comes along the better it will be for you" (144). The officer seems cynical as he tells Sue, "[H]e'll be right back—if he's innocent," but Tom must hold on to this possibility. He must believe that he can depend on the justice system to recognize his citizenship and value his testimony.

Whether Tom's faith is born of teenage naiveté, the stunned helplessness of already being in handcuffs, or irrational optimism, Johnson crafts the scene to suggest that he will not find justice, even if allowed to address the sheriff. When the officers rush in, they declare themselves judge and jury. They interrogate Tom about his whereabouts the previous night and treat his answers with suspicion, asking who can confirm that he had been at home. When Grandmother Sue and his brother Bossie corroborate his story, one officer shouts, "Shut up. Your word's nothing. . . . Nor yours either. Both of you'd lie for him" (143). Yet who would be better able to verify his claim than those who live with him? As black testimony is rejected, the scene does not inspire confidence that the sheriff would be more receptive to Tom's account. While the officers reject the word of black family members by claiming that it is biased, Johnson shows that the officers' own biases determine what they will accept. Before allowing the young white woman to utter a word, one officer proclaims, "We've got it figgered all out" (144). Then they feed the terrified woman the answers that they want to hear. They do not ask her to make a strong claim; they require only a confirmation—and they do not pause when she does not confidently provide even that. The officer insists, "You say he looks like him?" and she answers: "Y-e-s (*slowly and undecidedly*) I think so . . ." (144).

By recording this exchange, and the injustice it represents, the play preserves aspects of the encounter that matter to the family in the play and the communities reading in real life, but do not interest these officers of the law. Indeed, by juxtaposing the rejection of black witnesses with the instant acceptance of white ones, Johnson implies that African American testimony must be preserved because white testimony often works to make irrelevant what community members know. The existence of Johnson's script gestures toward African Americans' belief that black testimony must be given and recorded regardless of the fact that whites will reject it. Especially because it is a play that circulated in private circles, *A Sunday Morning in the South* registers the community's faith in the race's honesty and integrity, undaunted by how consistently the nation's discourses and practices deny it.

Because lynching dramas, even those that were not published, survive in the archive, modern readers have access to the self-affirming discourses and practices of African Americans who lived with lynching. Johnson's handling of black testimony operates in harmony with Du Bois's famous declaration: "All art is propaganda and ever must be . . . I do not care a damn for any art that is not used for propaganda. But I do care when propaganda is confined to one side while the other is stripped and silent" ("Criteria" 296). The voices of those who vouched for the honesty and integrity of black men, women, and children were constantly being silenced or diminished. African Americans thus used various venues for preserving and sharing community knowledge. These private plays of Johnson's suggest that she may have concurred when Du Bois said, "It is not the positive propaganda of people who believe white blood divine, infallible and holy to which I object. It is the denial of a similar right of propaganda to those who believe black blood human, lovable and inspired with new ideals for the world" ("Criteria" 297). Perhaps it is with this spirit that Johnson offers her play as a testimony with no pretensions of neutrality. She presents a portrait of honorable black manhood, and she does so forcefully. Like all lynching one-acts, hers would enter the community conversation to equip African Americans to assess mainstream discourse critically, enabling them to withstand the assault on their self-conceptions.

The playwrights knew that theirs was what Mikhail Bakhtin would call an inescapably "contested, contestable, and contesting" discourse (332). They did not have the luxury of pretending that theirs was the only perspective on lynching and black citizenship to be voiced, but that was all the more reason to speak boldly. Yet speaking boldly did not necessarily mean addressing the mainstream. Given the hostility of their historical moment, blacks' best opportunities for preserving community insights would emerge in private spaces. Accordingly, Tom's innocence is made clearest because he is depicted inside the black home where the audience is privy to family jokes about his early bedtime, before anyone knows that he will become a suspect. Such a play would have been appealing to black community members because the characters engage in activities not unlike those that take place in their own homes: black characters nurture each other and enjoy each other's company rather than shuffle and grin as they did in commercial theater. The familiarity of the scene would have been welcomed by African Americans who maximized alternative public spaces fostered by publications like *Crisis* magazine. The emphasis that black-authored one-act dramas place on ordinary, family-centered depictions of African Americans underscores the value of private spaces in the process of preserving community perspectives. As readers bring the script to life through performance or dramatic reading, they participate in embodied practices of black belonging inside spaces they control. Their doing so helps solidify the impressions they have of themselves and other members of their communities. In short, they verify for each other that they are honest citizens worthy of the best that the country of their birth has to offer. These messages must be articulated and reiterated to African Americans themselves if they are to withstand the assault on their self-conceptions long enough to make the case to anyone else.

As Johnson spotlights manipulation of testimony when black life hangs in the balance, her creative work resonates with the realities of her historical moment. Even when black men reached courtrooms in the early 1900s, these spaces did not prove receptive to black testimony. As historian William Henry Holtzclaw observed in 1915, "The fact is that . . . it is somewhat difficult to draw at this time a sharp line marking off distinctly the point where the lynching spirit stops and the spirit of legal procedure commences" (qtd. in McMillen 195). Especially in the South, confessions were coerced through brute force and admitted as evidence. As late as 1934, whites determined to extract a confession strung a black man up twice. Because he still maintained his innocence, a deputy took him from his house, wife, and children, forced him to cross state lines, and flogged him until he promised that he would say whatever they wanted to hear (McMillen 198). Two other black men charged under similar circumstances limped into court, could not sit, and had rope burns on their face and neck, but the affidavit made no mention of their condition (McMillen 198). Just as frequently, African American material witnesses, fearful of repercussions, would fail to appear in court, so judges would not have had to disregard black testimony as blatantly as the police officers in *Sunday Morning* do. And courts seldom summoned black witnesses for cases wherein their testimony would likely contradict whites' claims (McMillen 206–7). In fact, judges often valued speed over fairness in cases involving blacks because mobs used the justice system's purported sluggishness as an excuse for not letting black defendants live long enough to stand trial. Once again, the mob's claims shaped American definitions of "due process" much more than ideals about law, order, and equality.

Johnson's contribution to the community conversation bolstered blacks' self-conceptions by showcasing their honorable character through the figure of the aspiring lawyer. In the process, the text also extends, in creative form, the work of Ida B. Wells's ongoing antilynching campaign. Like Wells's pamphlets and speeches, Johnson's script acknowledges examples of black manliness and exposes the ways in which white men prove to be the true barbarians. Johnson even puts Wells's arguments in her characters' mouths. Before the police arrive, the family had been discussing lynching. Sue says, "I don't hold wid no rascality and I bleves in meting out punishment to the guilty but they fust ought to fine out who done it" (142). Similarly, in the preface of *Southern Horrors,* Wells had asserted that her statements are not "a shield for the despoiler of virtue . . . [but a] contribution to truth" (50). Later, Liza adds, "[B]ut you know a sight of times they gits the wrong man and goes and strings him up" (142). To the same effect, Wells had challenged American law from her podium in England to "prove your man guilty, first; hang him, shoot him, pour coal over him and roast him, if you have concluded that civilization demands this; but be sure the man has committed the crime first" (qtd. in Bederman 62). Finally, Tom comments that "they lynching you bout anything too, not just women" (142). This remark echoes Wells's proclamation that being "'sassy' to white folks" is enough of a crime (*Southern Horrors* 60). Because blacks could be lynched for any reason, Wells argued that American law was corrupt and that its perversion negated claims that the United States was a civilized, modern nation. Liza speaks of the law in similar terms when she says that it "ought er be er ark uv safty to pertect the weak and not some little flimsy shack" (142).

There were innumerable attempts to make American law an ark of safety for black citizens, and by 1918, one option was to support the Dyer Antilynching bill. The bill proposed capital punishment for members of lynch mobs and a fine for local governments that did not prosecute lynchers (Zangrando 43). In 1922, the bill was defeated by a filibuster in the Senate, and American law proved to be a "flimsy shack" for African Americans. Though her play would not undo the damage that the legislature had done, Johnson used her script to continue African American efforts to preserve community knowledge, including those of Ida B. Wells at the turn of the century.[16] Thus, the black woman of the 1920s offered dramatic testimony in harmony with the work of her literary and political foremother. The Dyer bill had been defeated by those who demonized black men and disregarded the testimonies offered in African American communities about the fathers, sons, and brothers within them. Even if the legislature further silenced these testimonies, lynching dramatists left their scripts to bear witness.

 II.

If Johnson's goal was to honor black manhood by preserving community testimonies about black male innocence, this is accomplished by the nearly identical sections of the black church and white church versions. Why then was Johnson invested in dramatizing segregation by offering two incarnations of *A Sunday Morning in the South*? Surely the answer lies in the scripts' differences, the most significant of which is setting. All of the action in the black church version takes place in the black home, but in the white church version, there is an abrupt scene change; the last moments unfold not only outside the black home but also outside the African American community.

When the police arrest Tom in the black church version, Sue's friend Liza begins praying aloud, and Sue joins her. In fact, Sue is praying through her sobs when another family friend, Tildy, rushes in, reporting that she had seen a crowd of armed white men in the street trying to take Tom away from the police who had him in custody. Sue and Liza begin brainstorming and decide that Sue should call on her "good white folks." Sue asks Tildy to hurry to Miss Violet, a young woman whom Sue nursed when she was a baby. Sue sends Tildy to Violet because her father is a judge with the power to intervene so that Tom is not kidnapped and lynched. Bossie says that he knows a shortcut to Miss Violet's house, so he volunteers to accompany Tildy, and they leave on the errand.

When they exit, the script highlights affection that readers would recognize as characteristic of the communities to which they belong. Sue "sinks back in her chair exhausted while Liza comes over to her and pats her on the back" (146). Liza tries to comfort and encourage Sue, while Sue continues to pray. When the congregation next door begins singing another hymn, "*the two women listen to the words with emotion*" (146). Then Sue admits feeling faint and asks for her bottle of camphor. She says that her heart is getting weak and Liza encourages her to relax and listen to the singing because "they all sho talking to the Lord fur you in that church this morning" (147).

The church is now singing another song, and the women continue to pray. Soon, Tildy returns, with Bossie in her wake and in tears. Tildy reports that it was no use going to Miss Violet because Tom has already been lynched. Sue screams, "Jesus," then "gasps and falls limp in the chair" (147). Bossie runs to her "crying afresh" while singing from the church begins again (147). Liza and Tildy work over Sue with the camphor bottle and finally shake their heads in grief. She is apparently dead and the church's singing pours in: "Lord have mercy . . ."

Just as music sets the tone in the black church version, it does so in the concluding moments of the white church version, but Johnson designates the latter as "a one-act play in two scenes," and the change of scenery goes to the heart of the difference between these scripts. In the white church version, Liza, the family friend who is by Grandmother Sue's side when the officers take Tom, is the character who informs the family that Tom is in danger. She looks out of the window and sees a mob following Tom and the police as soon as they leave. She also hears one of the men say that they will not wait for the courts to cheat them (133). When Liza shares this news, Sue, whom Johnson has made ten years younger than in the black church version, jumps to her feet asking her friend, "Whut kin I do?" (134). Liza says, "Ef I was you, I'd go and git some good white man to hep him right away—befo' it's too late" (134). Once Sue decides to call on Judge Manning, she approaches the door and Bossie follows, insisting that she take him with her. The next scene is outside of a small church from which the choir can be heard (134). Sue asks the usher to bring Judge Manning to her. The usher is reluctant, even after Sue insists that it is a life-and-death matter. Sue then threatens, "Ef you won't tell him, I'll go in myself" (135). The usher goes inside the church, and as Sue waits, the choir's singing continues. When Judge Manning appears at the door "looking vexed," the singing ceases and the preacher's voice can be heard in the background (135).

Sue begs the judge's pardon for interrupting him at church but explains that her grandson has been arrested and the mob has threatened to take him from the police. She asks the judge to take charge of Tom before something happens; after all, Tom has done nothing wrong (135). The judge says that he will look into the situation after service. Sue continues to plead, yet the judge insists, "But it's Sunday. Nobody's going to do anything to your grandson today" (135). Sue persists and Judge Manning agrees to leave, but only after getting his coat. While he is inside, two white men pass by, chatting about having just participated in a lynching. One of the men remarks, "Well we strung him up all right. But when he kept hollering, 'Granny, Granny' it kinder made me sick in the belly" (136). Moments later, Sue clutches her heart and collapses as music is heard from the church. When the judge appears on the steps, he is stunned to see the dead woman on the ground with Bossie crying beside her. The music continues.

The most significant differences between the versions of A *Sunday Morning in the South* arise from the realities of U.S. segregation. Yet Johnson does not offer a simple indictment of the custom; she uses it to underscore the importance of both belonging to a group and having one's rightful place within it acknowledged. On the most basic level, the two versions call attention to the fact that the black church is in Grandmother Sue's neighborhood and the white church is not. In the former script, she can be comforted by the church's singing by simply opening her window. However, when she is compelled to seek assurance from a member of the white congregation, she must travel across town.

Much more significant, juxtaposing Sue's experiences with these two churches highlights the extent to which the black church provides spiritual, emotional, and social support while the white church holds power that it refuses to use for blacks' benefit, failing to recognize them as members of its community. In other words, though Tom and Grandmother Sue die in both versions, Johnson does not seem invested in insisting that the churches fail equally to shape the nation's morality. Instead, Johnson points to the white church as a locus of power that could be used for justice while the black church is portrayed as a source of comfort that will remain invaluable partly because African Americans who survive the mob's physical attack will need support as they are forced to live with lynching. That is, even as Johnson does not depict the black church as capable of preventing the injustices that accompany the rejection of black testimony, it is a space that acknowledges black belonging by viewing experiences like Sue's and Tom's as not only legally unjust (they were not guilty of any crime) but also as morally and ethically undeserved.

Johnson distinguishes between these churches by maximizing the power of music to make meaning. The first song heard in the black-church version is the hymn that Sue sings to herself while waiting for her grandsons to come to breakfast. The lyrics include "Jes look at the morning star/ We'll all git home bye and bye" (140). It is a light-hearted tune to accompany the everyday joy of nurturing her family with a meal that they will appreciate. Next, the characters make mention of hearing "Amazing Grace" from next door and the script details these lyrics:

> I once was lost but now I'm found
> Was blind but now I see.

Amazing grace, how sweet the truth
In a believer's ear,
It heals his sorrows, heals his wounds,
And drives away each tear. (142)

Not long afterward, the lyrics from the church's next song are detailed:

Shine on me, shine on me,
Let the light from the lighthouse shine on me,
Shine on me, shine on me,
Let the light from the lighthouse shine on me. (143)

This call for light emerges right after the women have declared that Tom's good reputation would prevent false accusations that might lead to lynching. Also, it immediately precedes Tom's attempt to describe his plans to study law. The song thus helps give the impression that Tom's noble goals make him a light for his community and it emphasizes the hope that Tom has in his own heart about making a difference for his people.

Later, when Sue has been waiting a while to learn if Miss Violet will be able to help, she focuses on these lyrics from the church, which resonate with her current crisis:

I must tell Jesus, I cannot bear my burdens alone
In my distress he surely will help me
I cannot bear my burdens alone.
I must tell Jesus, I cannot bear my burdens alone
Jesus my Lord he surely will help me
Jesus will help me, Jesus alone. (147)

The listener is told that she is not alone while facing significant problems, but the final suggestion is that aid will not come from earthly brethren; "Jesus alone" will help. While those who sing along with the sufferer may not be able to alleviate his or her pain, they acknowledge the difficulty and insist that it is serious enough to require supernatural power.

Finally, after hearing that Tom has indeed been killed, Sue falls limp in her chair. As the others work over her and realize that she is dead, these lyrics float in from the church: "Lord have mercy,/Lord have mercy,/ Lord have mercy over me" (148). Every step of the way, then, the music is corroborating the anxiety, fear, and pain experienced in Grandmother Sue's household. The script therefore recognizes and encourages the various ways in which community was maintained among African Americans. Both the characters in the play and the readers who encounter them are invited to create "networks of affiliation constructed in practice" (Hartman 59). The lyrics do not slow the injustice but they provide a sense of communion; Sue and those in her home are not alone as they deal with the crisis. The larger black community seems to be in sympathy with them.

In stark contrast, the music in the white church version helps create a feeling of isolation. Even the song that Sue sings while waiting for Tom and Bossie to come to breakfast carries a different tone. This time, her song is more ominous than light-hearted. The lyrics include "Oh Poor Sinner, now is the time. . . . What you gointer do when the lamp burns down?" (130). The joy of the hymn she sang while cooking in the black-church version is replaced by ambiguous foreboding, creating a sense of uncertainty where only joy had been. The next time that music enters the scene is when Sue has traveled to the white church in search of Judge Manning. There is no mention of her living near a black church in this version; her only encounter with a congregation's singing is when she is compelled to find a powerful white man. The music that emanates from the white church creates irony; as she approaches, she is met by these lyrics:

> Jesus Savior, pilot me, over life's tempestuous sea—
> Unknown waves before me roll, hiding rock
> And treacherous shoal
> Chart and compass come from Thee
> Jesus Savior, pilot me. (134)

The irony here is striking because readers have witnessed the injustice that Sue's family has experienced in their own home and followed her on this desperate journey. One wonders how the challenges deemed "tempestuous" by these white congregants compare to Sue's crisis. The same song continues after the usher has left in a huff to summon the judge only because Sue has threatened to enter the church herself. Again, Johnson juxtaposes the white congregants' belief that they are facing stormy weather with the prejudice that Sue is experiencing on the steps of their church.

The next time that music enters the scene is when Judge Manning has insisted upon getting his coat rather than leaving immediately to help Tom. After Sue hears the men talking about their victim screaming "Granny," these words pour from the church, "Going home, going home, Yes I'm going home" (136).[17] Sue dies with these words from the white church underscoring the fact that Christians sat by not only as Tom died but also as she did. Their voices are not in sympathy with her pain or Bossie's as he mourns over her body at the bottom of the church steps. In this way, if the church should be a moral center for the community, this scene shows that white morality is defined without accounting for what blacks endure. Judge Manning's assumption about what blacks might encounter on a Sunday is painfully uninformed. Thus, "good whites" are shown to be clueless about what Sunday really is in this country. As Martin Luther King Jr. would later declare, it is a time when one can find citizens most divided along the color line. It is also a time—historians have discovered but Johnson already knew—when this sort of racial violence was most likely to occur. Because children were not in school and many laborers did not have to report to work, mobs could delight large crowds who were eager to be entertained, and they often took advantage of the leisure time by prolonging the victim's torture.[18]

Because blacks faced these sorts of realities on Sunday mornings, both versions of the play continue the genre's tradition of showcasing de-generation. As with so many of the plays, there is a grandmother and grandchildren but no mother and father in the middle. Indeed, the script makes much of the fact that Tom is an orphan. In the white-church version, Sue prays when he is in the officers' custody: "Oh Jesus! Hep my poor little motherless chile" (133). Likewise, when Liza is praying in the black-church version after Tom is taken by the officers, she reminds God, "You said you would hep the fatherless and motherless; do Jesus bring this po orphan back to his ole cripple grannie" (145). By emphasizing that the middle generation is missing, Johnson underlines the likelihood that the father (at least) suffered an unjust death because an actual crime is not necessary for a black man to lose his life. The mother's absence remains a mystery, but the script leaves open the possibility that she may have died of a broken heart, not unlike Grandmother Sue.

When black households are routinely dealt these sorts of devastating blows, the importance of sharing community testimony becomes even clearer. *A Sunday Morning in the South* did not see publication in Johnson's lifetime, so it circulated through private, informal networks, testifying to the solid black homes and good black men that the myth of the black male rapist denied existed. Along the way, it also acknowledged parallels between black men's experiences and that of Jesus Christ. When Tom leaves saying that he will speak to the sheriff, he exhibits arguably unreasonable optimism, but he also exemplifies black manliness, certifying its existence even in the face of white barbarism. As Tom leaves with his false accusers, he represents moral black manliness in the hands of brute white masculinity, not unlike the black men whom Ida B. Wells said "clung to [the] right of franchise" despite facing mob terror. Wells declared that African American men "believed that in that small white ballot there was a subtle something which stood for manhood as well as citizenship, and thousands of brave black men went to their graves, exemplifying the one by dying for the other" (*Red Record* 77). In this drama, Tom is willing to invest in the white paper of a diploma and in the letter of the Law. Meanwhile, white men (who are assumed to be civilized) are free to express a primitive masculinity that permits the barbaric practice of lynching.

As Ida B. Wells's pamphlets had, the play places uncivilized white violence alongside honorable black manhood and exposes the nation's hypocrisy as it allows lynching to go unchecked. In both versions, Sue dies upon learning that Tom is lynched before he could reach the sheriff. There is no justice for these characters, but by recording these injustices, Johnson suggests that black communities must speak their truths even if they are ignored by their white counterparts. Blacks must reiterate to each other that they are valued members of their own families and communities, and they must remind each other that they are rightful citizens of the nation. In the process, Johnson's script offers African Americans opportunities to rehearse mourning as the appropriate response to lynching. While mobs and their photographers insisted that their victims should not be mourned, lynching plays reminded blacks that their brethren are not targeted because they are rapists, but rather because whites have the power to reject community knowledge. Johnson insists that the resistance to black testimony makes its preservation all the more imperative. Blacks must bear witness for the sake of those who, in their own historical moment, must find a way to endure the assault on their self-conceptions and for those who will come generations later.

Figure 8. Picture of dramatist Myrtle Smith Livingston, author of *For Unborn Children*. *Crisis,* July 1926, p. 122. Used by permission from Crisis Publishing Co., Inc., publisher of the National Association for the Advancement of Colored People.

For Unborn Children

Like all of the plays of this study, *For Unborn Children* places a spotlight on a black household, but unlike most of the one-acts, this one features a middle-class black family, bringing into the one-act tradition a home reminiscent of that in Grimké's *Rachel*. The Carlson household is "tastefully, though not richly, furnished" and is occupied by a "refined" family (122). Their social status is well established, with even the grandmother described as "gentle" and "well-bred" (122). While Tom of *Sunday Morning* yearns for an education that will empower him to improve the legal system and help African Americans, the mob ensures that he never reaches his goal, but *For Unborn Children* focuses on LeRoy Carlson, who is already an attorney. His presence in the genre points to the existence of black professionals who have achieved even in the midst of Jim Crow repression. At the same time, by depicting this figure's words and actions inside his own home, Livingston's script preserves evidence that the race's most accomplished members are denied basic rights and freedoms.

For Unborn Children takes place in 1925 in the "living room" of "a refined family, evidently of the middle class," and as in other lynching scripts, familial relations are highlighted at the outset. The main characters are listed as: LeRoy Carlson, "a young lawyer," Marion Carlson, "his sister," and Grandma Carlson, "his grandmother" (122). The action begins with Marion reading the newspaper, but soon, "she throws it down and goes to the window, peering out into the night" (122). She and her grandmother are worried because it is nine o'clock and LeRoy is not home from work. Earlier, Marion had called the office and was told that he had left around 5:30. The worrying women know that he is with his white girlfriend, and they discuss how they wish they could convince the girl to stay away from LeRoy, because talking to *him* has not worked. As Marion looks out the window, hoping to see her brother, she and her grandmother can only hope that he is not in the mob's clutches because "that's what will happen . . ." (123). In fact, when LeRoy finally arrives, Marion is genuinely relieved as she says, "Well, thank goodness, it hasn't happened yet" (123).

As they gather information about why LeRoy is late, he explains that they will not have to worry much longer because he and Selma will soon elope. Marion runs from the room sobbing but only after making her stance clear: "Well, if you marry her, may God help me never to breathe your name again!" (123). LeRoy asks his grandmother if she feels the same way, emphasizing that he and Selma are very much in love. Grandmother Carlson is gentle but gives reasons for why interracial coupling is not a good idea.[19] LeRoy persists with his own logic about what is fair and right, until Grandmother Carlson offers her most important argument. She explains why she has been the only maternal force in his life: LeRoy's mother was white and "she could never stand the sight of you and Marion; she hated you because you weren't white!" (124).

LeRoy is stunned by this news, and it does not take long for him to change his mind about eloping with Selma; he will not risk giving his unborn children a mother like his. He declares, "That makes it different" (124). Suddenly, his fiancée Selma rushes in to warn of an approaching mob. In no time, the rumble of the crowd is heard along with cries of "Lynch him," "The dirty nigger," and "We'll show him how to fool around a white woman" (124). Marion emerges from her room to see what is happening, and Grandma Carlson falls to her knees praying. LeRoy tells Selma, "It has to be, sweetheart, and it is the better way; even though we love each other we couldn't have found happiness together. Forget me, and marry a man of your own race; you'll be happier, and I will too, up there" (124). He also asks his sister to forgive him and tries to comfort his grandmother by saying " . . . just think of it as a sacrifice for UNBORN CHILDREN" (124). A voice from outside demands, "Come out, you damned nigger, or we'll burn the house down!" (124).[20] LeRoy answers, "I'm coming, gentleman," and walks out to his death, "victorious and unafraid."

As with most lynching one-acts, much of the action in *For Unborn Children* comes in the form of conversation, and this family's intimate discussions revolve around rights and responsibilities. LeRoy often makes declarations about what he is entitled to do. The women in the house may not necessarily disagree, but they often add nuance. For example, when Marion says that it must have been a date with Selma that led LeRoy to arrive so late and forget to call, he responds, "Yes, it was; I still have the liberty of making an engagement with anyone I choose, Marion" (123). Stage directions call for LeRoy to say this while "trying to control his anger," but LeRoy's frustration seems misplaced. The reader cannot help but remember that Marion is far from the only one in the South who has an opinion about the company that LeRoy keeps. In fact, while Marion is hurt by his choices, others will use them to justify hurting him.

Even if the outside world can be ignored, Marion is not alone in believing that LeRoy may be delusional regarding the scope of his "liberty." Grandmother Carlson chimes in, "But you haven't the right, son, to cause us unnecessary worry and pain" (123). The women's distress stems more from the racist environment than from LeRoy's choices, but they insist that he behave in ways that acknowledge his surroundings.

Later, LeRoy pleads with his grandmother, "Selma and I can't help it because we don't belong to the same race, and we have the right to be happy together if we love each other, haven't we?" (123). Grandmother Carlson answers with sadness in her voice: "We have the right to be happy, child, only when our happiness doesn't hurt anybody else; and when a colored man marries a white woman, he hurts every member of the Negro race" (123). Also, because she insists that white women cannot mother black children, Mrs. Carlson makes her own declaration about entitlements: "Every child has a right to a mother who will love it better than life itself" (124). In these exchanges, LeRoy articulates his expectations of American life in personal terms while his female relatives insist upon family- and community-centered conceptions.

Livingston's black lawyer is surrounded by female characters determined to convince him that African American citizenship depends on black men remaining exemplars of manliness. As explained in chapter 2, at the turn of the century manhood could be expressed as either manliness, which was associated with high-mindedness and propriety, or masculinity, which emphasized corporeality and instinct. History has shown that white men responded violently to all expressions of black manhood, but the women in LeRoy's life make their preferences known. When LeRoy announces that he and Selma will elope, his sister Marion responds, "Have you lost all your manhood?" (123). For her, "manhood" means control of one's emotions and commitment to home and family. Immediately, Grandmother Carlson follows with: "Ah, boy, you've forgotten us! Don't you love us at all anymore since [Selma] came into your life?" (123). Then, more forcefully privileging manliness over masculinity, Marion asks in angry desperation: "Even if you do love her can't you find your backbone and conquer it for the sake of your race?" (123).

Marion is frustrated because she has watched her manly brother adopt masculinity. LeRoy's professional success points to his manliness, but his relationship with Selma leads him to make decisions more indicative of masculinity. Because he is an educated, accomplished lawyer who jeopardizes everything he has, Ida B. Wells would have described LeRoy as one of the many black Sampsons[21] who "had been manly towers of strength until they were ensnared and destroyed" by white women (Bederman 58). As LeRoy develops a relationship with Selma, he neglects his most basic responsibilities. He knows that his sister and grandmother expect him home at six o'clock, but even by nine o'clock, he does not call. When confronted, he explains: "I was on my way home when—her note was brought to me and I didn't have time to call you then" (123). A mere note from his white fiancée and LeRoy seems to forget everything else,[22] leaving his sister and grandmother disappointed that he is no longer making rational, responsible, manly decisions that benefit his family and community.

As black women characters privilege manliness, the script registers community awareness of the dilemma that black men faced when white men increasingly lost interest in manliness and embraced masculinity. The abstract ideals of manliness encouraged white men of social standing to disregard black men, but this became more difficult with corporeal masculinity. If physical strength helped identify "real" men, then even an uneducated black boxer could seem more powerful than a successful, but scrawny, white banker.[23] Black men's simple bodily existence therefore became more of a challenge to white men than when their identities rested mostly on abstract ideals. In this context, LeRoy's relationship with a white woman constitutes an expression of manhood that white men felt should be reserved for them. Because white men refused to tolerate African American masculinity or manliness, LeRoy's life would always be in danger, but the black women who love him are most disturbed by his masculine choices. From their perspective, LeRoy not only risks his life by adopting masculinity, rather than being man(ly) enough to discipline his desires; he also brings shame on the race by not choosing a black woman to love. LeRoy's grandmother and sister seem to agree with Du Bois's assumptions about how accomplished black men should not only behave but also feel: they should not want to mingle across the color line sexually or even socially; "natural race pride" should prevent such desire (qtd. in Ross 160–61). Viewing black coupling as the "natural" result of racial pride, the women in LeRoy's life seem to be as intolerant of his new-found expressions of masculinity as white men are.

By featuring a black attorney who incorrectly assumes that his loving relationship with a white woman will be successful, Livingston reflects and encourages intense debates about whether asserting African American citizenship requires strong black homes that are free of white influence. In the process, this script continues a tradition that literary historian Robert Reid-Pharr has identified in earlier black-authored texts. In *Conjugal Union*, Reid-Pharr suggests that many nineteenth-century intellectuals urged their brethren "to sever their sexual, romantic and familial ties to whites" (116). In harmony with those efforts, writers working to develop a distinctly African American literature often structured their texts around the creation of "purely" black homes. This tendency was meant to affirm African Americans' conception of themselves as independent citizens. It encouraged a community desire to move away from domestic arrangements that centered on serving whites and toward freedom and self-sufficiency.

In the 1920s, Livingston's work enters this tradition; though there is much to admire about the Carlson household, its members apparently enjoy a fraction of the success that accrues to black families whose men remain committed to community. In revealing the family secret, Grandmother Carlson testifies to the destruction that awaits black homes whenever whites are allowed to enter them. LeRoy's father had given his children a white mother, so Mrs. Carlson now pleads, "I couldn't go through it again! Boy, you can't make the same mistake your father did" (124). Long before LeRoy had ceased being a "manly tower of strength," his father had, by failing to guard against white influences. In this light, the father's absence becomes suggestive. His death is never fully explained, leaving open the possibility that he was lynched, especially since he had chosen to be with a white woman. Like other homes of the genre, then, this middle-class example contains no middle generation, and the mother is mentioned only because Grandmother Carlson wants to keep her grandson from repeating his father's mistakes. Through two generations of black men, Livingston encourages discussions about what fortifies or weakens African American families and communities.

In literature based on the assumption that white presence destroys black homes, "mulatto characters are either killed off or reinterpreted as black" (Reid-Pharr 11). Marion's and LeRoy's choices therefore gain significance. Their grandmother has worked to create a "pure" black household by not telling them about their white mother; she has tried to sever their familial ties to whites. As a result, Marion has become committed to the black community and pledges to disown her brother if he marries a white woman. LeRoy, on the other hand, has not broken his ties to whites; he forges a romantic bond with Selma, making his separation from the black community inevitable. Because racism shapes U.S. culture, either he will leave his family—as he plans to do—or he will be "killed off" by whites who are offended by his relationship.

While setting the stage for LeRoy's death, *For Unborn Children* is structured to detail his fall from grace, followed by his redemption. First, despite his professional success, the text shows that LeRoy has become what Ida B. Wells would have called a "Black Sampson." Livingston offers a Wells-inspired critique of LeRoy in Marion's explanation of miscegenation statutes: "[L]aws would never have been passed against it if states could have believed white women would turn Negro men down, but they knew they wouldn't; they can make fools out of them too easily" (123). Wells had been more diplomatic, but she too argued that "many white women in the South would marry colored men if such an act would not place them . . . within the clutches of the law" (*Southern Horrors* 53). In fact, Wells insisted that "white men lynch the offending Afro-American, not because he is a despoiler of virtue, but because he succumbs to the smiles of white women" (*Southern Horrors* 54).[24] Livingston corroborates Wells's critique by setting the action of *For Unborn Children* in the black home. There, readers/viewers see Selma rush in to warn her lover of the approaching mob. She cares for LeRoy, and Livingston underscores this fact by placing her inside the black home along with the black women who cherish him.

LeRoy and Selma's relationship is mutual and loving, but as it intensifies, LeRoy becomes less concerned about how his actions will affect others. Grandmother Carlson therefore explains that marrying a white woman is a disservice to his unborn children (124). Like Grimké's *Rachel*, this play insists that unborn children are in danger, but Livingston's work argues that a white mother is chief among those dangers. When LeRoy decides that eloping would be wrong, he joins Rachel in sacrificing happiness with a romantic partner in order to save innocent babies from a racist society. By then, it is too late; the mob is in front of the house.

Before LeRoy exits, Livingston redeems her protagonist; the script testifies to his transformation from weak Sampson to Christ figure. Because LeRoy decides to prioritize his family and community over his feelings for Selma, Livingston depicts him as a civilized gentleman while white men prepare to indulge their savagery. Hearing the mob arrive, LeRoy accepts his fate: "(a light breaks over his face and he is transfigured; a gleam of holiness comes into his eyes; looking heavenward he says): Thy will be done, O Lord" (124). With this portrayal, Livingston refuses to corroborate the images offered in mainstream newspapers. In addition to printing pictures of mutilated bodies, reporters often spoke of the "shivering Negro" or "grotesque beast" in opposition to the "orderly" white "citizens" who lynch him. In making LeRoy a Christ figure, *For Unborn Children* joins the countless artistic works that mark a similarity between the race's persecution and Christ's crucifixion.[25] The play testifies to LeRoy's manliness and innocence, and it survives as a record of his Christ-like demeanor at the moment when he faces the mob.

By not saving her manly character, Livingston refuses to simplify the issues that her text raises; the play is designed to provoke heated discussions among black readers similar to those depicted among LeRoy, Marion, and Grandmother Carlson. *Crisis* magazine rewarded this strategy, not only by publishing the script but also by granting its author a creative writing prize.[26] No doubt, Du Bois and his readers saw the value of debating the contours of black identity and citizenship with an eye toward interracial love. Black men's affection for white women was clearly of serious concern because, like LeRoy's, their love for these women was real. Recognizing that black men fall in love with white women, Livingston's drama, not unlike Wells's pamphlets, insists that their doing so makes them into black Sampsons. And if Marion and Grandmother Carlson are to be believed, African American men who involve themselves with white women risk helping the race's enemies, who insist that black communities lack solid homes built on a foundation of love and fidelity between black men and women. As Wells made clear, rape was alleged in only one-third of lynch cases, and very often it was not rape but a consensual relationship. Thus, a black man who consorts with a white woman enough to fall in love may be said to have failed to recognize lynching as master/piece theater. That is, he may have believed that because he is a beloved partner, not a rapist, he would be safe. In Livingston's view, such men are uninformed, and she offers her script as a model for the intervention that they need: not proscription but debate. Livingston's work seems to suggest that in order to see that lynching is not a legitimate scenario of exorcism, one must use family and community perspectives to filter the nation's rhetoric, which claims that mobs only target rapists.

On the question of interracial coupling, Livingston's script seems to resonate with the rigidity associated with the Black Power Movement that would later emerge; but more than that, it reflects 1920s debates about how African Americans can best assert their right to full citizenship. The text reflects community agreement that the black lawyer is an important figure whose accomplishment creates hope, but it also places him in a situation that illustrates the need to debate the link between personal freedom and community responsibility. LeRoy explains that he and Selma are in love and should be able to make a life together, but Grandmother Carlson insists, "Before we can gain that perfect Freedom to which we have every right, we've got to prove that we're better than they! And we can't do it when our men place white women above their own!" (124). Here, Livingston's character speaks in harmony with Fannie Barrier Williams, a leader of the black women's club movement: "Until the present stigma is removed from the home and the women of the race, . . . there will never be an unchallenged vote, a respected political power, or an unquestioned claim to position and importance" for African Americans (qtd. in White, *Too Heavy* 70).

Clearly, these were issues to be discussed, stances that were articulated but by no means passively accepted. As LeRoy's words and actions suggest, not everyone agrees with declarations like those made by his sister and grandmother. Nevertheless, alongside LeRoy's opinions, *For Unborn Children* preserves those of his relatives. In the process, the play records multiple perspectives that would not have been welcomed in the mainstream. The script therefore registers African Americans' commitment to reading against the grain of mainstream discourses.[27] As important, it indexes their tendency to grapple with the question of how best to help others to do the same. Intense discussions in the home would not necessarily protect black men from mobs, but this script's survival in the archive suggests that the authors and readers who were brought together by publications like *Crisis* participated in practices of black belonging—not the least of which was debate.

African Americans understood that conversation must continue because there are no easy solutions to the challenges that they encounter. Military service had not been the saving grace that many assumed it would be. Then, as communities placed more and more faith in the law, many hoped to become attorneys but were killed before they had a chance. Meanwhile, those who managed to practice law found that they often could not enjoy the most basic freedoms. For one thing, they lived with the threat of the mob, despite the fact that they were lawyers, not criminals.

※ ※ ※

The portrait of the black attorney set forth by Johnson and Livingston interacts with the historical moment in powerful ways, emphasizing that this figure embodied the race's simultaneous optimism and anxiety. While they lived lives of modern sophistication, blacks nevertheless found themselves cast in mainstream discourses as primitive and backward. In fact, many claimed that blacks made progress only by becoming better criminals.[28] In identifying with the black attorney, African Americans were asserting that they were honest and hardworking and that they loved law and order. At the same time, relating to the black attorney meant recognizing how often his integrity was disregarded by the country of his birth. Scholars have often marked the New Negro Era as one of tremendous confidence, but the optimism was accompanied by justified anxiety, and the black attorney embodies this tension because he at once represents significant accomplishment and profound limitation.

The figure of the black attorney becomes a symbol around which playwrights organize discussions of black citizenship in the mid-1920s, shortly after the failure of the Dyer Anti-lynching Bill. He points to both the archive and repertoire of a period in which African Americans continued their struggle to define themselves in public and private life as modern citizens. Though the black lawyer was sometimes honored in the pages of *Crisis*,[29] historians provide evidence of his painfully contradictory position. Because professional success required persuading judges and juries, whites' responses had serious implications. African American attorneys were often disrespected, and "word of their mistreatment . . . naturally reached the black community and caused potential clients to doubt the efficacy of black professionals" (Smith, *Emancipation* 15).[30] In short, black lawyers "experienced widespread hostility from courtroom and jury and faced a Negro public skeptical of their abilities" (Meier and Rudwick 131). African Americans "often used white lawyers at higher legal fees because they thought that justice could be obtained only in this way" (Smith, *Emancipation* 11). As a result, whether in the North or South, the black attorney often had limited opportunities to practice his skills. Very often, the work involved "only a few, very definite stereotyped situations: the errant spouse, the parent abandoning the children, . . . and petty criminal offences" (Houston qtd. in Meier and Rudwick 131). Gaining experience in areas beyond stereotyped issues usually required obtaining a white partner.[31]

Despite the insulting conditions under which they entered U.S. courtrooms, African Americans who had reached the point of practicing law had already proved themselves to be exceptionally capable. Law schools at the turn of the century were not welcoming to students who were not white, male, and Christian; the few African Americans who were admitted generally had prominent white sponsors. Then, if one survived the grueling years of study and untold number of racial incidents along the way, one might secure the degree. The next hurdle was admission to the state bar, without which one could not practice. Because the bar examination was administered in person, outright discrimination often characterized these exchanges in which the black professional's livelihood was at stake. As James Weldon Johnson shares in his autobiography, one examiner "blurted out in my face . . . 'Well, I can't forget he's a nigger and I'll be damned if I'll stay here to see him admitted'" (*Along This Way* 143). For those who managed to overcome all of these obstacles, membership in the profession's national society, the American Bar Association, was a reasonable expectation. Yet African Americans met so much opposition that they founded their own national organization in 1925,[32] the year that *Sunday Morning* and *For Unborn Children* were composed. Given the barriers that black lawyers had overcome to appear in the courtroom, the abuses encountered there must have been especially demoralizing. Just as important, their treatment was a reminder that they belonged to a people whose citizenship was not acknowledged.

Besides the disregard for their accomplishments (and for the idea that they and their clients were citizens guaranteed equal protection under the law), black attorneys often worked knowing that their vocation placed their lives in danger. As one turn-of-the-century black lawyer put it, to expect "economic security and reasonable protection" for himself and his family was unrealistic (Smith, *Emancipation* 14). Especially "in the South, black attorneys were sometimes assaulted, run out of town, or even killed for practicing their profession" (Finkelman 194). Furthermore, "lawyers defending black men charged with rape in Tennessee were, on occasion, forced to flee the state after their clients were lynched" (Smith, *Emancipation* 353).[33] Even the lynching of one's client did not always satisfy whites determined to communicate who should or should not feel legally protected.

The fact that both Tom of *Sunday Morning* and LeRoy of *For Unborn Children* die at the hands of the mob accords with the precarious position even accomplished lawyers occupied. They are not criminals, but the power of the black rapist myth within U.S. culture makes that fact seem irrelevant. By preserving evidence of these men's words and actions in their homes, the plays survive to mark the value that black communities placed on their own perspectives. Only by valuing the insights of the community conversation might one see that the rapist myth enabled criminal treatment of innocent, law-abiding black men.

Recording and encouraging embodied practices of black belonging, lynching playwrights helped African Americans to rehearse understandings of themselves as more worthy of citizenship than the whites who already enjoy its privileges and abuse its power.[34] Ultimately, Tom's death shows that blacks are prevented from becoming active citizens because whites insist on segregating and disfranchising them, but LeRoy's predicament is also designed to illuminate the unfair limitations placed on black citizenship. LeRoy has achieved the education that should empower him in courts of law, but he is isolated from them by a court of public opinion that robs him of the most basic freedoms.[35]

As LeRoy initially focuses on individual rights and entitlements, he operates more out of a sense of national belonging than community citizenship. His assumptions about freedom are rooted in the country's purported respect for everyone's inalienable right to life, liberty, and the pursuit of happiness. In this way, his story parallels the justified attempt to assert Sergeant Edgar Caldwell's federal rights. However, the nation refused to recognize Caldwell, despite his service to it. Meanwhile, his allies acknowledged his belonging—they insisted that he had a rightful place in their communities *and* in the nation. In doing so, they operated out of a tendency to affirm black citizenship despite the nation's denials. As I argued earlier, African Americans could not rely solely on mainstream acceptance if they were to see themselves as upstanding individuals and worthy citizens.

African Americans might manage to do without the nation's affirmation but not without community connection. Both the Caldwell case and black-authored lynching dramas illustrate that as long as the United States does not truly acknowledge African American citizenship, blacks will need to continue to affirm each other. Heated debate is an important part of that affirmation. After all, the exchanges between LeRoy and the women in his life are fueled by the connection they feel and the value they place on each other. Because it springs from mutual recognition, intense discussion helps African Americans to hold on to their belief that the race is composed of honorable individuals and worthy citizens.

This communal ethos, more than a focus on national acceptance, would shape the kind of black lawyer that Charles Hamilton Houston wanted to see. For Houston, becoming an attorney was a significant achievement, especially for blacks who faced incredible odds to do so, but it was not enough. Those who focused on personal accomplishment were likely to "stay in the less controversial fields of strictly civil work and office practice" (52). But African American attorneys could no longer afford to avoid volatile issues. The modern black lawyer must become a "social engineer" who is unafraid to "fight for true equality before the law" (51–52). To take on that sort of responsibility, he must be informed by the community conversation that preserves valid testimonies that would be disregarded in courts of law and the court of public opinion. Only community connection will keep him attuned to his people's honesty and integrity while he is bombarded with declarations of their depravity. Armed with this knowledge, he can become the soldier of the new era.

CHAPTER FIVE

THE BLACK MOTHER/WIFE
NEGOTIATING TRAUMA

In all conversations about lynching and citizenship, including those centered on the soldier and lawyer, black women were crucial. Because mobs so often negated black citizenship by targeting men, African American women routinely survived the physical attack and were left to face a forever-altered future. In *Mine Eyes Have Seen*, *Aftermath*, *A Sunday Morning in the South*, and *For Unborn Children*, the surviving black women are sisters and grandmothers. However, the plays written in the later 1920s by the genre's most prolific author, Georgia Douglas Johnson, focus on black wives and mothers. Angelina Weld Grimké had inaugurated the genre by placing a spotlight on Mrs. Loving—a grieving wife and mother whose experiences lead her daughter to reject marriage and maternity. When Johnson revisits this figure, she uses the black mother/wife to illuminate the most tragic dimensions of the mob's attack on black families. Because she so often survives to suffer in the home from which her husband or son is removed, the black mother/wife is the witness that those content with the racial status quo most want to silence. She bears witness to what it means to live with lynching. Through this figure, authors and readers access the conversation and conduct of those who lived with the "traumatizing shock of a commonly occurring violence" (Caruth 6).[1]

Though "mother/wife" is a bulky term, it highlights a figure that has not shaped the historical record to the degree that lynching drama suggests it should. Historians have typically relied on archives that bear the imprint of mainstream discourses and practices, which seldom prioritized depictions of African American mothers and wives in their own homes. Yet, as I have argued, it is the black home scene that oppressive forces sought to erase. As black women asserted themselves as citizens, they were portrayed as either asexual and unappealing or oversexed and unscrupulous.[2] Harkening back to the "good old days" of slavery, mainstream discourse often cast black women as mammies; they were believed to love the white children in their care far more than their own offspring, and they were imagined to have no romantic ties to black men. For the black mother/wife, who was neither a single mother nor mammy figure, it would seem undeniable that she enjoyed a sense of belonging within her family, yet national rhetoric downplayed her homebuilding success by asserting that she was naturally promiscuous. At the turn of the century, mainstream discourse often "portrayed all black women as sexually available and subservient to all white men" (Rosen 8). Thus, the nation embraced mammy figures and images of unwed black mothers but rejected the idea that black women could sustain respectable marriages.

Because lynching plays reflect and encourage community conversation, the emergence of the black mother/wife as a central figure registers the degree to which her experiences informed discussions of black identity and citizenship. Rather than portray a black woman in a white family's house where she dotes on white children, the genre presents black women characters in ways that emphasize their love for their own children as well as for a romantic partner. In the process, African Americans participated in, and preserved evidence of, embodied practices of black belonging. As discussed, the genre showcases black belonging by virtue of the plays' family-centered content as well as their one-act form, which made them conducive to practices of communal literacy. By engaging in and recording discourses and practices of black belonging, African Americans sustained themselves, even as they watched their homebuilding efforts negated in the mainstream.

Reading their surroundings accurately, blacks understood that the nation encouraged the denial of African American familial ties by tolerating lynching and the circulation of photographs that cast mob victims as isolated brutes. At the same time, private violence worked to destroy all evidence that there had ever been bonds of love in the first place.[3] In fact, while whites declared blacks to be homeless brutes and whores, vigilantes often attacked African Americans in distinctly domestic ways. As historian Hannah Rosen establishes, "Although schools and churches were occasional targets for arson . . ., the vast majority of violent encounters occurred in and around homes" (189). Whites could have terrorized blacks by shooting at them from afar, but they often preferred invading their victims' households, and these intrusions "lasted at times for hours and involved prolonged interaction and dialogue between assailants and victims" (180). In other words, whites invaded black households and forced occupants to perform their powerlessness—reveling in "creating circumstances under which black fathers and husbands could not prevent the violence against their family members" (Rosen 8). Thus, African American clubwomen often remarked that black men's "inability to protect black women in slavery . . . had carried over into freedom" (Feimster 116). Accordingly, in 1917 and 1919, the bloodiest race riots were characterized by what Anne Rice calls "homefront violence." In East St. Louis, Illinois, whites "set entire residential areas alight," and one witness saw "the mob chasing a colored man who had a baby in his arms" ("White Islands" 76).[4] While these violent practices worked to obliterate African Americans' conception of themselves as citizens, lynching drama continued to depict black households from the community's vantage point.

Within their homes, African Americans affirmed their identities, marking their roles as husbands, wives, brothers, sisters, daughters, and sons, so the black home scene in lynching drama becomes evidence of black belonging and of white responses to it. In essence, African Americans continued traditions of affirming their self-conceptions through the black home scene, and in response, mainstream attempts to deny black homebuilding success intensified. Antiblack efforts became especially important as the nuclear family was increasingly valued as the key to the country's progress and as individuals were said to demonstrate capacity for citizenship through personal discipline and propriety.[5] White intrusions upon the home space index the success with which blacks affirmed themselves there; direct attack seemed necessary to whites who wanted to negate black citizenship in the most fundamental, painful way.

Whites used segregation to claim public space as their own, and they often rejected blacks' claims to private space too. As activist Mary Church Terrell declared in 1904, "[T]he negro's home is not considered sacred by the superior race. White men are neither punished for invading it, nor lynched for violating colored women and girls" (865). In this climate, if African Americans were to maintain their sense of themselves as citizens, they must lay claim, through words and actions, to their right to assert the sanctity of the spaces that were theirs by virtue of segregation—black homes and civic centers, black churches and schools. Put another way, as mainstream discourses and practices took every opportunity to construe "the U.S. landscape as always raced white and gendered male," African Americans viewed their management of black spaces, especially domestic ones, as opportunities to critique "white terrorism and Jim Crow segregation" (Rice, "White Islands" 76, 80). In this spirit, black women activists emphasized the order and cleanliness of "black-inhabited physical space" (Higginbotham 202). Investing in the "politics of respectability," African Americans exemplified propriety even in the privacy of their own homes;

they lived by morality, purity, and efficiency. In doing so, they demonstrated that racial hierarchy was "socially constructed rather than derived by evolutionary law or divine judgment" (Higginbotham 192). By their actions as much as their words, African Americans "condemned white America for failing to live up to its own rhetoric of equality and justice as found in the Constitution" (Higginbotham 222).[6]

While African American activism often underscored the value placed on the sanctity of black spaces, so did African American literature.[7] In the case of lynching drama, as I have suggested, using the black home as setting called attention to the conversation and conduct that sustained African Americans as the United States permitted antiblack violence. At the same time, using the one-act format made black-authored scripts conducive to informal "production" in private spaces. Lynching plays encouraged African Americans to rehearse their understanding of themselves as worthy citizens, and it is no surprise that many self-affirming rehearsals took place in black households.

Indeed, to understand the lynching plays that foreground the black mother/wife, one must consider a home in the nation's capital that was used for racially affirming literary and theatrical work: the S. Street residence of Georgia Douglas Johnson. Like the alternative discursive space represented and fueled by *Crisis* magazine, Johnson's literary salon proved to be a figurative and literal space in which various viewpoints could be shared. When guests gathered in Johnson's living room, "they read their writing aloud, exchanged criticisms, talked about the latest books they had read, and argued their views on literature, art, and politics" (McHenry 269). They also read magazines together and discussed their content (272). Though it is not clear when the "Saturday Nighters" salon was officially launched, regular meetings may have been in place by September 1922.[8] Even if the group had not congealed that early in the 1920s, the salon grew out of the fact that Johnson was already a mentor and friend to many artists and intellectuals. Her correspondence with a young Jean Toomer dates back to at least 1920, and her house was among the places that many visited when traveling (270). In 1922, her visitors included Toomer, Jessie Fauset, and Zora Neale Hurston. Both before and while the group met regularly, Johnson created an environment similar to those nurtured by black literary societies of the nineteenth century. Reading was not passive; "it was an invitation to participate" (102). This sort of space proved to be relevant even in the 1920s, and even for writers. When facing the doubts and fears that accompany a writing life, owning one's identity as an author required having support and affirmation.

Thus, the creative works that Johnson generated in the 1920s should be seen as products of the community conversation that her home helped to facilitate as she made it an alternative public space. In Washington, D.C., blacks were reminded that they were not wanted, no matter how skilled or educated, and the plays Johnson wrote proved to be "an outlet for the unnaturally suppressed inner lives which our people have been compelled to lead" (Matthews 131).[9] Johnson's *Blue Blood* (1926), *Safe* (1929), and *Blue-Eyed Black Boy* (c. 1930) did not appear in print for years, so they circulated primarily through intimate interactions.[10] Much more than indexing Johnson's individual interests, these plays reflect a community conversation about black women who were both wives and mothers in the midst of racial violence.

Plays featuring the black mother/wife foreground the terror with which too many women lived, acknowledging emotional and psychological pain beyond that illuminated in discussions of the black soldier and lawyer: she is depicted as the embodiment of what it means to live with lynching. When the black mother/wife becomes lynching drama's key figure in the late 1920s, she represents the haunting nature of black citizens' vulnerability. It is therefore important that Johnson writes three plays that foreground this figure; its recurrence registers community trauma. As literary historian Daylanne English suggests, in the context of lynching drama and fiction, "repetition . . . is not an individual psychological response or symptom and certainly not a writerly error" (*Unnatural* 121). Cathy Caruth has found that trauma manifests in literature as "recurring words or figures" that mark "the oscillation between a *crisis of death* and the correlative *crisis of life*" (7). The black mother/wife's existence revolves around attempts to delay death. Her roles as wife and mother are shaped by the desire to escape lynching while never being able do so.

Johnson offers portraits of the black mother/wife in *Blue Blood, Safe,* and *Blue-Eyed Black Boy,* but despite different circumstances, this character's every action is motivated by the fact that her loved ones are constantly in danger. In *Blue Blood,* the mother/wife prevents the murder of the men in her family by hiding the fact that she has been raped by a powerful white man. In *Safe,* she becomes desperate to avoid what she believes to be the inevitable fate of her newborn son: humiliating death at the hands of a mob. In *Blue-Eyed Black Boy,* she protects her adult son, but her success in stopping the mob ultimately illuminates her family's vulnerability to white whim. Simply put, the mob's unchecked power shapes the environment in which the black mother/wife struggles to create and sustain romantic and parental bonds.

As she hosted a literary salon in her home in the nation's capital, where antilynching legislation had been defeated, Johnson offered the black mother/

wife to expose contradictions between American claims about valuing nuclear families and stable homes and responses to black examples of both. The three plays Johnson penned in the late 1920s demonstrate that black mother/wives created romantic and parental bonds despite a painfully unjust reality: white men's power to take black men's lives and claim sexual access to black women. Together, Johnson's *Blue Blood, Safe,* and *Blue-Eyed Black Boy* suggest that the nation's disregard for black citizenship—through its denigration of black womanhood and attack on black manhood—continued in the 1920s, making for a barbaric modern era indeed.

Blue Blood

Composed in 1926, Georgia Douglas Johnson's *Blue Blood* looks back to the late 1800s and acknowledges African Americans who built solid homes against all odds. Mrs. Temple is a mother/wife whose domestic success has come at a high price: silence about rape. Indeed, her silence comes to an end only to prevent an incestuous marriage. Mrs. Temple and Mrs. Bush are preparing for their children's wedding, which is only minutes away, when they discover that the same white man fathered the bride and groom. The script corroborates what community members know, that black women often keep quiet about their encounters with white men because they are "wives who [seek] to protect their husbands from assault and murder" and "mothers concerned with protecting their children from violence" (Rosen 233). Mrs. Temple had established her domestic tranquility by keeping her rape a secret, so Johnson uses this mother/wife to acknowledge, and show respect for, the many African American couples who nurtured romantic bonds despite humiliating circumstances.

The action takes place in "Georgia" and "shortly after the Civil War" in the kitchen of Mrs. Bush, whose daughter May will soon marry John Temple. Randolph Strong enters with a bundle of white roses, and it is evident that he and May's mother are fond of each other. He calls her "Mother Bush" and she insists that, in refusing his marriage proposal last Christmas, May had "turn[ed] her back on the best fellow in this town" (63–64). Mrs. Bush is not thrilled with May's decision to marry John Temple; she says that he is a "stiff-necked, good-looking dude" and a "high-falutin' nothing"(64). Furthermore, Mrs. Bush would have chosen Randolph to be her daughter's mate because he has a dark complexion: "I never did believe in two 'lights' marrying, no how, it's on-lucky" (64). John and May are "jest exactly the same color," with hair and eyes "alike too" (64). Randolph does not disagree. Still, he insists, "If she's happy, that's the main thing." Mrs. Bush doubts that May will be happy because she suspects that May has been swayed by John's financial standing. Mrs. Bush predicts, "She'll re'lize some day that money ain't everything" (64). Randolph sees no point in hoping that May will change her mind, but he admits, "[S]ometimes I think May cares for me" (64).

Soon, Mrs. Bush is boasting that everything is ready, and she shows Randolph the gown that she is wearing underneath her apron. Then she realizes that the person responsible for bringing the mayonnaise for the chicken salad is thirty minutes late (65). Randolph volunteers to go get it, and Mrs. Bush says, "Oh, what a son-in-law you would've made!" (65). When he leaves, she notices the package that he had brought. It is a gift for the couple, a lovely vase. After admiring it, she calls May downstairs. May loves the vase as much as the white roses and she places one of the flowers in her hair.

As May begins to return upstairs to finish getting dressed, the mother of the groom arrives, and the happy anticipation of wedding preparation becomes dramatic tension. Mrs. Temple enters in an uproar because family friends in other areas of the house had tried to keep her from entering the kitchen. She has persisted, determined to help with the arrangements because "everything must be right" (67). When she learns that Mrs. Bush is waiting on Randolph to return with mayonnaise, she insists upon making it from scratch. She also says, "Why, May, are you not dressed yet! You'll have to do better than that when you are Mrs. John Temple" (66). Later, when May has gone upstairs, she tells Mrs. Bush, "You'll have to admit that the girls will envy May marrying my boy John" (67). Mrs. Bush quickly grows competitive and declares that if she told Mrs. Temple who May was, she would be "struck dumb" and would "fall flat" (67).

With prodding from Mrs. Temple, Mrs. Bush reveals that May's father is "Cap'n Winfield McCallister, the biggest banker in this town, . . . 'ristocrat uv 'ristocrats" (67). At this, Mrs. Temple almost collapses. Speaking "softly and excitedly," she responds, "You . . . terrify me. . . . Captain McCallister can't be May's father!" (68). Mrs. Bush takes offense when Mrs. Temple asks additional questions, and she finally exclaims, "I'm telling you that my daughter—May Bush—has got the bluest blood in America in her veins. Jest put that in your pipe and smoke it!" (68).

Mrs. Bush remains impatient with Mrs. Temple because it is now eight forty-five and the wedding should be beginning soon. Mrs. Temple is struggling to make Mrs. Bush be still and listen, and she is having trouble finding the words to articulate what she must. Mrs. Temple pleads, "Oh, where can I begin? Let me think—," but Mrs. Bush insists, "This ain't no time to think,

I'm going to act" (68). With that, she *takes [the] mayonnaise from Mrs. Temple's apathetic hands*" (68). Mrs. Temple confesses first, "Oh, oh how I've tried to forget it!" (69). Then she explains that when she was nineteen and saving for her wedding, she met a man at the bank where she kept her money and "he helped me" (69). When he began writing her letters, she saw that "he wanted his pay for it" (69). She ignored the advances, but he bribed the woman in charge of where she boarded. As a result, "he came into my room—. . . I cried out. There wasn't any one there that cared enough to help me" (69).

While struggling to find the words to share this secret, Mrs. Temple had declared, "I'm just a broken-hearted mother," and it soon becomes clear that she is not alone. Up to this point, Mrs. Temple has emphasized her social standing. She acknowledges that her presence in Mrs. Bush's kitchen is unexpected: "We have not called on each other in the past, moving around . . . in somewhat different social circles" (66). Nevertheless, she says, "Since our two children are determined to marry, . . . my place to-night is right back here with you!" (66). Mrs. Bush does not want the help and says that Temple might ruin herself "doing kitchen work" (67). She reasons, "Sich folk as you'd better go 'long in the parlor" (67). Johnson emphasizes the class distinction by signaling that Mrs. Bush's speech is not exactly "properly" pronounced "standard" English and by giving Mrs. Temple white gloves to go along with her snooty attitude. She is willing to help in the kitchen not for Mrs. Bush's sake but because she does not trust her to make tasteful preparations: "This is my son's wedding . . . he is a Temple and everything must be right" (67).

Yet, the story that she is forced to share reveals that John is not a Temple at all. The pride of that name, the name of the man to whom she was engaged when she was raped, cannot be claimed biologically, as she has led everyone to believe. She was robbed of the identity that she claimed for herself, that of a traditionally respectable woman, and her son was deprived of the paternity that she would have chosen for him. Rather than have the "blood" of a man who offered his mother stability, he carries that of the man who offered only shame. Though Mrs. Temple enjoys a loving and financially stable union, her marriage does not signify the propriety and protection that it should. She had been living apart from her fiancé until they were married and it was "proper" for them to cohabitate, but the dignity of entering into wedlock with untainted virtue was denied to her. Mrs. Temple succeeds in forming a nuclear family with the man she loves, but there is an unwanted element woven into the romantic bonds upon which their family is built.

Though Mrs. Temple has "tried to forget it," her past comes back to remind her that she has more in common with Mrs. Bush than she would willingly admit. Mrs. Temple ends her story thusly: "You know yourself, Mrs. Bush, what little chance there is for women like us, in the South, to get justice or redress when these things happen" (69). Mrs. Bush responds, "Sure honey, I do know!" (69). Suddenly, these bickering women have much in common— despite having moved in different social circles, "not being," in Mrs. Temple's words, "thrown very close together" (66). With her confession, Mrs. Temple's refined white gloves lose significance, as do her many comments about May needing to rise to the occasion of sharing her surname. Johnson's script shows that vulnerability to white men makes Mrs. Temple's experiences parallel to those of the less refined, dialect-speaking Mrs. Bush.

Just as *Blue Blood* traces black women's similarities across social classes, it pinpoints connections that span generations. Mrs. Temple says that her own mother had discouraged her from trying to expose Captain McCallister: "[Mother] said I'd be the one . . . that would suffer." Mrs. Bush agrees, "[W]hut your ma told you is the God's truth" (69). Not only do these two recognize the injustice that follows black women, but Mrs. Temple's mother had also testified to it. Next, May—representing a third generation—will discover the extent of society's disregard for "women like us." Decades of experience certify that black women's morality will be questioned, not that of their assailants.

With a spotlight on black women's words and actions, *Blue Blood* demonstrates that sexual vulnerability forces them to make painful decisions if they are to have any chance of enjoying romantic attachments. Mrs. Temple has never publicly accused Captain McCallister, but she shared the truth with her fiancé, Paul Temple, even while refusing to reveal her attacker's identity. Mrs. Bush affirms her: "That wuz good sense." Without Mrs. Temple's secrecy, her fiancé "would've tried to kill [the Captain] and then they'd have killed him" (69). Significantly, she is sure of the black man's death, even if he had simply *tried* to punish the white rapist. Thus *Blue Blood*'s spotlight on black women's vulnerability simultaneously bears witness to the emasculation of black men. The script reflects awareness in the community conversation that white men prey on black women in order to negate their citizenship and that of the black men who want to protect them.

Again and again, black women keep secrets in order to preserve the romantic bonds that will become the foundation for their nuclear families. Through the black mother/wife, the play gives voice to the pain of knowing that black men can stay alive only if black women do not speak the truth about the injustices they endure. Mrs. Temple had been able to establish a home and gain social standing because she had been willing to shield her fiancé from the truth. She confides, "He understood the whole thing—and he married me. He knew why I wouldn't tell him the man's name—not even when—when that man's son was born to me" (69). Because her fiancé had been understanding rather than treat her as a guilty concubine, they could create a home together. Revealing the assailant would have placed Paul Temple in the position of choosing one of two paths. He could either appear to substantiate what white men assert about black men, that they are "uninterested in preventing their wives' and daughters' denigration" or he could be chivalrous and protective by seeking vengeance, which would get him killed and leave his wife a widow. An alternative has been produced by the black woman's silence; it prevents lynching and allows a measure of black domestic fulfillment. These are unjustly limited choices, but by recording this predicament, the play gives verbal and embodied recognition to the many unknown black mother/wives whose silence offered a measure of stability to black families in a racist society.

In addition to operating as evidence of the existence and experiences of such women, the text demonstrates that romantic bonds between African Americans flourished despite the uniquely unjust conditions under which they were forged. The script's survival in the archive registers embodied practices of black belonging; Mr. and Mrs. Temple managed to move past the humiliating start to their life as husband and wife. Johnson's work declares that in a nation that deemed wedlock to be the foundation of modern citizenship, African Americans built marriages despite the worst odds. Black women proved themselves to be devout mother/wives even as they were denied the honor and protection of those roles. The plight of black women was a part of the community conversation, even as it was erased in mainstream discourse; Johnson's work reflected that fact and helped to ensure that it would continue to be the case. When *Blue Blood* initially circulated, mostly privately, it no doubt empowered African Americans to question the mainstream insistence that black women existed only as whores and mammies. As mainstream discourses and practices sought to erase their stories, Johnson worked to preserve them, thereby acknowledging, honoring, and affirming those brave soldiers in American homes, black mother/wives.

Mrs. Temple's choices had been limited by the mortal danger that surrounds black men, and the same proves to be true for the next generation. Ultimately, Mrs. Bush and Mrs. Temple agree that May must know the truth, and John must remain ignorant of it: "We can't let [John] know or he'll kill his own father" (72). The mothers tell May that she must be strong and do her duty: "It's the black women that have got to protect their men from the white man by not telling on [white men]" (73).

Black women are often deprived of the ability to make decisions based on their own desires, as becomes most apparent when May must begin a new life with Randolph Strong. The script modifies the genre's tendency toward representing de-generation in that marriage is not altogether prevented, but the impending union relies on disregarding the woman's will. Indeed, Johnson uses May and Randolph's reunion to critique further the nation's refusal to respect or minimally protect black women. Having returned from his errand, Randolph Strong is present when May learns that John is her brother. Because May cannot marry John, Mrs. Bush asks Randolph to help. He had proposed to May the previous Christmas, and she had rejected him; now she has no choice. The play's ending is worth recounting here because Johnson shows through deliberately choppy dialogue that May's desires simply do not matter.

Everyone agrees that May's fiancé, John, cannot know the truth, so all responsibility falls on her shoulders:

MRS. TEMPLE: What are you going to do, May?

MRS. BUSH: Yes, May, what are you going to do?

RANDOLPH STRONG: We are going to run away and get married, aren't we, May? Say yes, May—say yes!

[. . .]

RANDOLPH STRONG: May! Come with me *now*!

MAY: Randolph—do you want me?

RANDOLPH STRONG: I want you like I've always wanted you.

MAY: (*shyly*) But—I don't love you.

RANDOLPH STRONG: You think you don't . . .

MAY: Do you want me now?

RANDOLPH STRONG: I want you now.

MAY: Ma, oh, ma!

MRS. BUSH: (*in tears*) Quick, darlin'—tell him.

MAY: My coat.

MRS. BUSH: I'll get your coat, honey.

MRS. TEMPLE: Here May, take my coat!

MRS. BUSH: What are we going to tell John—and all the people?

MAY: Tell 'em—Oh God, we can't tell 'em the—truth?

RANDOLPH STRONG: Mother Bush—just tell them the bride was stolen by Randolph Strong (*Strong puts the coat around her and they go out the door, leaving the others staring at them.*) [Curtain]

Randolph Strong is a good man who has long loved May, but their life together will be shaped by the secret that she is keeping and the vulnerability that made it necessary. In contrast to earlier plays, the women here have prevented lynching with their secrecy, so the mob does not extract a successful head of household. Nevertheless, the threat of mob violence and the rape of black women facilitated by that threat, place May in impossible circumstances. May feels violated as she cries, "Oh God—I've kept out of their clutches myself, but now it's through you, Ma, that they've got me anyway. Oh, what's the use" (72). May cannot afford to reject Randolph Strong; he is her only viable option now. They cannot reveal the rape that caused these siblings to want to marry each other because it would ruin much of what the Temple family has paid so dearly to have, and it could lead John to attack or kill his own father. Therefore, May must disappear with Strong because, without a man in her life, she is even more vulnerable to white men. After all, McCallister had gotten to nineteen-year-old Mrs. Temple because she was living alone until her wedding day.

Like Mrs. Temple, just when May is about to marry the man of her choice and act upon her own sense of decency and sexual integrity, her plans are destroyed by the actions of a white man who cares nothing for her. Through no fault of her own, May's morality will be brought into question. How could she be moments from marrying John Temple and then disappear with Randolph Strong? Though May has not been exploited in the way that Mrs. Temple and Mrs. Bush testify is so common, a white man has nonetheless created circumstances that make her appear to be a bit too sexually available. Thus, when May asks, "What's the use," she is partly addressing the fact that she will seem like a woman of ill repute despite having been able to physically avoid white men. If a mother/wife of pristine reputation like Mrs. Temple ultimately proves the power of white men to rape and murder with impunity, what hope do women without claims to married motherhood have?

By closing the action with the obliteration of May's will, Johnson seems most interested in black women's agency and the circumstances that threaten to make it irrelevant. Many readers take miscegenation to be the theme of this play, but interracial sex simply serves to foreground violence against black women—the violence of having one's sexual and reproductive choices stolen. To make matters worse, the sexual license that white men claim creates a hostile atmosphere for the romantic love upon which black nuclear families are formed.[11] Black women remain silent about their exploitation because they want to keep their loved ones alive, and *Blue Blood* suggests that the sexual vulnerability of black women, which had undergirded slavery, continued to cast a shadow long after Emancipation.

Written in 1926, the play registers blacks' understanding that the country's racial hierarchy depends on dehumanizing tendencies that did not disappear in the postbellum era or dissipate as the United States declared itself to be modern. As generations of women in *Blue Blood* keep secrets from the men that they love, Johnson's text echoes insights offered by Harriet Jacobs in *Incidents in the Life of a Slave Girl* (1861). As literary historian Catherine Clinton insists, though everyone knew that white men victimized black women, speaking that truth would upset the power structure and expose the fiction of southern honor (205). Jacobs emphasized the cost of *not* remaining silent: "But did the mothers dare to tell who was the father of their children? Did the other slaves dare to allude to it, except in whispers among themselves? No, indeed! They knew too well the terrible consequences" (31). Within such a system, Jacobs finds it difficult to have any semblance of virtue. To discourage her master's advances, Jacobs decides at age fifteen to "give herself" to another white man, Mr. Sands. Jacobs reasons, "It seems less degrading to give one's self, than to submit to compulsion. There is something akin to freedom in having a lover who has no control over you, except that which he gains by kindness and attachment" (47). Given that Jacobs is fifteen years old and a slave, it is not clear that she could have truly consented to any relationship. Thus, as she writes as an adult, she emphasizes that judging her sexual conduct is impossible and indeed inappropriate.

Since the women in Johnson's work often choose black men as partners when given a real choice, the script reminds readers that, even outside of slavery, questions of agency arise around relationships between blacks and whites. Because virtually limitless political and economic power ensured white male access to black women, white men created a troubling continuum of "consent" from black women. As one adult child of an interracial union puts it, "I don't know if it was rape or money or lust or affection . . . that caused the mingling up. In my mother's case, I don't know. I've spent a lot of my life trying to know, but I don't" (qtd. in Clinton 207). This testimony helps illuminate the complexities underpinning interracial unions, just as Jacobs does by discouraging readers from judging her sexual behavior. Acknowledging similar complexities, Johnson's *Blue Blood* leaves many mysteries in place as she writes in the 1920s about black women's experiences with powerful white men. The reader knows very little about how consensual Mrs. Bush's relationship with the Captain had been. She commiserates with Mrs. Temple about her violation, but she also brags that her child has the blood of an "aristocrat." Are we to assume that she had consented to her relationship with the Captain? Or had she simply learned to repel the shame because she knew resistance to be futile? The ambiguity surrounding Mrs. Bush's complicity comes into focus when it is clear that May's paternity has destroyed her life. Mrs. Bush pleads, "God forgive me

. . . God forgive that man. Oh no . . . I don't want Him to forgive him" (72). This leaves the possibility that, like Jacobs in *Incidents,* she had "given herself" because she knew she would be forced otherwise.[12] Not insignificantly, Johnson's drama *Blue-Eyed Black Boy* also refuses to clarify the nature of the relationship that the black mother/wife had with a governor.

Prominently displaying these sexual ambiguities allows Johnson to emphasize that black women continued to struggle, long after Emancipation, to control their sexuality and create homes that honor it. In slavery, they nursed white women's children and kept the identity of their own children's fathers a secret. Emancipation made them optimistic that their homebuilding efforts would be respected, but white men still showed little regard for black women's marital bonds. Because white men went unpunished, rape and lynching kept black women from being safe in their own homes, kept them from truly choosing their lovers and remaining faithful to them, and it could keep their daughters from choosing their husbands.[13]

Johnson uses the mother/wife in *Blue Blood* to insist that as long as white lust runs amok, African Americans' discipline and propriety do not bring the safety and citizenship that it should. Mrs. Temple lived apart from her fiancé until their wedding day in order to enter marriage with dignity. That right was stolen, but the couple put the injustice behind them, built a respectable life, and reared their son to be independent and proud of his identity as a Temple. The silence around the fact that he was not a Temple was not mere pride on his mother's part; it was a practical decision based on the understanding that white men kill black men with impunity. Mrs. Temple was protecting her husband and son, not just appearances. Even though she succeeded in keeping them alive and by her side, there is no denying the trauma that she suppressed or the pain of having to do so.

By exposing the sacrifices made by a mother/wife like Mrs. Temple, Johnson ensures that posterity will have access to the words and actions of the countless black women who enjoyed abiding by traditional standards of sexual propriety but encountered powerful white men who made it impossible. When these women share their testimonies, it becomes clear that whites make their own sexual conduct irrelevant in national discourse by labeling black women "whores" and black men "rapists." Also, relying on the hierarchies sustained by racial violence, whites free themselves to create impropriety in black homes—and at the same time accuse blacks of being incapable of monogamy, thus challenging their claims to citizenship. Exposing this tendency, *Blue Blood* insists that African American freedom is limited, but not because blacks fail to behave responsibly. By depicting the stable families who exist despite absurdly unjust circumstances, lynching dramas insist that if blacks have limited access to the rights, privileges, and safety that citizens should enjoy, that fact indicts the nation, not the race.

Safe

In 1929, Georgia Douglas Johnson continued placing a spotlight on black domestic success and the rights nevertheless withheld, but this time the mother/wife figure illuminates the limits of black citizenship by demonstrating that black parenthood is robbed of its joy, saturated with anxiety and fear instead. Like other lynching plays, Johnson's *Safe* spotlights a black home to detail its destruction, but it also uses the black mother/wife to bear witness to the reverberating damage associated with a famous lynching. Johnson takes her 1929 contemporaries to "1893" and introduces a victim named Sam Hosea, to retell the story of Sam Hose, who was lynched when he was suspected of killing his boss.[14] The Sam Hose case captured much attention in the 1890s, and historians have uncovered details about the murder and its aftermath.[15] For instance, the knuckles of the real Sam Hose were displayed in a store window in Atlanta. When W. E. B. Du Bois decided to visit the offices of the *Atlanta Constitution* to complain about the newspaper's biased coverage of mob violence, he walked past that window and saw Hose's knuckles. Horrified, Du Bois turned around and became convinced that his sociological studies could not help the race (Lewis 226). At that moment, Du Bois the scholar became a relentless civil rights agitator—joining the ranks of Ida B. Wells, whose antilynching campaign was well underway.

Du Bois's decision to dedicate himself to activism confirms that Hose's murder touched black community members besides those in his family, but Hose's familial ties are undeniable. Once whites claimed that Hose had raped his boss's wife, reward money was offered, and he was captured because he was "lying low, taking meals in his mother's cabin" (Dray 9). In his time of trouble, the twenty-one-year-old went back to the farm on which he grew up because his mother still worked there. Hose's body parts were carelessly displayed in a shop window, suggesting that he had been an isolated brute, but history tells us that those knuckles came from a man who was connected to family and a larger community, which included people like Du Bois. This community did not distance itself from Hose's memory but worked to uncover and preserve the truth about what had happened, knowing that he was not a "monster in human form," as white newspapers had claimed.[16]

To similar effect, Johnson's dramatic rendering of the story emphasizes that Hosea's murder affected the larger community. *Safe* is set in the home of Liza and John Pettigrew, whom Johnson labels "the wife" and "the husband." John is reading the newspaper and Liza, happily pregnant with their first child, is sewing. Liza is also trying to convince her mother, Mandy, to stop doing housework; she is grateful that Mandy has come to help prepare for the baby's arrival but believes that she should rest while she can (110). John shares the news that he is reading: Sam Hosea has been in jail since morning. Liza asks, "'Twant no woman mixed up in it, was it?" and John elaborates, "No, seems like he and his boss had some sort of dispute about wages—the boss slapped him, and Sam up and hit him back" (111). Mandy's response is telling: "[T]hat's mighty unhealthy sounding business . . . Hittin a white man, he better hadder made tracks far away from here I'm er thinking" (111). Clearly, having physically defended himself will be treated as a crime, no less than getting "mixed up" with a white woman. Hannah, a family friend, arrives to check on Liza but also to share the news that she has heard, which is worse than what has been reported thus far. A member of the community told Hannah that a mob has formed downtown and "there'll be hell to pay tonight" (112). John asks, "Ain't they gointer call out the soldiers, did he say?" Hannah's response is unsettling: "No, he jest said the crowds was gathering and it didn't look good in town" (112).

John decides to go and see "what they knows by Briggze's store" (112). When he leaves, the women discuss white men's violent contempt for dignified black manhood and Liza says that she hopes that she never has a boy child. Suddenly, they hear a gunshot, followed by noise that seems to be moving in their direction. Hannah peeks out the door and reports that a crowd is indeed approaching the house. Mandy says that they had better "put out the light and pull that curtain way down" (112). Growing anxious, Liza asks, "They wouldn't come in here? Would they?" Her mother tries to comfort her but another shot is heard and *the women jump and look at each other in fear*" (112). They also begin to worry about the fact that John has not returned. Mandy *peeps cautiously out from behind [the] shade*," Hannah follows her, and so does Liza, but the older women tell her to stay back; she should not see such things in her delicate state (113).

As Liza wonders what is happening, she paces restlessly and asks questions. The older women try to comfort her, but it is no use because they can hear all of the commotion. Mandy says, "You hadn't ought to hear all this screeching hell" (113). Then, seventeen-year-old Sam Hosea's voice is heard above the mob, "Don't hang me, don't hang me! I don't want to die! Mother! Mother!" At this, Liza *runs to the door and looks out*" (113). Mandy and Hannah drag her away and sit her down; she is "*shivering, her teeth chattering*" as she says "Oh my God, did you hear that poor boy crying for his mother?"

Before the chaos subsides, Mandy asks Hannah to find help for Liza. "I hates to ast you," Mandy admits to her friend, "but John ain't got back and we ought to git a doctor" (113). While Hannah is gone, Mandy watches as Liza paces, occasionally peeks out of the window, and often doubles over in pain. The noise outside diminishes but there is occasionally the sound of curses and laughter as men leave the scene. Mandy asks Liza to lie down and assures her that the doctor will arrive soon. Liza seems to ignore her mother's words and asks, "Did you hear him cry for his mother? Did you?" Mandy insists, "Yes, honey chile, I heard him, but you musn't think about that now. Fergit it. Remember your own little baby—you got him to think about. You got to born him safe!" (114).

Liza goes into her bedroom looking "wild-eyed." John finally arrives, explaining to Mandy that he has been hiding from the mob. He goes into the bedroom with Liza. Soon, there is a knock at the door; Mandy calls John to answer it. He escorts the doctor into the bedroom, then he joins Mandy in the living room. They worry about how having seen and heard the violence will affect Liza and the baby, and John regrets not having been by his wife's side when she was most afraid.

Suddenly, John and Mandy hear the baby's healthy cry. They step forward but wait for the doctor to emerge. When he steps out of the bedroom, "*his face looks distressed*" as he gives his report: "She's all right and the baby was born all right—big and fine. You heard him cry" (115). However, Liza had asked whether the baby was a girl and the doctor had informed her, "No, child, it's a fine boy" (115). He continues, " . . . then I turned my back a minute to wash in the basin. When I looked around again she had her hands about the baby's throat choking it. I tried to stop her, but its little tongue was already hanging from its mouth. It was dead! Then she began, she kept muttering over and over again: 'Now he's safe—safe from the lynchers! Safe!'" (115). At this, "*John falls down on a chair sobbing, his face in his hands*" and Mandy goes to be with her daughter in the bedroom. Meanwhile, the doctor stands, "*a picture of helplessness as he looks at them in their grief*" (115).

In Johnson's text, the grief inspired by Sam's death is felt in the home of John and Liza Pettigrew as much as in the Hosea household itself. When the action begins, the Pettigrews are enjoying each other's company as they prepare for the baby's arrival, but it is also clear that they value their connection to the community. When they learn that Sam is in jail, John immediately thinks of the boy's mother, saying "I reckon his ma is plum crazy if she's heered they got him" (111). Liza responds, "I knows her. . . . Belong to our church. She use to bring Sam along pretty regular all the time. He was a nice sort of motherly boy, no mor'n seventeen I'd say" (111). In fact, since his father died, Sam has been "working hard to take kere of his widder mother, doing the best he kin" (112). When they realize that a mob is forming, John goes to a community meeting place, Briggze's store, to inquire, leaving his wife with her mother and a family friend. These older women identify with Sam's mother as they share their experiences of living in fear for the men they love. Agreeing that mobs especially target black males, Liza confesses that she never wants to give birth to a boy.

Being privy to community conversations allows African Americans to read mainstream discourses and practices critically. Despite what the newspaper might imply, these characters know that Sam is not an angry, irrational brute who hit a white man. He lands in jail because he had been "trying to be a man and stan up for hissef, and what do he git? A slap in the face" (112). Those in the Pettigrew home know this pattern well. The text suggests that because they have intimate knowledge about Sam and his family, and his connection to the church and community, they understand that this could befall any of them because white men hate to see a black man "trying to be a man."[17] Thus, Liza's pessimism about having a male child suggests that she has no illusions about being able to rear the kind of boy who will not be targeted. Because she reads her surroundings accurately, she knows that the entire community is under siege, not just a "bad" segment of it.

The script suggests that while dominant discourses deny the possibility of honorable black manhood, whites actively work to destroy evidence that it already exists. Johnson's account of the Hose case exposes the hypocrisy undergirding the nation's rhetoric about manliness and civilization. At seventeen, Sam has become man of the house. He lives with and provides for his mother, who is a widow. The text never reveals the circumstances of his father's demise, leaving open the possibility that he had been a lynch victim, given how easily black men are deemed criminals. Members of the community testify to Sam's impeccable character and suggest that his success helped to ignite his boss's primitive masculinity. Sam is offered less-than-fair pay, and his boss assaults him when he will not accept it (111). After being struck, the otherwise manly Sam physically defends himself. This masculine response is answered with death at the hands of a mob—the ultimate manifestation of white masculinity. In this play, whether a black man expresses his manhood with quiet manliness or self-preserving masculinity, white men seek to destroy him.

With these tendencies shaping her environment, Liza cannot assume that parenthood will enable her to determine her child's life chances. Her decisions to rear her son to be God-fearing, churchgoing, and hardworking (like Sam) may be the very reasons that his life will enrage white men. Only now, before her son has had a chance to become an honorable black man who is embraced by his community but hated by whites, does the black mother/wife have any hope of parenting—that is, of shaping her child's fate.[18] When she learns that she has given birth to a boy, Liza strangles her baby to death, convinced that she is actually protecting him (115).

Traumatized by the sights and sounds of racial violence, Liza sees little hope in the future and in fact sees guilt. If her son were ever to become the mob's prey, she would feel responsible because she had seen (and heard) it coming. Sam had called for his mother and Liza's son might call for her, and like Sam's mother, she would have no power to change the situation. From her perspective, the best Liza can do is keep her son from dying at the hands of men who will laugh as they leave the lynching site.

Liza's actions are not offered as a solution but as an expression of black parents' despair; likewise, Johnson's text is not suggesting that African Americans should feel guilty for having children. The critique is of the society that makes the world dangerous for black children, not of the parents whose romantic love produces them. As Daylanne English asserts, "The abnormal symptoms here are not Liza's . . . but the modern lynching culture's" (*Unnatural* 129). When Sam calls out for his mother, Johnson does not strive to have readers agree with the guilt that Liza anticipates. Instead, his screams illustrate the strength and importance of the parent-child relationship, which the mob has worked so hard to destroy while claiming that it does not exist. Hannah Rosen reminds us that "freedpeople went to great lengths" not only to legitimate their marriages after Emancipation but also "to assert parental rights over their children" (191). White supremacist violence targeted black households in order to deny "black people public recognition of their identities as husbands and wives, parents and children" (Rosen 225). Black men were not to be seen as empowered to protect their wives, "nor were black men and women to appear to be providing for their children" (Rosen 186).[19] In this climate, *Safe* preserves evidence of the identities that whites sought to erase by destroying black homes and the familial bonds between children and parents nurtured within them. The pain articulated when Sam cries out for his mother becomes evidence of embodied practices of black belonging.

Safe highlights the problems African Americans face while living in a society that denies their domestic success and citizenship. The play gives voice to the despair that black women feel about living in a country that disregards their homes and their husbands' and sons' lives. The mob's intention of negating black homebuilding efforts and stealing black parents' joy is best exemplified by Liza's question to the older women who try to keep her from witnessing the violence. When the mob passes her house, Liza asks: "They wouldn't come in here? Would they?" (112). Her mother Mandy replies, "No, they wouldn't, but then we better keep it dark" (112). Mandy's response captures the irony of the situation. She consoles her daughter by claiming that the mob would not actually come into her home, then immediately admits that they should make their presence less conspicuous. But more than that, the action of the play makes clear that the mob invades Liza's home *without* physically entering it. Vigilantes have not stepped inside—they have not even murdered her husband, only kept him away—yet they have certainly violated her domain. They have shown her that domestic success will not make her home a safe haven for her children.

While offering a community-centered account of the Sam Hose case, *Safe* suggests that mob victims are not isolated brutes whose deaths inspire no sorrow. Just as Sam (the character and the man) stood up to his boss, black women playwrights refused to accept the stereotypical portrayals undergirding mainstream discourses and practices. Johnson suggests—as Ida B. Wells had—that white men are the real savages. However, while Wells published pamphlets and lectured internationally, there are no records that *Safe* was formally staged, and it was not published until 1990, long after Johnson's death in 1966. While Johnson lived, then, it was in private spaces that this work addressed mainstream accounts of the Sam Hose case; in such spaces, African Americans could affirm their own sense of themselves and of the events that shaped their lives.

Discussions in Johnson's Washington, D.C., literary salon about the Sam Hose case could have inspired the play and become the foundation for its dialogue. Then, once drafted, the conversations that Johnson created in her text would have sparked further discussion in her living room. Whatever the specific circumstances of the performances or dramatic readings, the text both reflected and contributed to discussions and debates about what it means to be black and a citizen, especially in a nation that allows lynching—to the point of rejecting antilynching legislation.[20]

In the process, Johnson's black mother/wife exposes lynching as not just a weapon against black bodies but as a tool for preventing African Americans from being protective parents who can determine the direction of their children's lives. Partly because Liza's sanity deteriorates, she represents the community's recognition of the intensity of black familial love even in the face of the mob's efforts to deny its existence. When Liza's attempts to escape the power of racial violence claim her sanity, the community conversation that was reflected and encouraged by Johnson's play suggested: blacks may find ways to live with lynching, but there is no diminishing the severity of the wounds they suffer.

Blue-Eyed Black Boy

Like Mrs. Temple (the mother/wife in *Blue Blood*), Pauline Waters in *Blue-Eyed Black Boy* has gained domestic success by keeping secret her sexual encounter with a white man. However, while the secret harms the next generation in *Blue Blood*, it proves to be the saving grace in *Blue-Eyed Black Boy*. Because Pauline has had a relationship with the governor and has been quiet about it, she is able to call on him when she needs someone powerful to intervene with the mob and police. It seems that Pauline's relationship with the governor had been consensual. As a result, Johnson ensures that the community conversation will continue to recognize not only black women rape victims who had "screamed out" but also those who had been otherwise coerced. Both of these mother/wife figures encourage complex conversations about the nature of African American citizenship because their experiences demonstrate how vulnerable to white whim black domestic stability is. At any moment, the mob can strike. These women live with an awareness that as long as their loved ones are alive, it is because they have avoided a lynching that has taken someone else's husband or son.

The action of *Blue-Eyed Black Boy* takes place in the home of Pauline Waters, whose daughter Rebecca will soon marry a young black physician, Dr. Grey. Rebecca is pressing her wedding gown and wishing that her brother Jack would come home so that she can clear the dinner dishes. Soon, Dr. Grey arrives, and he attends to Mother Pauline's foot; she has stepped on a rusted nail. Dr. Grey says that it is healing well, but she must stay off of it for another week (117). He also mentions having seen "some mighty rough looking hoodlums" on his way to the house, so he suspects that there may be trouble. Rebecca and her mother Pauline admit that whites are always disturbing the peace in their neighborhood. Suddenly, Pauline's best friend Hester arrives, struggling to catch her breath. She brings news that Jack, Pauline's son, has been arrested, accused of "brush[ing] up against a white woman" (118). Pauline does not believe the charges, saying, "It ain't so! . . . He's a gentleman" (118). Hester presses on to share the worst of the news: "They, they say there's gointer break open the jail and string him up!" (118).

At this, Dr. Grey offers to drive to the judge's house, but Hester says that they should not put any faith in that judge because "he's a lyncher his own self. [. . .] Ain't he done let 'em lynch six niggers in the last year jes' gone?" (118). Rebecca asks Dr. Grey if he has any other powerful contacts, but Pauline interjects, "Wait, wait. I know what I'll do. I don't care what it costs" (118). She instructs Rebecca to bring a silver ring from her jewelry box. She gives the ring to Dr. Grey and tells him to take it to Governor Tinkham's house. Her exact instructions are: "Just give him this ring and say *Pauline sent this. She says they goin to lynch her son born 21 years ago. Mind you, say 21 years ago. Then say, listen close. Look in his eyes and you'll save him*" (118).

When Dr. Grey leaves on this errand, wagons of armed white men begin passing in front of the house. Rebecca and Hester watch and grow anxious, but Pauline turns away from the window as her lips move in prayer (119). Finally, her prayers become audible and she says, "Lord Jesus, I know I've sinned against your holy law, but you did forgive me and let me hold up my head again. Help me again, dear Jesus. Help me to save my innocent child . . ." (119). As the women continue to wait for Dr. Grey's return and the commotion outside seems unceasing, Pauline suddenly hears above her own sobbing "the sound of many feet" (120). Rebecca and Hester confirm that the noise marks the arrival of state troopers. They also see Dr. Grey approaching the house. Once inside, his words end the play: "He's saved, Miss Waters! Saved! Did the Governor send the troops?" (120).

As discussed, playwrights prioritized depictions of black women who were both wives and mothers because mainstream discourse acknowledged black motherhood only if it appeared to be outside of wedlock. Black mothers who are also wives call attention to the promise of citizenship because they have exhibited the personal discipline that the nation claims to reward. In *Blue-Eyed Black Boy*, Johnson combines the exploration of romantic love that characterizes *Blue Blood* with the emphasis on parental love that shapes *Safe*. Pauline and her husband had established strong romantic bonds upon which they built a successful nuclear family, but the true test of citizenship comes with the attack on the ties between parent and child.

Despite evidence to the contrary, Pauline's friends and family act as if Pauline's now-deceased husband was the only man who could have fathered blue-eyed Jack, and while their naiveté is hardly believable, it points to the strength of the romantic ties that Pauline had established with her life partner. The text leaves no doubt that Jack is the product of a relationship that Pauline had with the governor, but her friends and family act as if they are ignorant of this fact. Not unlike the situation that Harriet Jacobs witnessed on slave plantations, it seems that blacks can live relatively peacefully even if everyone knows about their sexual ties to whites—as long as it is never discussed. For instance, when speaking of how handsome Jack is, his sister

Rebecca says, "It's funny that he's the only one in our family's got blue eyes though." She continues, "Pa's was black, and yours and mine are black too. It certainly is strange . . ." (117). When Mother Pauline sends Dr. Grey to the governor to say "Look in his eyes and you'll save him," Rebecca asks, "Mother, what does it all mean?" and Pauline's best friend Hester declares, "Well, . . . I don't know what you mean but I recon you knows what you is doing" (119). To make their obliviousness even more untenable, a distraught Pauline begins to pray aloud, pleading "Save him, Lord. Let his father . . . (*she stops and looks around at the two women, then cautiously speaks*) You understand all I mean, sweet Jesus" (119). For the rest of the play, even when the governor apparently sends the state militia, no questions are asked about how Pauline could have so much influence over him. Even if the others suspect the truth, they do not dare speak it, largely out of respect for Pauline, her dead husband, and the life they built together.

The characters' reticence is appropriate because what is infinitely more important than the secret is what it has enabled: romantic bonds and black homebuilding success. Pauline claims to have "sinned" in her past, but because God forgave her, she managed to establish a strong marriage with a black man; they built a respectable life and enjoyed social standing in their community. As her daughter Rebecca looks forward to her wedding, she believes that it must be exceptional because "everybody in the Baptist Church" looks up to their family (116). Pauline agrees, and she notes that the community's admiration is only appropriate: "I ain't carried myself straight all these years for nothing" (116).[21] Yet her blue-eyed son is evidence that she does not have a spotless record—even if it is not clear whether her lapse had been voluntary or coerced. Either way, it is her silence that had enabled her proud husband to keep her "on a pinnacle" (116). As with the women in Johnson's *Blue Blood*, if Pauline had insisted on revealing the identity of her child's father, or if her husband had insisted on knowing, they would not have been able to live peacefully as a family.

After featuring the black mother/wife in *Blue Blood* and *Safe,* Johnson offers Pauline, ensuring that the community conversation about black citizenship would acknowledge even black women who may have consented to interracial sexual encounters. As historian Hannah Rosen has found, black women who called on the state to protect them from whites' sexual advances did not assume that being worthy of such protection required "denying past sexual relations considered illicit" (223). Civil rights should accrue to a black woman without her "attempting to craft her story to fit into a conservative vision of the 'virtuous' woman," which was defined by "willingness to risk even death to prevent coerced sex" (Rosen 223, 9).

Whereas Johnson offered Mrs. Temple as an example of those who were physically forced, she leaves open the possibility that Pauline consented to her relationship with the governor, when her prayer includes an admission that she had sinned. However, as Rosen's research makes clear, in a society based in rigid racial hierarchy undergirded by violence, consent is difficult to define in relationships between white men and black women. One woman who testified before the Freedman's Bureau in the years following Emancipation did not deny having had a long-standing relationship with the man that she was now seeking protection from; she had even had children with him. Nevertheless, now that she was no longer a slave, Mrs. King was determined to control her own sexuality. As Rosen puts it, this woman was now "publicly naming [the relationship] as unwelcome and abusive by enlisting the bureau's aid" in resisting it now that she was free (Rosen 223). The fact that Pauline pursues a life with a husband rather than remain a white man's concubine—even one with a ring—may suggest a similar situation.

Pauline puts the encounter behind her and establishes a home that allows her to embody the private discipline and virtue that, according to the nation's rhetoric, yields public respect and rights, but it is not that stellar reputation that provides leverage in a time of crisis.[22] Her son's life is not spared because of her respectable household and the civil rights it should bring. Further, her son is not rescued because of his own innocence and good character. Rather, though Jack did not commit the crime, he avoids dying for it only because his mother is able to call upon a white man with social and political power. This power benefits Jack because this white man chooses to acknowledge quietly his biological link to the blue-eyed youth. Ultimately, then, Pauline's ability to save her son derives from the illicit sexual encounter that she had had with the governor. Her romantic bond with an honorable black man may have been the basis of the marriage that allowed them to prove their readiness for citizenship, but civil rights did not spring from it. The governor could have just as easily refused to acknowledge his connection to this black woman and her son, or he could have simply chosen not to help. The fact that he did brings this family some relief, but it does not diminish the anxiety that they may have reason to feel tomorrow.

By spotlighting Pauline and the apparently open secret that she has kept, Johnson's *Blue-Eyed Black Boy* corroborates testimonies that mainstream discourses and practices are designed to erase.[23] The young man targeted by the mob is not an isolated brute rapist. He is a loyal son who works to provide for his mother and sister now that his father is dead. When Pauline's best friend Hester comes to tell the family that Jack has been arrested, her report illuminates the difference between African Americans' intimate knowledge and what the majority of Americans believe. She begins: "*They say* he done brushed a white woman on the street," but she immediately adds: "They had er argument and she *hollowed out* he's attacking her" (118, emphasis added). On the one hand, there is what "they say" happened; on the other, there is what Hester knows—that the white woman was not attacked but *hollered out* that she was. Yet Hester shares both versions because African Americans must always deal with both.

While everyone outside of the black home focuses on the rumor that Jack "brushed against a white woman on the street" (118), the action of this play spotlights a real case of miscegenation that never makes headlines. The drama thus suggests that circumstances like Pauline's exist (without remark) in countless black homes at the exact time that lies about white female victimization abound. In other words, lynching is not about protecting white women or even about miscegenation; as Ida B. Wells often suggested, "the faces of the million mulattoes in the South" prove that whites have few objections to interracial sex (*Red Record* 80). Instead, racial violence is about ensuring that white men can control the sexuality of both black and white women. There is no difference, many activists asserted, between "the mobs of Southern white men who tortured and murdered black men for allegedly assaulting white women [and] those who raped and lynched black women" (Feimster 116). Based on a similar insight, *Blue-Eyed Black Boy* highlights the sort of miscegenation that never inspires the "chivalrous" white mob,[24] thereby allowing the experience of the black mother/wife to illuminate the power dynamics that lynching creates and perpetuates.

Just as lynching is not about sexual liaisons across the color line, neither is Johnson's play; above all, the script preserves evidence of African Americans' commitment to home and family. Without claiming that she has never had a misstep, Pauline nonetheless proves to have moved beyond her "sin" to carry herself "straight all these years." Clearly, she is proud of the life that she had built with her husband. And her adult children are evidence of her success and the values she instilled. Rebecca is helpful, pressing her own wedding gown and waiting to clear the dinner dishes, and Jack has grown to be a "gentleman." In fact, when Jack is an hour late for dinner, his mother and sister know that it is not because he is "running after girls" (117). The reader soon discovers that they are right; he is late because whites have imprisoned him. While the mob responds to lies about his character, Johnson emphasizes the testimony of the women inside the black home. They speak of his determination to become an engineer. He plans to go to school as soon as his sister gets married. As Pauline explains, "He's been mighty tied down since your father died taking care of us" (117).[25]

In effect, Johnson takes readers into intimate spaces, where community conversation equips African Americans to withstand the assault leveled when they are characterized as rapists and whores. Creating an imprint of community members' words and actions required preserving what black women sometimes refused to speak publicly. Johnson's late 1920s scripts articulate that which, in Harriet Jacobs's words, African Americans did not "dare to allude to, except in whispers among themselves" (31). One-act dramas were appropriate outlets, then; there are no records that *Blue-Eyed Black Boy* was formally staged, and it was not published until 1989, so it circulated in private arenas. In black homes, churches, and schools, African Americans could use drama to verify for each other that black women and men had already proved worthy of citizenship. Doing so was crucial because blacks still found themselves vulnerable to whites whom the nation allowed to decide arbitrarily whether they would respect black life. African Americans needed a way of assuring each other that these scenarios were not reflective of their failures but of those of their countrymen.

✳ ✳ ✳

It seems that Johnson's Washington, D.C., location made her especially attuned to the country's hypocrisy. While lawmakers mobilized to address white female vulnerability to prostitution,[26] they never questioned the assumption that black women should be perpetually available for sex. Likewise, while arguing that black men were rapists who deserved lynching, most Americans ignored the frequency with which white men raped African American women. How were blacks to understand themselves as citizens when being female made them white men's playthings and being male made them targets? Further, how were they to cling to their sense of citizenship when their government placed little value on their lives, virtually forcing blacks either to refuse to have children or to accept that they were bringing them into a society bent on destroying them?

As African Americans grappled with these questions, they understood the gendered nature of racial violence, which enabled it to terrorize black women and men with equal intensity. By engaging rape in her late 1920s scripts, Johnson acknowledges how successfully white men had made their exploitation of black woman irrelevant within national discourse. African Americans knew that "the myth of the black rapist reinforced the idea of the immoral and hypersexual black woman and vice versa" (Feimster 117). Yet, even while aware that these images "were intricately linked and would have to be tackled simultaneously," there remained a desire to shield black women. Accordingly, though the direction of the community conversation demanded that lynching drama address black women's rape, the texts ensure some modesty; it is a long-kept secret that is revealed only out of necessity.

Lynching drama therefore contributes to what Darlene Clark Hine calls the "culture of dissemblance" among black women[27]—a tradition of "achieving a self-imposed invisibility" (382). However, the genre's dissemblance manifests in areas other than its treatment of rape. This woman-initiated genre refuses to depict, or thoroughly describe, physical violence. This tendency enables the plays to illuminate the less corporeal, more enduring destruction that the mob accomplishes, but it also allowed women authors to distance themselves from the sort of graphic language that led many to question whether Ida B. Wells was a "proper lady."[28] Just as important, the genre contributes to a "cult of secrecy" by avoiding any mention of female lynch victims.[29] By including black women as victims only in that their homebuilding efforts are destroyed, women lynching dramatists created "the appearance of openness and disclosure, but actually shielded the truth of their inner lives and selves . . ." (Hine 380). Surely, black women lived with a traumatic fear about their own mutilation and death as much as they worried about their loved ones.

In lynching drama, the black mother/wife emerges to illuminate the vulnerability of romantic and parental bonds, but this figure's most striking real-world corollary would have been Mary Turner, who was killed in May 1918 for threatening to report the men who had lynched her husband.[30] Johnson constructs the black mother/wife without reference to Turner; Sam Hose and the 1890s seem to have made more of an impression. Yet Johnson's circle had certainly been touched by Turner's story; Angelina Weld Grimké had written several treatments, and Turner haunted Jean Toomer's *Cane*.[31]

The fact that Johnson's plays do not depict women who fall prey to the mob is worth noting because Mary Turner's vulnerability as a wife and mother made her tragedy possible. Mary's husband, Hayes Turner, was accused of conspiring to kill his boss, despite the murderer's confession to the contrary. While police transported Hayes from one jail to the next, he was kidnapped and lynched. Mary Turner declared that she would identify the mob in a report to the authorities, so within a few days she was lynched in the most spectacular, humiliating manner—in her eighth month of pregnancy. Walter White reported in *Crisis*:

> Her ankles were tied together and she was hung to the tree, head downward. Gasoline and oil from the automobiles were thrown on her clothing and while she writhed in agony and the mob howled in glee, a match was applied and her clothes burned from her person. When this had been done and while she was yet alive, a knife . . . was taken and the woman's abdomen was cut open,

the unborn babe falling from her womb to the ground. The infant, prematurely born, gave two feeble cries and then its head was crushed by a member of the mob with his heel.[32]

Lynching plays written during the height of mob violence and its photographic representation differ dramatically from this *Crisis* magazine account of what can befall African American wives and mothers. Thus, if lynching drama uses the black mother/wife to index repeated attempts to delay death, perhaps the death most persistently deferred is the black woman's own.

Black-authored lynching plays of the 1910s and 1920s do not evince awareness of the Mary Turner story, but this should not be interpreted as an oversight or flaw. Rather than encourage what Eve Sedgwick calls the "policing of literature for its failings," I am arguing for "an appreciation of the daunting complexities of the attempt to represent . . . the most freighted and fraught social, political and psychological problems" (qtd. in Davidson 14). In that spirit, I reiterate that Johnson's mother/wife plays are not so much an expression of her individual negotiation of the trauma of living with lynching, but a reflection of a larger community conversation that included more direct representations of the Turner story, including Grimké's and Toomer's. Taken together, these works demonstrate awareness not only that black women were violated and murdered, but also that they were sometimes raped before being lynched . . . and lynched for resisting rape.[33]

In the final analysis, the black mother/wife registers the words and actions of women who negotiated the trauma of racial violence by trying to minimize its impact on their families. There were women who kept rape a secret to protect black men; women who used their sexual liaisons with white men to gain access to social power; and women who buckled under the weight of their desperation, killing their babies as some had done in slavery.[34] As these women represented individuals oscillating between "the crisis of death" and "the crisis of life," their behavior gestured toward an unspeakable fear and dread, born of their understanding that the mob could as easily turn on them as claim the men in their families. Ultimately, because Johnson's black mother/wife does *not* resemble Mary Turner, these scripts suggest that African American communities grappled with an enduring question: "Is the trauma the encounter with death, or the ongoing experience of having survived it?"[35]

CHAPTER SIX

THE PIMP AND COWARD
OFFERING GENDERED REVISIONS

Lynching plays by African American women preserve a remarkable diversity of opinion, but considering black men's contributions to this unique genre reveals additional variety. Black men began writing lynching plays in 1925,[1] several years after Angelina Weld Grimké initiated the genre, and Alice Dunbar-Nelson and Mary Burrill began revising it.[2] Lynching drama therefore contradicts the expectation that men establish literary traditions and women revise them. Often, modern readers assume that genres expand when women offer "gendered critiques" of the silences in men's texts, and this understanding often involves a hierarchical view in which authors who address perceived silences occupy a lower position. Earlier writers are treated as "artists" while successors are often interpreted as "activists" whose artistry may go unnoticed. Rather than assume that lynching drama reverses expected patterns, I question the logic of hierarchical approaches, guided by an appreciation for how thoroughly African American literature bears the imprint of the vernacular. In the black vernacular tradition, when a preacher's sermon launches into rhythmic excitement, it cannot continue without the congregation's enthusiastic *amen*s. The group's response proves to be as important as the preacher's call.[3]

Black literary revision works the same way, so its traditions take shape through dynamic interaction that troubles the tendency to speak of "leaders" and "followers" or "major" and "minor" voices. Therefore, though black men's lynching dramas emerged later, their contributions are not secondary. Instead, they illuminate the genre's reliance on intertextuality—the concept that Henry Louis Gates highlighted with his theory of "signifying," and that Patricia Liggins Hill usefully re-figured as "call and response." Acknowledging intertextuality demands considering the possibility that revisions are not supplementary but complementary. We are driven to ask: Must revisions inspired by differing gender identifications be reactionary and therefore secondary? Might revision be a mark of relationship, an egalitarian acknowledgement of linked destiny?

Ultimately, men's lynching dramas confirm the intensity of the turn-of-the-century community conversation. Male dramatists joined women authors in recording existing discussions about identity and citizenship. In the process, black men's scripts offer figures that are strikingly different from those featured in women's plays: the pimp and coward.

Especially when compared to the male characters in women's plays, the pimp and coward may not inspire admiration, yet they spring from much the same impulse that yielded the black soldier, lawyer, and mother/wife. When depicted in their own homes, all of these figures encourage discussions about conceptions of black identity and citizenship, but plays with less traditionally admirable figures also illuminate how differing gender identifications fueled the intertextuality through which this genre developed. As we have seen, in women's plays, telling the story of those who survive the mob's attack often means recording the testimony of everyone but the man of the house. Women's plays typically feature homes from which male adults are missing. Also, because they account only for honorable heads of household, women's plays suggest that the strength and stability of black homes can be compromised only if men are taken from them. In contrast, lynching plays written by black men present homes that seem to be "castrated" even when male family members survive. In short, black male playwrights altered lynching drama as much as the women who turned away from Grimké's example of creating genteel black characters for integrated audiences.

This chapter examines the two earliest plays by black men that use the home as setting: G. D. Lipscomb's *Frances* (1925) and Joseph Mitchell's *Son-Boy* (1928). By examining scripts that share women's concern with domesticity, one can better identify those elements that men revised.[4] These scripts place as much emphasis on the black home as women's plays do, but in *Frances*, the head of household is a pimp; in *Son-Boy*, he is a shameless coward. The emergence of these figures registers the community's understanding that lynching is master/piece theater designed to make white men into masters, even after Emancipation. The scripts suggest that, even without killing every black man, whites solidify their social position; especially because photographs continue the work, the mob's violent performances need not physically alter the composition of all black households to have the intended effect. The threat of the mob can make some black men lose all desire to become head of household.

Whether spotlighting the black soldier, lawyer, or pimp, lynching dramatists maximized the alternative public spaces fostered by periodical culture.
Periodicals both reflected and encouraged discursive spaces whose physical
corollaries could often be found in African American churches, schools, and
homes. Lipscomb's *Frances* emerged in the discursive space fostered by *Opportunity* magazine, the official organ of the National Urban League, and
Mitchell's *Son-Boy* appeared in the *Saturday Evening Quill,* published by a
black literary society in Boston. These scripts remind readers that black men,
no less than mother/wives, found ways to live with lynching. The pimp and
coward offer access to the words and actions of those who did not cling to
either manliness or masculinity as they faced the reality of racial violence.
Recognizing that either expression of manhood could get them killed, some
tried to avoid both. At the same time, by giving these figures a place within
the genre, the playwrights of this chapter join women authors in recording
African Americans' understanding that lynchers always sought to "castrate"
black homes, but they insist that mobs could sometimes do so without killing
the man of the house. Male playwrights offer their communities the pimp
and coward in order to encourage difficult conversations—within the plays
and among African Americans reading them.

Frances

Black men and women lynching dramatists used the home in different ways
as they testified to the impact that lynching had on African Americans. Both
depicted "castrated" black homes, but women did so by emphasizing the
mob's determination to kill strong heads of household while men placed a
spotlight on emasculated characters who survive. G. D. Lipscomb's *Frances*
initiated this generic revision by portraying a home that is anything but
traditionally successful because it is under the leadership of Frances's ma-
terialistic uncle. Nineteen-year-old Frances lives with her uncle Abram on a
farm in the Mississippi Delta. Frances's homebuilding efforts are on display
as she keeps her surroundings clean, but her uncle has been prostituting her
to the white man who holds the deed to their farm and their house. Like the
women playwrights, Lipscomb thematizes manhood, but his work spotlights
a despicable head of household whose behavior illustrates that the mere
threat of lynching can destroy a black man's desire to live according to the
ideals of patriarchal honor.[5]
    Set in the winter of 1925, all action takes place in the "shot-gun house"
that Frances shares with her uncle Abram. The play opens with Frances

"seated near the bed, with a book lying open before her" (148). The tranquility that she steals for herself is disrupted when her uncle enters, warning Frances not to let anyone near the kitchen when he leaves because many of the town "niggahs" would tell whites that he is "makin' gosh" (illegal liquor). He also says that he hopes that the new black teacher, George Mannus, will leave town. George has made life harder by telling "niggahs" what they should not tolerate from whites (148). Abram also reports that county officials are pulling resources from the school because George Mannus has upset whites "wid his smaht talk" (148).

Abram leaves the house, and Frances is left alone to worry about the news that she has just heard. Soon, George appears, and we discover that he and Frances are involved. He tells her that Charles Thawson, the planter who holds the deed to Abram's farm, has been harassing him. George admits that he normally tolerates Thawson's abuse, but could not do so that day because Thawson had insulted Frances's honor. In fact, George assaulted Thawson, who vowed that the mob would come for him within twenty-four hours. George Mannus plans to leave for Chicago and wants Frances to accompany him. She resists because she feels indebted to her uncle and believes that it would be disloyal to leave him. Soon, she asks, "George, would my life really mean anything to you in the North?" and he answers by declaring his love for her. Frances confesses her love for him, and they share a kiss. Then Frances promises that she will meet him at nine o'clock. George objects, but Frances reasons that they will travel farther without arousing her uncle's suspicion if she leaves after he is asleep. Because a neighborhood woman sends her nephew to ask for Frances's help whenever she is sick, Frances comforts George by telling him to send little Andy if she is not at their meeting place ten minutes early.

George Mannus is gone when Uncle Abram returns to tell Frances that Thawson will visit her tonight and that he expects her to be friendly. When she objects, Abram reminds her that she had always been cooperative until George Mannus put foolish ideas into her head. Frances admits that she had not known better before, but she now refuses to be involved with a white man who has a wife and children in Memphis (151). Unlike women's plays, this script does not avoid direct discussion about the sexual activity of a black woman. Abram insists that Thawson's marital status is of little concern; besides, he does not believe it anyway. Frances says that he chooses to ignore many things that are obvious to everyone else, including the fact that Thawson has no intention of letting him pay off the mortgage on the farm (151). Their argument is interrupted by Thawson's arrival, but as she had promised, Frances is not friendly.

Abram tries to assure Thawson that Frances has missed him, but she calls him a liar. When Thawson flaunts the fact that he has threatened George Mannus's life, Frances begins, "Oh, you dirty . . .," but Abram warns her to hold her tongue. Thawson and Abram talk and drink, and Frances leaves the room. When she reemerges, she has her coat and hat, and Thawson is furious to know that he will not be spending the night with her. He demands the deed to the land, Abram pretends not to remember where it is, but Thawson knows its location and orders Abram to place it in his hands. Thawson then reveals that it has never been recorded (152). The rest of Thawson's declaration comes as no surprise to Frances but devastates her uncle: "This property is mine. I've been acceptin' payments from your uncle, but I didn't intend that he should buy it with anything but you. You're my woman!" (152). Thawson also shouts "you can get out of my house tonight" (152). He begins ripping the papers, and Abram falls to his knees begging him to stop.

The heartbreak that Abram feels about losing his property yields lynching drama's most direct depiction of physical violence. The frank discussion of a black woman's sexual activity is matched by rough-and-tumble action that ends with murder. When he realizes there is nothing left to lose, Abram attacks Thawson and they fight fiercely. Frances runs to the door, calling for help. Then, she hears gunfire and rushes back to find that Thawson has shot Abram. Frances bends over her uncle, but when a knock is heard, she looks up and sees Thawson facing the door, "ready with his gun" (153). It is now ten minutes before nine o'clock. Frances snatches the pistol from Thawson, but he pushes her against a table and twists her wrist until she drops it near Abram. To Thawson's surprise, Abram is still alive and is now taking aim. Abram gasps, "De Lawd has puhserved me fo' dis one pu'pose" (153). He shoots and kills Thawson and falls back to the floor himself. Frances holds her uncle's head in her arms and buries her face in his hair (153). She looks up when the clock chimes nine times; she is supposed to be leaving with George Mannus at this very moment. The play ends with her lowering her head as she resumes grieving over her dead uncle. As Lipscomb leaves us with this image of a young woman mourning the loss of the uncle who prostituted her, Frances offers a model of audience response; like her, the reader/viewer cannot simply despise Abram. Her affection toward her uncle as she buries her face in his hair is matched only by her confession of love to Mannus and their shared kiss. All of these are embodied practices of black belonging, and the pimp is not excluded.

Uncle Abram is the main male character, present for most of the action. The script thus prioritizes the pimp's conversation and conduct, using others mostly to illuminate his perspective. Though readers may find Abram to be less than admirable, the text leaves no mysteries regarding how his beliefs and attitudes developed. Above all, he is a pimp because he believes that only men with material means can access the economic independence that citizens enjoy, so he must maximize the resources and commodities within his reach. He has devoted many years of toil to making the forty acres on which he lives profitable. In fact, he has made monthly payments for so long that the mortgage should soon be paid in full (152). As he explains to Frances, he works day and night because he wants to "get in de cleah" and save for when he is too old to work (150). In addition to farming long hours, he tries to gain financial footing by making illegal liquor (148).

Clearly then, when he urges Frances to help him, he is speaking out of desperation; his hard work does not seem to be enough. He wants Frances to understand what he has come to accept, that "you got to do a heap o' things dat don't jes' please you 'till you kin git independent of folks" (150). His attitude toward using his niece is practical in his view: "'T ain't gwine hurt you to treat Cap with respect an' keep him feelin' good 'til we gits in de cleah" (150). He believes that he is not asking a lot of Frances: "Now why kain't you go long an' keep Mistah Chahles in good humah 'til we gits in de cleah an' gits ouah nose off de grin'stone?" (150). Frances just happens to be a valuable asset to which he has access. Because she's a "good lookin' wench," Thawson desires her.

It seems that, if he could, Abram would keep Thawson "in good humor" himself. After all, when it is in Abram's power to appease whites, he does. When Thawson knocks, Abram's demeanor changes; stage directions indicate that he "shuffles to the door, opens it, and bows low" (151). This is a very different posture from that which, only moments before, characterizes his exchange with Frances. Also, in order to keep Thawson from getting upset, Uncle Abram lies to protect Thawson's ego. When Frances is not friendly, Abram declares that the only thing wrong with her is that she is "lonesome." He claims in fact that she has been in a bad mood, assuming that Thawson had forgotten about her. Abram swears that Thawson had punished Frances lately by not visiting regularly (151). Determined to sell this story, he says to Frances, "You little ole big-eyed, good-lookin' rascal, you knows you wants to be right in Mistah Chahles' ahms" (151). Thawson does not seem to believe him, but he nevertheless declares that he is spending the night and asks if Abram has anything "stimulating." Abram serves whiskey and drinks with Thawson as a sign of courtesy and accommodation.

As demonstrated throughout this study, the black home scene in lynching drama reveals that whites respond violently to black success and self-affirmation; *Frances* accomplishes the same, even while showcasing a pimp's household because the mob's wrath is ignited by George Mannus's attempt to protect a black woman's honor, not by the pimp's immorality. In fact, George's manliness not only places him in danger; it also limits his access to resources. George Mannus has angered the planters by teaching classes when they want black workers in the fields, so "de County ain't gwine to fix dat road up pas' de school like dey had 'cided" (148). As Abram puts it, "[J]es like I tole you—dat niggah done broke his own neck wid his smaht talk" (148). The reference here to hanging, or neck breaking, is significant because it indicates Abram's keen awareness of the unbalanced power between blacks and whites. In other words, Abram believes in performing submission because he has read his surroundings critically and sees that society grants a level of power to whites that cannot be ignored. He believes that he must go through whites to access power and resources, and he has no doubts about the behavior that they require. It is through Abram that readers discover that whites have limited Mannus's capacity to do what he believes is important, make the school a success. For Abram, this predicament proves that George does not understand his surroundings and how best to navigate them. Because Mannus has not been submissive to whites, "he ain't got nothin' but his hands" (151). Abram therefore scoffs at Frances's desire to go north with George Mannus: "Wheah kin he tek you? What is he got?" (151).

Abram is the script's central male figure, so George Mannus serves mainly as a point of comparison; Abram's question—"What is he got?"—therefore proves significant. Mannus sacrifices social and financial capital. He has already seen authorities renege on promises to improve the road near the school, and they are withholding his pay (148). Furthermore, because he has enraged the planters, and Thawson has vowed to have a rope around his neck within twenty-four hours, George is now willing to move to Chicago and leave the school altogether. Though he claims to believe that the townspeople will not let the school fail, he seems willing to abandon the dream that brought him south. George risks everything because he refuses to leave an insult to black womanhood unchallenged. In other words, George Mannus represents the strong, patriarchal spirit that exists among black men despite the fact that it puts them, and everything they love, in danger. He also believes that personal dignity takes precedence over not only access to money but also access to education. When Frances insists that she is indebted to her uncle because he has borrowed money from Thawson to send her to school, George fires back, "What good is it, Frances, to have an education and not be free?" (149). The loan has tied Frances to Thawson, so George's goal is to "snatch [her] from eternal degradation" (149).

This declaration is telling because it reveals that, for George, manhood is about patriarchal status—about becoming "head of household" in the most traditional sense. George Mannus had moved south to uplift "this mass from ignorance and depravity at any cost," but he has now abandoned that dream. He will not feel like a failure, though, if he can have Frances by his side: "To win you means more than to atone for my lost ideal" (149). This race man had come to the South to uplift scores of blacks, but he believes that creating a home, and serving as patriarch of it, would be an equal achievement. Yet this is just one perspective acknowledged within the community conversation reflected and encouraged by this script. Abram would wonder how Mannus's stance benefits anyone. If Mannus is lynched, how can he protect Frances? From Abram's point of view, just as Mannus's refusal to appease whites leads him to abandon the school, it may very well leave Frances alone and financially destitute.

It is important that Lipscomb's script depicts Uncle Abram and George Mannus inside the black home; in that private space, they articulate their beliefs and act on them, especially in relation to black womanhood. The threat of lynching rather than its realization drives the action, and that threat—though directed toward Mannus—has everything to do with Frances. The white planter has long enjoyed a relationship with Frances, but because Mannus has convinced her that she is being re-enslaved through that affair, she has begun resisting it. Unhappy that he is losing sway over Frances, Thawson threatens George. Rather than appease Thawson, as Uncle Abram does, George defends Frances's honor. White male power manifests itself in the desire to own black womanhood, and black manhood expresses itself through its response to that predicament. In a patriarchal society, a true head of household is motivated to protect his loved ones, whether the bond is romantic or familial. Because both George and Abram know that a protective black man is a dead black man, their character is defined by their response to that truth. Like Georgia Douglas Johnson's later plays, Lipscomb's work demonstrates that the conflict between black and white men often revolves around black women. The action is driven by sexual desire for Frances (Thawson), the need to use her as a pawn (Abram), and the urge to protect her (Mannus). Placing Frances at the center reiterates the extent to which turn-of-the-century struggles for "manhood rights," also known as "citizenship," were staged in and through domestic spaces.[6]

While depicting this struggle, Lipscomb seems determined to establish that George's willingness to migrate does not spring from fear. George tells Frances that he will remain with her in the South if that is what she wants; he will see the dispute out to the bitter end (149). Also, knowing that George's life has been threatened, Frances offers George her uncle's gun, but he refuses it, explaining that he will stay out of Thawson's way. However, when she leaves the room, stage directions call for him to briefly examine the automatic that he is carrying in his pocket. Clearly, George is ready to defend himself but would rather not parade that side of his manhood. Given his traditional values, he prefers shielding Frances from harsh realities. Indeed, his goal is to place her in a situation where these predicaments do not emerge. He is ready to abandon his life's work of uplifting the masses in order to undertake his new mission: offering her love and protection.

George places nothing above his conception of self-determination and decency, and the script depicts his values in order to emphasize that not all black men share them. For Abram, having a "degraded" black home is not the issue; losing the house itself is his breaking point. Lipscomb therefore refuses to deny that some black men respond to racism by refusing to become heads of household who protect black women. Readers may find Abram despicable, but he represents an important perspective for those discussing black citizenship at the turn of the century. After all, property ownership was not irrelevant to making citizenship claims.[7]

Abram's tactics are not offered as a model, but if lynching drama is to engage the many issues that arise as African Americans discuss the quality of their citizenship, then the views and strategies of such a figure could not be ignored. The staff of *Opportunity* magazine saw the value of sparking debates among readers that the pimp would inspire. Not only was this script published in the May 1925 issue, but it also won first prize for drama in the periodical's literary contest.[8]

As the pimp is acknowledged within the community conversation, he raises questions to which there can be no easy answers. Abram suggests that if citizenship includes economic power, then claims to manhood that are not accompanied by wealth are worthless; they are not claims to citizenship at all. Accordingly, there is no reason to invest in personal stances of integrity, morality, or manliness if they will not bring economic independence. One can almost hear Abram ask, "Who cares about manly postures from those with no material resources?" By extension, "Who cares about the despicable character of men with money?" Accordingly, when confronted with the idea that Thawson has been pursuing Frances while having a wife and children in Memphis, Abram insists that it does not matter. Frances declares that his reaction proves how little he knows of decency. However, Abram's life experience has taught him that decency in black men is not necessarily practical and certainly not profitable.

Son-Boy

Interpretations of Joseph Mitchell's *Son-Boy* emphasize the fact that the character pursued by the mob is not lynched. Noted theater scholars James Hatch and Leo Hamalian call this a "happy ending" (74),[9] and Judith Stephens reads the play as ironic and humorous: "*Son-Boy* introduces elements of humor into a genre in which humor is rare and unexpected" ("Performance Strategies" 664).[10] When we leave underexamined the definition of a "happy" ending, certain aspects of the play can be read through a lens of optimism when neither the text nor context support that approach. After all, much of the humor that Stephens identifies arises from the constant "bickering" between Dinah and Zeke, the parents of the potential lynch victim. Their verbal sparring is much more than marital bickering, however. All of their arguments stem from the fact that Zeke's every word and action mark him a shameless coward. The arguing therefore suggests that, especially in the eyes of his wife, the living man of the house can be as "castrated" as lynch victims who hang from trees.

Son-Boy is set in the home of Zeke and Dinah. The year is 1900, and they live in a shack in the South, where Dinah takes in laundry. Dinah's is the first voice we hear; she is singing as she works, "Before I'd be a slave/ I'd be buried in my grave/ And go home to my father and be saved" (77). Soon, Dinah and her husband are disagreeing about the song, because Zeke distances himself from all suggestions of militancy. In fact, for the first third of the play, the action revolves around the couple's quarrels. Lynching begins overtly to drive the plot when a family friend arrives, reporting that a mob is looking for Son-Boy (82). As Dinah prepares to search for her son, she and Zeke argue some more. Zeke wonders what she thinks she can do to stop the mob, and Dinah calls him a coward for not wanting to try. Dinah then boasts that her ancestors had never been passive slaves and that Son-Boy has inherited their noble characteristics, not Zeke's worthlessness (84).

Just as Dinah reaches the door to leave, Son-Boy rushes in asking for a weapon to protect himself, but Zeke has apparently hidden the family gun and razor (85–86). When Dinah resolves to go find another gun, someone knocks urgently. Everyone assumes that it is the mob, and Zeke proves that he is not a protective father; he locks one door and blocks the other so that Son-Boy cannot escape. Dinah urges Son-Boy to hide in the pile of laundry and insists that Zeke answer the door. Zeke seems to cooperate, but he speaks to Son-Boy for no apparent reason, except to alert whoever is outside to Son-Boy's presence. After this betrayal, Zeke hides in a closet without answering the door (87). Fortunately, it is Son-Boy's friend Joe, not the mob. Dinah pretends that she knows nothing about the threat in order to obtain information. Joe reveals that an unidentified man had entered a white girl's room to steal. When she screamed, he ran out of the house, and a black man named Snow-Ball saw him. When the growing mob asked Snow-Ball who it was, he said that he did not know but that the man's face and hands were black. One of the men suggested that it was Son-Boy and told Snow-Ball that they would "string [him] up" if he did not agree. Fortunately, Joe reports, they soon caught the real criminal—a white man who had blackened his hands and face (90).[11]

By this time, Zeke has come out of hiding, and he and Dinah begin a new argument. As usual, Dinah berates Zeke, and now that he is safe, Son-Boy joins his mother in insulting his father, agreeing with her that he will be a better man than Zeke is (91). Next, Dinah, Son-Boy, and Joe begin calculating what age nineteen-year-old Son-Boy will be when he completes the twenty years of schooling that they believe becoming a doctor requires (91). When they finish, Dinah tells Son-Boy to make a fire in the stove because Zeke has eaten all of the food that she had prepared. The play ends as Dinah cleans the mess made during the scare, while repeating the refrain that she had been singing at the outset: "Before I'd be a slave/ I'd be buried in my grave/ And go home to my father and be saved."

When readers assume that Son-Boy's survival constitutes a happy ending, it is easy to overlook the significance of the script's structure, but the play ends as it began—suggesting that very little has changed as a result of the mob's threat. Dinah sings the same militant song, Zeke continues to be a self-preserving coward, and Son-Boy's dreams show no signs of coming true. The lynch threat creates dramatic tension and helps build momentum that engages the reader/viewer, but it ultimately yields nothing extraordinary. The question is, does the threat fail to alter the family's future because they have been spared *or* because the threat itself is nothing unusual? After all, the family may avoid physical violence, but there is little reason to rejoice. No one pretends that Son-Boy's innocence factors into whether or not he may be killed, so surviving this time does not guarantee survival next time. As in *Blue-Eyed Black Boy,* the characters' relief does not diminish their vulnerability to white whim. Furthermore, Son-Boy's being spared does not mean that another innocent black man has not unjustly died.[12] When the drama closes, everyone knows that the threat remains for this family and the entire community.

Under these circumstances, not only is there no happy ending; there may be no ending at all. As Dinah sings the same song that begins the action, the play's circular structure becomes especially suggestive. The script ends, but the lyrics take the audience back to the beginning. The song therefore works in harmony with other elements of the play because *nothing* points to a better future—or even a different one. Indeed, Dinah's militant melody may be the best indication that the play is merely a snapshot of an ongoing cycle of fear and stale mobility. When Dinah begins singing after the crisis has passed, she utters only the refrain—a few lines meant to be repeated. Because refrains appear between verses, they can mark the end of a verse or signal that one is about to begin. Furthermore, the audience could be hearing the refrain for the first time that it occurs in the song or the last. The refrain alone gives no clues about where in the song it appears, and this play both begins and ends with a refrain.[13] As Dinah sings while putting the house back in order, the song could come to a close at any moment, or it could go on forever.

Much of the play's action corroborates this sense of perpetuity. The characters speak of the education that Son-Boy will obtain, but the glimpse of his life that Mitchell provides offers little evidence that the cycle of illiteracy, hard labor, and subjugation will end.[14] After all, Son-Boy cannot do the simple arithmetic needed to calculate how old he will be when he finishes medical school. Likewise, Dinah's life has an air of trapped circularity, made painfully ironic by her militant diatribes. She claims a proud heritage based on her family name, but she has married into another family. Moreover, she and her son bear Zeke's last name—no matter how much she claims that Son-Boy is more "Battle" than "Johnson." Also, despite berating Zeke, she not only has married him, but she also makes no plans to leave him. Finally, while listing all of the benefits of migrating north, Dinah remains in a shack in the South—doing white people's laundry. Like her soulful refrain and the laundry she folds, Dinah's complaints mark the irony of her situation but never give the illusion that it will improve.

The family's inability to alter its circumstances suggests that the mob can sometimes achieve its purpose without killing the head of household; because Zeke shows no signs of wanting to be a strong father and husband, this play revises the genre's representation of de-generation. Lynching drama depicts the removal or prevention of generations to register African Americans' understanding that racial violence is designed to neutralize the most productive generation of black families, which would otherwise guarantee the race's healthy survival and progress. Mitchell is similarly committed to representing the "castration" of black households, but he does so—not by removing the middle generation—but by giving a thorough picture of Zeke's emasculation. Zeke speaks and behaves in ways an honorable husband and father never would. When the family learns that Son-Boy's life is in danger,

Dinah launches into action. While she frantically dresses, Zeke calmly walks around the room with a pipe in his mouth and says that he would help, but he just does not know where Son-Boy is (83). Then, as she tries to arouse his sense of responsibility by declaring that Son-Boy is as much his child as hers, he admits "I'se skeered de white fo'ks'll lynch me" (83). He reminds her that angry whites will "take any nigger dey see an' string 'em up" (83). Later, when Son-Boy arrives looking for weapons to protect himself, Zeke basically admits hiding the gun: "I kno'd yuh'd come heah lookin' fer it . . . I ain't gwine ter let no whar fo'ks fin' no gun in heah when dey gits heah—an' den dey kills us all" (85).

Emasculating fear shapes Zeke's behavior, so while Mitchell offers a traditional nuclear family, it does not represent domestic success. Unlike most of the plays of this study, the middle generation in *Son-Boy* not only survives but also remains together as a couple.[15] However, Dinah does not respect her husband,[16] and her husband does not love her or his son enough to want to protect them. Also, Dinah's domesticity primarily benefits whites, and Zeke is more concerned with remaining in the good graces of those who hold the economic reigns than with gaining financial power himself. At one point, he tells Dinah that he has no time for her because he needs to see "Mars Ross" about some work (90). Slavery has ended, and the Johnsons have their own home, but as his calling Ross "master" indicates, Zeke's family remains subservient to whites. In fact, before the lynching scare, Zeke had preached contentment with their lot in life. When Dinah complains about their low wages, Zeke answers, "What you's an' Son-Boy's makin' is 'nuff fer poo' ignunt fo'ks lak y'all is" (79). According to him, their expectations should be more in line with slavery than citizenship.

If Zeke were to resist his social and economic position, he would encounter frustration or death—like the characters who assert themselves in other lynching scripts. Despite their militancy, Dinah and Son-Boy are not on the verge of radical change, so the text suggests that their approaches to living with lynching—and the racial hierarchy that it secures—are not necessarily better or worse than Zeke's. Together, these three characters gesture toward a recognition within the community conversation that African Americans responded to similar circumstances differently.

Besides pointing to a diversity of coping mechanisms among African Americans, Mitchell's coward figure must be read as part of both the archive and the repertoire. Because Zeke fears whites, he will not defend his family, ask for higher wages, hold up his head and walk straight, or dress nicely when he goes to town (78). As a coward, Zeke understands that he communicates his acceptance of his "proper" place not just through words but also behaviors, postures, and modes of dress. Just as the nation's racist rhetoric was never limited to language, his demonstration that he understands its message cannot be simply linguistic. In this way, the presence of the coward figure marks the existence of real-life black men who performed submissiveness in everyday life. Because Zeke conforms to white demands, he offers historical context for mainstream depictions of black men at the turn of the century. The emasculated buffoon has always provided comic relief, and Mitchell uses Zeke to illuminate the violent circumstances that created this popular figure. If Zeke's cowardice sparks laughter, then Mitchell both invokes and critiques the enduring legacy of minstrelsy, supporting Stephens's assertion that this script brings humor into lynching drama. Zeke understands that he must act in ways that please whites or he may be forced into a theatrical production called lynching.[17] Those who reject the role of emasculated buffoon risk becoming the mob's muse, antagonist, and stage prop.

Mitchell places the coward figure in the archive by publishing the script in the *Saturday Evening Quill,* and his presence points toward a repertoire of embodied practice; at the same time, because it is a play available for amateurs to read or act out in spaces that they control,[18] *Son-Boy* both reflects and becomes part of the multivalent community conversation about identity and citizenship. The play may depict the lack of respect that Dinah and Son-Boy have for Zeke, but it does not allow his perspective to be dismissed. Instead, the text suggests that Zeke's fear is legitimate, given what happens to Snow-Ball and Sambo, two black men whose experiences are discussed in the Johnson household. Through a community conversation within the script, the characters discover that Snow-Ball acts out of fear and stays alive. When a white man threatens to kill him if he refuses to incriminate Son-Boy, Snow-Ball tells whites what they want to hear (88). In this respect, Mitchell's work, like Georgia Douglas Johnson's *A Sunday Morning in the South,* suggests that whites do not seek the truth; they consider black testimony only when it serves their purposes. In contrast to Snow-Ball, Sambo was run out of town for educating himself.[19] As Zeke explains, town whites had said that Sambo "wuz gittin' too much learnin' to be a 'good nigger'" (79).

Here, the script preserves a conversation in a private space, and a cowardly black man shares that he has received an important message: peacefully remaining in town requires submitting to whites. Zeke makes observations, draws logical conclusions about the limits of black citizenship, and shares them with members of his family and community. He also notes that Sambo's mother has never been the same mentally since whites ran her son out of town (79). From Zeke's perspective, partaking in behavior that hearkens the mob may not only leave an individual homeless; it can damage his loved ones' psyches. Therefore, Dinah and Son-Boy may owe their bravado to Zeke; perhaps his cowardice has decreased the frequency with which tragedy threatens to enter their home, break their spirits, and destroy their sanity.

Because black cowards recognize that whites require submission, Mitchell must portray Zeke in a private space; only there might he reveal his true thoughts and feelings. In public, Zeke would work to behave in ways that suggest that he believes in the natural superiority of whites. However, in the black home, he is freer to emphasize his awareness that white men's "master" status is asserted through violence—running Sambo out of town, for example. Zeke recognizes that whites violently fabricate their social position, but the script does not suggest that his emasculation is any less real, that the coward is merely pretending. In fact, because his cowardice emerges from critically reading his surroundings, Zeke's prominence in this script demands that the community conversation engage his perspective.

Readers are encouraged to grapple with the words and deeds of a black man of whom some might be ashamed, not just those considered models for the race. Lynching drama's black soldier had been presented as unquestionably honorable, but he promoted intense debate because the country had shown itself unworthy of his sacrifices. For different reasons, the coward could also generate considerable conversation. After more than a decade of *Crisis* magazine's "Men of the Month" column,[20] which featured those deemed exemplary members of the race, Mitchell used his literary society's publication to ensure that discussion would also be fueled by other representations of black manhood. In Mitchell's work, readers encounter a black man who may not meet certain standards of propriety and honor but who articulates practical, commonsense reasons for his behavior.

Like Lipscomb's pimp, Mitchell's coward is surrounded by characters who bring his perspective into stark relief. Zeke is on stage for most of the action of the play, so even Mitchell's title character, Son-Boy, seems to emerge mainly to provide a contrasting image of black manhood.[21] Son-Boy's life is in danger, yet he is fearless compared to his father. In fact, though Son-Boy is not in a position to change his life chances, he believes in his own worth. When pursued by the mob, he comes home looking for a weapon, convinced that his life is precious (90). He apparently agrees with Ida B. Wells, who had argued that "the more the Afro-American yields and cringes and begs, the more he has to do so. . . . When the white man . . . knows he runs a great risk of biting the dust every time his Afro-American victim does, he will have greater respect for Afro-American life" (*Southern Horrors* 70). Also, while Zeke pledges to stay alive at any cost, insisting, "Don't tell me dat a good run ain't better'n a bad stand," Son-Boy feels that it is better to die than to live with diminished dignity. Echoing the sentiments of Dinah's song, he would rather be "a dead dog" than a "no-count dog" who is of little use to his own kind (90–91). Yet the script illuminates Zeke's character—even his manhood—not just with the contrast between him and his son, but also in the difference between him and his wife.

Dinah's protective instinct and her willingness to bear arms make her better suited for fulfilling a traditional "head of household" role, but Mitchell does not allow her to assume that position.[22] In Mitchell's text, even a strong, hard-working woman can never compensate for a weak man. Despite her determination, Dinah is unable to change her or her son's life chances. She insists that her slave father had bought his family's freedom on an installment plan, and with Battle family blood in her veins, she intends to do the same (84). The piles of laundry in the house indicate that she is sincere, but her stagnation, which Mitchell underscores with the text's circularity, suggests that lynching interferes with black success—not just by taking men out of the home (as women dramatists had demonstrated), but also by infusing some black men with emasculating fear. Zeke's approach to life makes sense, and it seems to have kept him alive, but it is also a testament to the efficiency of mob terror.

✷ ✷ ✷

Like women authors, black male playwrights depict racial violence as an attack on black households. In all lynching dramas, homes, not just bodies, are victimized. Revisions emerge in *how* the destruction is represented. Whether portraying black men's deaths or their emasculation, the genre registers African Americans' recognition that the mob's aim is to nullify black homebuilding efforts, which are linked to conceptions of modern citizenship. Given the mob's goals and tactics, even behavior typically believed to bring shame on the race proves to be quite logical. After all, it is traditionally defined success, not criminality, that inspires the mob's wrath. As W. E. B. Du Bois declared when writing in 1915, "There was one thing that the white South feared more than Negro dishonesty, ignorance, and incompetency [*sic*], and that was Negro honesty, knowledge, and efficiency" (qtd. in Litwack xiii–xiv). As long as African Americans were successful, they would encounter repressive violence.

By accepting plays featuring the pimp and coward, *Opportunity* and *The Saturday Evening Quill* registered the existence within the community conversation of a "critique of normalizing narratives of racial and sexual identity" (Vogel 5).[23] These figures gesture toward the notion that because blacks are often prevented from, or punished for, fulfilling gender norms, "one strategy of attacking the [Jim Crow] regime entails resistance to masculine normalization itself" (Ross 2). The pimp and coward embody this resistance. And they could emerge as subjects worthy of portrayal partly because some publications made depicting the race in its "best" light secondary to encouraging artists to perfect their craft. At a time when uplift ideology remained a guiding force for many African Americans,[24] many also agreed with Langston Hughes's famous 1925 declaration, that art should reveal that blacks are "beautiful. And ugly too" (1314). Even if African Americans accepted conventional conceptions of who represented the race's "best and brightest," they could also value the artistic depiction of "low-down folks" (1314).

Because black male dramatists entered lynching drama by giving the pimp and coward a place within it, the genre offers access to an archive and repertoire that suggests that some black men did not live according to widely accepted ideals of moral manliness. American society constantly attempted "to unman, and thus discredit, black men as influential leaders,"[25] and many activists would have agreed that the existence of a single African American pimp or coward represented a victory for the race's enemies. However, black men's lynching dramas ensure that even the "unmanned" are heard—their voices and perspectives are not "discredited" in the community conversation.

Documenting Black Performance

Key Considerations

Of what use is fiction to the colored race at the present crisis in its history? . . . Fiction is of great value to any people as a preserver of manners and customs—religious, political, and social. It is a record of growth and development from generation to generation. No one will do this for us: we must ourselves develop the men and women who will faithfully portray the inmost thoughts and feelings of the Negro with all the fire and romance which lie dormant in our history, and, as yet, unrecognized by writers of the Anglo-Saxon race."
—Pauline Hopkins, September 1900 prospectus for her first novel, *Contending Forces*

Drama, more than any other art form except the novel, embodies the whole spiritual life of a people; their aspirations and manners, their ideas and ideals, their fantasies and philosophies, the music and dignity of their speech—in a word, their essential character and culture and it carries this likeness of a people down the centuries for the enlightenment of remote times and places.
—Theophilus Lewis, October 1926, theater critic for *The Messenger*

Novelist Pauline Hopkins,[1] quoted above, argued in 1900 for the value of writing fiction even when crises, such as mob violence, demanded African Americans' attention. She insisted that creative writing preserved the race's religious, political, and social customs by depicting the "inmost thoughts and feelings" of members of the group. I want to suggest (along with 1920s theater critic Theophilus Lewis) that black drama became increasingly important at the turn of the century for the same reasons.[2] Yet drama was perhaps even more attuned to the historical moment; it directly addressed the fact that theater was strengthening the assault against African Americans' conceptions of themselves as worthy citizens. In the early 1900s, the mainstream stage acknowledged blacks' existence with images that were denigrating and dehumanizing or comical. As an increasing number of African American authors began writing plays, their depictions of blacks did not match those created by mainstream theater. Black dramatists presented their communities as they knew them to be, and while doing so, several used their scripts to address lynching.

By portraying black bodies participating in ordinary activities inside their own homes, these playwrights helped to (re)define what was "dramatic"—what was worthy of dramatic portrayal. Blacks at home? Not singing and dancing? You can almost hear a 1920s theater manager ask, *Is that theatrical?* Black playwrights answered a resounding *yes!*[3] In doing so, they worked to alter what theater accomplished. They understood that the mainstream stage perpetuated a discourse that defined African Americans as "problems" that must be contained, if not eliminated. In this climate, blacks could not use existing dramatic conventions or rely on American theater's aesthetic tendencies. They had to transform theatricality in the United States from a mode that solidified blacks' position as noncitizens to one that further asserted their right to citizenship.[4]

As we have seen, African Americans recognized lynching as a theatrical production, and when they engaged the mob's destructive power, black dramatists preferred the less corporeal evidence of testimony to the physical evidence with which they were surrounded. Black-authored lynching scripts direct the gaze away from the brutalized body, finding its representational capacity to be insufficient. Committed to conveying the experience of devastated communities, the genre insists that truth cannot be gleaned from bones and charred flesh, mutilated corpses, or pictures of them. African Americans who lived with lynching left accounts of the violence that differ from the focus on "strange fruit" that modern Americans have come to expect.

Likewise, lynching dramatists and their allies left different kinds of evidence than historians typically hope to find in the wake of theater practitioners. Often, there are no playbills, programs, or box office receipts. Yet even without such records to prove that lynching plays were performed, these scripts served black communities. This unique genre challenges us to re-evaluate our assumptions about what creates theatrical power and what counts as proof of the impact that a production had on those who experienced it. One-act lynching dramas were most suited for informal productions among family and friends, and amateurs were more invested in participating in cultural activities than in documenting them. We must therefore recognize that a dearth of traditional documentation does not mean that the plays were not successful. Formal publicity and recordkeeping might have made participants more vulnerable to the violence that they critiqued, but there were other reasons for small theater groups to avoid publicizing their activities. Here, I propose just a few ways to, in James Hatch's words, "hear the 'silences' in theatre history."[5]

Aware that his including plays in *Crisis* was inspiring amateur productions, W. E. B. Du Bois wrote in July 1926 that theater groups should acknowledge the playwrights' labor with a tangible reward: a royalty check. In a notice called "Paying for Plays," Du Bois scolded those who were staging works without paying for the use of the script:

> We have published in *The Crisis* a number of plays and shall publish more. Most of them are adapted to amateur production. We would like to have them produced. But we have laid down the rule: Anyone who wishes to produce a play printed in *The Crisis* may do so upon payment of $5. Of this money, $2.50 goes to the author and $2.50 to *The Crisis*. To our surprise there has been almost unanimous objection; and that shows the singular attitude of our people toward artists and writers. Plumbers, carpenters and bricklayers we pay without question; the workman is worthy of his hire. But if a man writes a play, and a good play, he is lucky if he earns first-class postage upon it. [If the play is] about the kind of Negro you and I know or want to know . . . it cannot be sold to the ordinary theatrical producer, but it can be produced in our churches and lodges and halls; and if it is worth producing there it is worth paying for. It seems to us that $5 is not an exorbitant charge. Of course what is going to happen is that a number of our loyal friends are going to steal these plays, reproduce them without paying for them, and ask us impudently what we are going to do about it. And we can assure them pleasantly that we are not going to do anything. If they can stand that kind of encouragement for Negro artists, we presume we can.

Dramatist Willis Richardson agreed with Du Bois's philosophy but wanted to see its application expanded. Eulalie Spence's *Foreign Mail* won a 1926 *Crisis* prize, and the Washington, D.C., Krigwa theater troupe staged the play in early 1927. Representing this group, Richardson sent royalty to Du Bois. In the letter accompanying his check, Richardson mentioned looking forward to receiving funds for his own play *Compromise,* which the New York Krigwa group had staged. Du Bois's response made no mention of an intention to pay Richardson for the New York rendering of his work; indeed, Du Bois explained that royalties were not paid unless *Crisis* had published the text. Richardson did not have to pay for Spence's work, Du Bois reasoned, because *Crisis* had not published it but simply listed it as a winner of the 1926 contest (and then provided the script to groups that inquired). Richardson responded, "We of the Krigwa Group in Washington are already paying royalty for each play we use, and I think, as you do, that it is a plan all Krigwa Groups should adopt. Besides encouraging the young playwrights to do more and better work, such a course will make them know that we really value what they do. Following our usual custom I have sent the royalty check to Miss Spence at her home address."[6] Clearly, Richardson did not feel that publication in *Crisis* (and the requisite sharing of royalties with the magazine) should determine whether amateurs felt a duty to pay for plays.[7]

If African Americans had to be convinced that they should pay for a playwright's labor, scholars cannot assume that the majority of amateur productions would have been accompanied by documentation that would help us to trace them today. We must therefore be willing to recognize the importance of productions that were "under the radar" of the Little Negro Theatre movement that Du Bois was promoting. Yet recognizing the value of "underground" productions need not require agreeing with Du Bois's characterization of such activity. What Du Bois calls "stealing" may be better understood as communal literacy. African Americans routinely read the *Crisis* aloud, whether at home or in a barbershop or beauty salon. The same impulse could lead to a dramatic reading of a one-act play. As I have been arguing, the community conversation was never limited to words; it included tones of voice, gestures, and movement. For African Americans to read a play with their family and friends—even if they did so at school or church with costumes and props—may be best understood as participation in the dynamic community conversation that periodicals like *Crisis* encouraged. Du Bois's complaints suggest that many African Americans did not see the matter as he did. Some may have reasoned: *When we read an essay or short story aloud, and animated debate ensues, there is no expectation that we send* Crisis *a check, so why should amateur use of a one-act play be any different?* Evidently, there were enough "unauthorized" amateur presentations for Du Bois to complain about his missing royalties, so whether production records remain or not, it is clear that black communities were invested in performance.

While African Americans valued performance, the "productions" endorsed by black theater enthusiasts could be quite unceremonious. "Hearing the silences" therefore requires conceiving of theatricality and theatrical power broadly, and blacks who lived at the turn of the century point the way. Noted black theater critic Theophilus Lewis[8] refused to judge performances on the quality of their staging. He insisted, "But the staging of amateur performances doesn't mean anything. Anybody with money enough can hire expert property men and stage carpenters" (*Messenger,* Aug. 1926, 246). For Lewis, the most important element was the acting, the amateur's embodied practices. Lewis's reluctance to emphasize formal production reflects lessons learned at the turn of the century. As we saw in chapter 2, privileging technical production elements could change the content of African Americans' theatrical work. For example, the Lafayette Players wanted to demonstrate that they were "as good at drama as anybody else had been or could be," so they often presented the same shows that had been popular on Broadway, sometimes using the costumes that Broadway actors no longer needed. Because the troupe allowed its definition of quality to be influenced by commercial theaters with large budgets, black culture and blacks' ordinary lives became artistically unimportant. Given that they were surrounded by technically impressive theater that denigrated African Americans, it makes sense that many would prefer a rudimentary presentation that features "the kind of Negro that you and I know or want to know."

This commitment to the depiction of black culture, rather than formal staging, is evident as Du Bois plans for a theatrical presentation at a civic center. In a November 1927 letter to Eulalie Spence, Du Bois informs her that she has won a playwriting award. He will present her prize money at a Girls Club in New York City and asks that she be prepared to stage her play *Hot Stuff* that evening. He advises, "There would be no scenery or costuming. *You and your two sisters* might take three of the parts. . . . You could train and rehearse at home."[9] By deeming such a minimalist presentation to be legitimate, Du Bois embraces the tendency that cultural critic bell hooks would later identify. hooks argues: "Throughout African-American history, performance has been crucial in the struggle for liberation, precisely because it has not required the material resources demanded by other art-forms" (211). Here, hooks is highlighting embodied practice, using one's body to convey meaning—even if simply by speaking. Indeed, she describes the power of what we might call *word-based performance*: "The voice as instrument could be used by everyone, in any location" (211).

At the turn of the century, the investment in "word-based performance" also took the form of privileging playwriting over acting. As we saw in chapter 2, Du Bois believed that black theater must be built on the work of writers who "understand from birth and continual association just what it means to be a Negro" ("Krigwa" 447). Though he supported amateur theater efforts, he was concerned that they were not committed to black-authored scripts. He therefore declared in *Crisis*: "Some excellent groups of colored amateurs are entertaining colored audiences in Cleveland, in Philadelphia and elsewhere. Almost invariably, however, they miss the real path. They play Shakespeare or Synge or reset a successful Broadway play with colored principals" (July 1926, 134). To correct this tendency among amateur performers, Du Bois initiated Krigwa, The Crisis Guild of Writers and Artists, in large part to elevate the status of black playwriting.[10]

Lynching drama emerged before Du Bois formalized the promotion of black playwriting, so Du Bois and Krigwa joined early lynching playwrights in valuing "the performative power of the word"—even when a play simply appears in written form.[11] By identifying the absence of the black playwright as the reason that existing black theater fell short, early dramatists and philosophers insisted that those who wrote plays offered noble service to the race. Believing that they were answering a higher call—perhaps for posterity—was necessary, because they undertook this work at a time when black-authored "Negro" drama appeared to be the only form that did not bring financial rewards and widespread recognition.[12] Their efforts were to ensure that black-authored dramas were written and therefore *existed* rather than to allow mainstream plays to stand in for the whole truth. In doing so, they proved that the word could change the cultural landscape and alter material reality. Their labors changed the content of the archive, thereby preserving a fuller impression of the repertoire that shaped the era in which they lived. Early dramatists and their allies invested in the ability of the written word to perform—to effect change—simply by being available on the page.

If anyone could conceive of performance in all of these broad terms, African Americans could. As Du Bois affirmed in 1897 (*Atlantic Monthly*) and again in 1903 (*Souls of Black Folk*), many blacks lived with the sensation of always looking at themselves through others' eyes. For better or worse, "double-consciousness" was an acknowledgment that many African Americans went through life cognizant of how they appeared to others—as if they were on a stage. This awareness was especially high during the last turn of the century because blacks were more intensely asserting themselves as "New Negroes." Many focused on demonstrating that they were sophisticated, modern, and ready for full citizenship.[13] During these decades, black newspapers offered readers guidance on how to act in ways that represented the race well. As cultural critic Jacqueline Stewart demonstrates, the black press treated all public spaces as sites for engaging the politics of representation. For instance, columns routinely outlined the standards for "streetcar deportment," suggesting that "the streetcar function[ed] as the exemplary *stage* for black urban *performance,* an important corollary to the *theater*" (Stewart 663, my emphasis).

Theatrical portrayals never stayed on the stage, so seeing a black person in real life often became occasion for comparing them to familiar images. The prominence of the minstrel mask and the brute and whore stereotypes therefore made all the world a stage for African Americans.[14] Just as important, virtually every space felt like a stage because performance had played such an important role in African American survival. As Saidiya Hartman's analysis of the slave coffle demonstrates, performance has always been central to black life in the New World. Slaves were often made to sing and "step lively" as they marched to be auctioned; if they lagged behind or did not convey happiness and youth, they could expect punishment.[15]

For better or worse, then, black life in the United States has been shaped by performance, and the popularity at the turn of the century of the minstrel mask and the brute and whore stereotypes helped ensure that blacks appeared as if on stage—whether they donned burnt-cork masks or not. Whether in a store, on a sidewalk, on a train, or at home, African Americans offered impeccable performances in everyday life as an expression of how they saw themselves, of who they believed themselves to be. Blacks understood, as fully as the lynchers who maligned them, that you don't need a raised platform to make a stage.

NOTES

Introduction: Whose Evidence? Which Account?

1. Disagreements abound regarding how many blacks died by lynching, and I do not insist that my numbers are more accurate than anyone else's. Numbers seem less significant for the period I study because the violence reverberated through photography. For lynching history and statistics, see Tolnay and Beck; Brundage; White; Dray. For why statistics vary, see Waldrep.

2. Lynching plays are still written today, but this study focuses on those that emerged before 1930, pinpointing the period that historians agree constituted the height of mob violence. My goal is to understand how blacks—those who lived and wrote with the form of lynching represented in the photographs in *Without Sanctuary* (Allen et al.)—survived the violence and its implications. To my knowledge, there is only one extant, pre-1930 lynching play not examined here: Garland Anderson's *Appearances*. As mentioned in chapter 6, that play stands outside the tradition I trace, given its lack of interest in how lynching affects the black family. Set inside a hotel and insisting that a black man's innocence will save him, this script promotes the author's beliefs in Christian Science more than it enters a critical discourse on racial violence. I should also note that the present study includes a text that most have not considered a lynching play: Georgia Douglas Johnson's *Blue Blood*. As I explain in chapter 5, I engage it because the action is predicated on the threat of lynching; it thereby fits Perkins and Stephens's generic parameters.

3. See Foucault, *History of Sexuality, Volume I,* especially 94 and 95. These ideas have been widely influential; my thinking is shaped by how they figure in the theories of Stuart Hall and Hazel Carby.

4. The tendency to read texts that expose injustice, especially by black authors, as "protest" may have begun with James Baldwin's critique of Harriet Beecher Stowe's *Uncle Tom's Cabin,* which transitioned into criticism of Richard Wright's *Native Son.* However, Baldwin's critique would not apply to lynching drama. For Baldwin, Stowe's work falls short because "sentimentality . . . is the mark of dishonesty, the

inability to feel" (12). Therefore, Stowe's novel is "a catalogue of violence" that focuses on atrocities rather than "what moved her people to such deeds" (12). Lynching plays do not generally focus on physical violence; they are attempts to understand and overcome it. Baldwin's critique of Wright takes many forms, but his main issue is that Bigger Thomas accepts society's judgment so that he is "defined by his hatred and his fear" (18). Ultimately, "the failure of the protest novel lies in its rejection of life," the insistence that only "categorization" is real and "cannot be transcended" (18). Lynching plays do not concede to mainstream categorizations of African Americans.

5. Blacks are not the only lynch victims depicted, but they were often mutilated. The nonblacks killed by mobs were usually covered, not naked, and they were not typically castrated and burned beyond recognition.

6. Virtual exhibition located at www.withoutsanctuary.org. The Senate passed Resolution 39 on June 13, 2005. Full text of the apology on the sponsoring senator's website: http://landrieu.senate.gov/lynching/index.cfm.

7. The song was written by Lewis Allan (Abel Meeropol) but was made famous when Billie Holiday lent her voice to it in 1939, ultimately inspiring numerous renditions. See Margolick.

8. Many have visited exhibitions of the photographs, making for another embodied practice that intensifies their effect. The photographs were first displayed at the Roth Horowitz Gallery in New York City as *Witness* in January/February 2000 but proved too popular for this intimate space. A larger selection of images arrived at the New York Historical Society on March 14, 2000. Originally scheduled through July, the exhibition's run was extended several times, amounting to a stay of nearly seven months. Next, the Andy Warhol Museum in Pittsburgh scheduled its display for September 22 through December 31, 2001, but extended it to January 15, 2002. The Martin Luther King Jr. Memorial Site in Atlanta presented a selection of photographs from May 1 to December 31, 2002. This run was complemented by an international academic conference titled "Lynching and Racial Violence in America: Histories and Legacies" at Emory University, October 3–6, 2002. Curators of the Atlanta exhibition used dimmed lighting and somber music to encourage contemplation. A similarly thoughtful exhibition was mounted in Cincinnati, Ohio, at the National Underground Railroad Freedom Center January 19 to May 31, 2010.

9. Performance Studies has evolved many ways to acknowledge and examine the centrality of performance in human societies. Representative approaches include Victor Turner's three-part classification and Richard Schechner's capacious definition of performance as "restored behavior." Work on performativity that expands speech-act theory has also been influential. For overviews of some of the field's foundational premises, see Madison and Hamera as well as Bial. For examples of how these concepts figure in African American culture, see Elam and Krasner, eds.

10. The preference for lynching photography reminds me of Wendell Phillips's 1845 preface to *The Narrative of Frederick Douglass*, which begins, " . . . I am glad

the time has come when the 'lions write history.' We have been left long enough to gather the character of slavery from the involuntary evidence of the masters."

11. The pictures were created and preserved because they advanced white supremacist perspectives, so lynching scholarship must read against the grain of the photographs, lest it extend the violence and its implications. Very often, photographs of black lynch victims appear in Apel's work and are accompanied by description (more than analysis), perhaps with the presumption that the murderers are condemning themselves. However, because Apel simply makes matter-of-fact statements of how events unfolded and were justified, little analytical pressure is placed on what the white citizenry did or the justifications it offered. The scholarship makes no attempt at redressing the violence or questioning the reasons for which it was perpetrated; the violence and justifications are simply described, and the logic is left undisturbed. This pattern is especially evident in Apel's contribution to *Lynching Photographs* (University of California Press, 2008).

This approach is quite different from Ida B. Wells's commitment to letting the murderers condemn themselves when she included gruesome details of the mob's work. In the 1890s and early 1900s, Wells used white newspaper accounts to demonstrate that the mob's justifications were fabricated, and to expose how newspapers were complicit in the violence. Many have analyzed the brilliance of Wells's brave rhetorical moves, including Royster; Goldsby.

12. Shawn Michele Smith demonstrates that lynching photographs consolidated white identity, so not all scholarship on lynching photography leaves the perpetrators' logic unexamined. Smith asserts, for example, "As white subjectivity is foregrounded against a black corpse, these photographs make very clear that the power of whiteness is not only invisible and dispersed but also particular and embodied in U.S. culture" (139).

13. For an excellent discussion of the cultural work of souvenirs such as bones and charred flesh, see Young.

14. Kevin Gaines's influential characterization of uplift ideology leads many to approach literature of this period in ways that I want to complicate. His insights are well taken, so my goal is to add to them. Rather than simply say that this genre is an example of blacks' attempts to prove themselves worthy, I work to uncover the other purposes that this genre's "positive" representation of black families could serve.

15. Some African Americans understood escalating white violence to be a sign that the race was making substantial progress (and therefore inspiring white ire). See Litwack, esp. 309–30.

16. With the exception of Livingston, these playwrights not only lived near each other, they were also close in age, though varying birth years have sometimes been recorded in the scholarship because women artists of this period often felt compelled to mislead the public about their age: Angelina Weld Grimké (1880–1958); Alice Dunbar-Nelson (1875–1935); Mary Burrill (1884?-1946); Georgia Douglas Johnson (1880–1966); and Myrtle Smith Livingston (1902–74).

Grimké became a teacher in Washington, D.C., in 1902 when she was in her twenties (Hull 116). She remained there until her late fifties and enjoyed the camaraderie of the area's literati, galvanized by Johnson's literary salon (Hull 151). In the July 1927 issue of *Crisis*, Grimké was reported to have been a delightful addition to the salon's always-lively crowd (Hull 212). Alice Dunbar-Nelson moved to Washington, D.C., around 1898 to be with her new husband, Paul Laurence Dunbar (Hull 43). By 1902, they were separated, and she moved about 100 miles away to Wilmington, Delaware. She taught at Wilmington's all-black Howard High School until 1920, but she often traveled, spending some summers at Cornell University as a special student (Hull 60). In 1916, also while teaching at Howard High School, she married Robert Nelson, and beginning in 1922, Robert lived and worked in Washington, D.C., after the newspaper that they co-edited collapsed (Gaines 210).

Mary Burrill was born in the District and remained there until she attended the institution now known as Emerson College in Boston. She graduated in 1904 and returned to Washington in 1905 to begin her teaching career (Perkins and Stephens, *Strange Fruit*, 80). She taught at Dunbar High School until her retirement in 1944, when she moved to New York City only a couple years before her death.

Georgia Douglas Johnson moved to Washington, D.C., in 1910, at age thirty-three (Hull 156). When her husband died in 1925, she faced financial hardship but also ratcheted up her involvement with the area's writers and intellectuals, especially by hosting her famous "S" Street Salon.

Little is known about Myrtle Smith Livingston, but she was a student at Howard University when she wrote her lynching play *For Unborn Children* in 1925. When it was published the next year, she was likely already in Colorado attending a teacher's college. For more on Livingston, see *African American National Biography*.

17. Grimké's debut is significant not because she was the first to write serious drama, but because hers was the first black-authored drama to be executed by black actors for a broad audience on a semi-professional stage. Before *Rachel*, black-authored dramas were either not produced or were brought to life by amateurs in churches and schools. Of course, such productions are important. In fact, lynching plays would not have proliferated without these small shows. Nevertheless, the impact of Grimké's work stemmed from the fact that it drew a relatively large interracial audience to formal theatrical productions about African Americans. As important, it was a "non-musical" show. Some musicals were explicitly political, but the form's popularity hinged on its entertainment value. Political musical performances included the Hyers Sisters' *Out of Bondage* and *Peculiar Sam* in the nineteenth century. Nevertheless, these shows add to a musical tradition that diverges from the "legitimate" drama that African Americans felt was necessary at the turn of the century.

18. When referring to "drama" and playwrights' achievements, as opposed to "theater," which includes performers' accomplishments, scholars often overlook works that emerged before the 1920s. This trend began with the assumption that black characters did not enter the "legitimate" American stage until white dramatist

Ridgeley Torrence used black actors to portray African American characters in his *Three Plays for a Negro Theatre*. This moment did not rely on black playwrights, so many deemed African American dramatists irrelevant, a sentiment solidified with Alain Locke and Montgomery Gregory's 1927 drama anthology *Plays of Negro Life*. In that volume, Locke credits white playwrights Torrence, Eugene O'Neill, and Paul Green with the "pioneering genius" that made 1917 to 1927 an "experimental and groundbreaking decade" (i). Similarly, Gregory says that the production of Torrence's plays "marks the first important movement in the development of an authentic drama of Negro life and the establishment of Negro Theatre" (Gregory, "Chronology"410).

Of course, my work is indebted to theater scholars who avoid treating the mid-1920s as the beginning of significant African American drama. Yet much of that work has come in the form of anthologies rather than monographs. For example, James Hatch's *Black Theatre U.S.A.* and *Lost Plays of the Harlem Renaissance* contextualize early plays, and collections such as Kathy Perkins's *Black Women Playwrights* and Elizabeth Brown-Guillory's *Wines in the Wilderness* ensure that women's contributions receive serious treatment. Yet few monographs rigorously engage the texts preserved in these classic anthologies; those that do offer a strong foundation, but their findings must be updated. For instance, Leslie Catherine Sanders's *The Development of Black Theater in America* begins its exploration in the late 1920s and focuses on five men: Willis Richardson, Randolph Edmonds, Langston Hughes, Amiri Baraka, and Ed Bullins. Men are centered in a way that skews our understanding of black drama's development.

Elizabeth Brown-Guillory engages women artists in *Their Place on the Stage*. The study centers on late-twentieth-century dramatists Alice Childress, Lorraine Hansberry, and Ntozake Shange, but Brown-Guillory's thorough introduction has shaped perceptions of the early playwrights I examine. Writing to recuperate these women at a time when their value was questioned, she understandably resorted to arguing that they deserve attention because "they provide the feminine perspective" (4). The work that her book enabled allows me to demonstrate now that these women pioneered a literary movement; they did not offer "feminine" revisions to a tradition that men established.

Finally, Samuel Hay frames *African American Theatre* with the philosophies of Alain Locke and W. E. B. Du Bois, who disagreed about whether black drama should be "purely artistic" or political. Hay's study remains foundational and informs my project, but I have found that Grimké set the agenda for these debating intellectuals, not the other way around.

19. *The Mulatto* began this record-setting run after it was revised without Hughes's permission. James Hatch and Errol Hill explain that the director "turned tragedy into a sex melodrama" by adding "a gratuitous rape of the daughter" (313). This version received 373 Broadway performances.

20. Richardson often said in interviews (with James Hatch, for instance) that he returned from seeing *Rachel* determined to write drama of his own; he felt certain that he could do better. Also see Gray.

21. Most assume that Du Bois motivated Grimké. For example, as he introduces *Black Thunder*, theater historian William Branch calls *Rachel* "the first produced play to result from Dr. Du Bois's call . . ." (xv). Samuel Hay uses letters between NAACP drama committee members to show that Grimké's play was chosen when the organization wanted to improve race relations through theater. Indeed, he suggests that Grimké's work may have been chosen because her father was an officer for the Washington, D.C., branch. Though Hay does not insist that the drama was *written* in response to the committee's desire to stage a play for "race propaganda," later scholars have read his work in exactly that way. For example, Lisa Anderson's *Mammies No More* (1997) and Carol Allen's *Peculiar Passages* (2005) argue that the play was penned in response to the committee's call, but years earlier in 1987, Gloria Hull's *Color, Sex, and Poetry* made clear that Grimké's script was written before Du Bois founded the drama committee because a draft was circulating as early as January 1915 (Hull 117–23).

22. It is therefore telling that Willis Richardson's *Chip Woman's Fortune*, hailed by historians as the first black drama on Broadway, was characterized as a "curtain raiser" and "a light comedy of colored folk life" when *Crisis* celebrated this milestone (*Crisis*, June 1923, 74–75). Also see Chansky on the tendency to need three one-acts to make a bill.

23. Turn-of-the-century national rhetoric linked domesticity and citizenship in myriad ways. Citizenship was figured as "manhood rights," which required not only independence but also the ability to handle dependents, such as a wife and children. Black men were therefore said to be incapable of both, as many historians have shown. For example, see Lentz-Smith. Just as important, citizenship was consistently figured as a terrain of intimacy; citizens needed to be able to protect what was most private and vulnerable. Under these assumptions, black political equality was cast as an invitation for black men to have sex with white women. See Feimster; Rosen; Hodes.

24. Scholars have often viewed the turn of the century as a period in which artistic production became less important for African Americans because simple survival was so difficult. However, the 2006 essay collection *Post-Bellum, Pre-Harlem* encourages a reassessment of the period, and this study continues that effort. See McCaskill and Gebhard's introduction for an overview of traditional approaches to the period.

25. In this way, this study takes inspiration from the scholarship included in the 2002 collection *No More Separate Spheres!* edited by Cathy N. Davidson and Jessamyn Hatcher.

26. Given the frequency with which freedpeople overcame obstacles to reunite families and legalize marriages, this black soldier's wedding day exclamation represented the sentiments of many: "*I praise God for this day*! The Marriage Covenant is at the foundation of all our rights" (qtd. in Hunter 38). Clearly, these assumptions persisted into the early twentieth century.

Chapter 1. Scenes and Scenarios

1. I borrow "reading aright" from Frances Harper, whose novel *Iola Leroy* (1892) declares: "But slavery had cast such a glamour over the Nation, and so warped the consciences of men, that they failed to read aright the legible transcript of Divine retribution which was written upon the shuddering earth . . ." (14).

2. While not relying on the term "semiotics," this study understands that virtually anything can become a sign in the various sign-systems that shape societies. Because they account for layers of signification in both theater and society, the works of Erika Fischer-Lichte and Ric Knowles have been helpful.

3. I coin this term to maximize insights gained from placing in conversation Trudier Harris's study of lynching in literature, *Exorcising Blackness* (1984), and Diana Taylor's performance theory, as articulated in *The Archive and the Repertoire* (2003).

4. As James Cutler established in the first scholarly study of lynching, anyone who went against public opinion between the late 1700s and early 1800s could be lynched, although they were seldom killed. They were usually whipped and ordered to leave town (Cutler 3, 9, 32, 40). Physical punishments became more severe through 1830, but "lynching" was not synonymous with death until after 1830, when abolitionists were more often targeted. Though Cutler marks this shift and notes that it coincided with the rise of organized abolitionism, he does not acknowledge racial subordination as the primary aim of this change. Yet neither whipping nor tarring and feathering seemed harsh enough punishment for abolitionists, so mobs began killing them (Cutler 91). These new methods emerged to quell the abolitionists' willingness to acknowledge the human rights of African Americans. Thus, although these victims were white, their lynching was spurred by the desire to keep blacks oppressed—to ensure that a black body signified property.

By underscoring the antiblack work accomplished by lynching, I am not suggesting that people of other races were not lynched or that those lynchings were not as effective as tools of white supremacy, but it matters that black bodies were the ones most often put on display and circulated as picture postcards. As Ken Gonzales-Day demonstrates, some of the work of understanding the racialized murder of Latinos and others includes recovering what has been lost to the archive because pictures of these atrocities did not circulate like those of blacks did.

5. See Jacquelyn Dowd Hall; Patterson; Dray.

6. Reputable studies of lynching acknowledge that black men were the mob's main targets. The black male body was figured in ways that made its brutalization cathartic for white mobs. See Wiegman.

7. Many postbellum developments encouraged re-defining American identity. More detail about the role of modernization and industrialization later in this chapter.

8. See Kenneth Goings's classic study of black collectibles, esp. xiii, 14, 20.

9. Characters engage in heated debate, which should be understood as another

practice of black belonging. Debate suggests that one takes another's ideas and beliefs seriously enough to try to influence them. More in chapter 3.

10. Even lynching scripts that were not published in periodicals reflect the genre's debt to community-centered opportunities fostered by periodical culture, including literary societies. For instance, Georgia Douglas Johnson's plays were often published after her death, but they were surely related to conversations had in her Washington, D.C., literary salon. More in chapter 5.

11. Wells used the *Chicago Tribune*'s statistics to establish that rape was not even alleged in two-thirds of lynch cases, and historians have corroborated these findings. See Dray; McMurry.

12. Historians of lynching generally agree on this time span. For example, see Dray, iii.

13. Americans often approach this history assuming that blacks primarily responded to oppression, but W. E. B. Du Bois insisted that whites responded to black success. Writing in 1915, Du Bois observed: "There was one thing that the white South feared more than Negro dishonesty, ignorance, and incompetency [*sic*], and that was Negro honesty, knowledge, and efficiency" (qtd. in Litwack xiii–xiv).

14. Hale makes many of these claims in relationship to the South. However, she shows that "Southern culture" proved nationally influential as the North and South found common ground in the postbellum era (7, 22).

15. There were concerns that reprinting lynching photographs advanced the mob's work. Du Bois and the NAACP sought to minimize that danger. See Carroll; Wood; Markovitz.

16. "Camerawork" is Jacqueline Goldsby's term. She reads photographs as texts with recognizable representational strategies, not unlike literary conventions.

17. Lynching was addressed in myriad genres, as demonstrated by Anne Rice's anthology *Witnessing Lynching*.

18. As the official organ of the NAACP, *Crisis* had an integrated audience, and its contents were not all black-authored pieces. Still, Castronovo and Carroll, respectively, rightly analyze this magazine as representative of Du Bois's vision; he was editor for twenty-four years, from 1910 to 1934. I have no interest in claiming that the target audience was 100 percent African American or that black readers mattered more than others. However, accounting for the impact that the magazine had on its black readers requires us to attend to nuances and possibilities that scholars have been slow to consider—arguably because most conceive of the audience as interracial, with the magazine's effect resting mostly in the fact that it reached white readers. This tendency remains, despite the fact that *Crisis* magazine's readership was primarily black. As Carroll explains, "Readership of the magazine was estimated to be only 20 percent white in 1912 and 1916, which led to efforts to bring in more white readers" (231n9).

19. As Carroll says, these periodicals combined "visual texts—photographs, portraits, black-and-white drawings, and reproductions of paintings and sculptures— with written texts—news stories, essays, editorials, fiction, poetry, drama, transcriptions of music and folktales, biographical sketches, and bibliographies" (4).

20. It is important that Carroll recognizes that the magazine accomplished *both* affirmation *and* protest and did so simultaneously, but she sees these as two distinct strands.

21. Castronovo acknowledges this in several instances. He explains that "the crowds that gathered [at lynchings] made racial horror a grotesque distortion of *sensus communis*" and that "As an aesthetic object, the victimized black body becomes the focal point of white subjectivity" ("Beauty" 1451). Similarly, because "lynching was an aesthetic performance," "aestheticization revealed that beauty and art could not be trusted in the campaign against white injustice" ("Beauty" 1451).

22. Stage productions inspired by Harriet Beecher Stowe's *Uncle Tom's Cabin* (1852) were notoriously spectacular, borrowing from her famous characters but not her noble intentions. What became known as "Tom Shows" drew crowds as late as the 1920s. As Alain Locke asserted in 1940, "A plague of low-genre interest multiplied the superficial types of uncles, aunties, and pickaninnies almost endlessly, echoing even today in the minstrel and vaudeville stereotypes of a Negro half-clown, half-troubadour. The extreme popularity of these types held all the arts in so strong a grip that, after seventy or more years of vogue, it was still difficult in the last two decades to break through this cotton-patch and cabin-quarters formula." See *The Negro in Art*.

23. The Madonna as virgin mother is also featured to emphasize Rachel's love of children.

24. Scholars see the 1890s as a time when black women novelists in particular created characters who exemplify sexual propriety and familial stability. Key examples include Frances Harper's *Iola Leroy* (1892) and Pauline Hopkins's *Contending Forces* (1900). See Carby; Tate.

25. By highlighting "rehearsal," I encourage readers to view the cultural work that the plays performed for black communities as a precursor to Augusto Boal's "Theatre of the Oppressed." Boal urged collapsing the barrier between actor and audience, and his techniques are designed to allow people to rehearse resistance to oppressive situations so that, when they encounter them in real life, they will have already imagined empowered responses. Rather than the catharsis for audiences that Aristotle prized in tragedy, Boal valued creating circumstances in which "spect-actors" maximized "rehearsal." Theatre of the Oppressed techniques help individuals see the world in ways that both expose oppressive forces and equip them to believe that they can alter their experiences of those forces—through their "performances" in daily life. As African Americans read their surroundings at the turn of the century, lynching plays helped them to rehearse understandings of themselves and their brethren that enabled them to see lynching as unjust, not as a horrible but necessary disciplinary tool for the "bad" members of their race.

26. I say that theater was becoming more relevant to nationalism to remind readers that the extraordinary success of play versions of Thomas Dixon Jr.'s *The Clansman* coincided with the rise of stage realism in the United States. Although American theater histories have not claimed Dixon as a founding father, his plays emerged at

the same time that critics were insisting that the American stage should instruct, not just entertain. In other words, it was time to use theater to shape national identity, to stop mounting European plays and use "native" drama. Critics felt that American writers of fiction and poetry had reached a standard that represented the nation well and distinguished it from England; it was now time to dramatize American exceptionalism. As William Dean Howells and others promoted the development of a uniquely American stage realism, Dixon's work did not exist in a separate realm but was helping to define realism's conventions and its strategies for encouraging audiences to take physical features to be indicative of an inner truth. On Dixon's theater success, see Cook.

27. For brilliant analysis of smell at lynchings, see Patterson.

28. As this discussion makes clear, I use the term *theatricality* while avoiding "ahistorical and laissez-faire uses of the concept" (Davis and Postlewait 3). Elements of theatrical production can create powerful meanings and affective responses even if far removed from the formal stage. Thus, the mob used body parts as props, as a theater practitioner might, and often chose locations that provided crowds with unobstructed views of the killing. Throughout the study, I demonstrate that formal staging was not necessary for theatrical power, but I do not use "theatricality" as a metaphor or theoretical concept completely unrelated to an understanding of theater history.

29. The plays represent women as mob victims solely in terms of their familial losses. None of the plays features a woman who dies at the mob's hands, though the authors knew that women were lynched. (More on this in chapter 5.) Similarly, the genre emphasizes the nuclear family, but the authors' lives suggest that they did not blindly accept the politics of propriety. As is well known, Grimké, Dunbar-Nelson, and Burrill did not conform to expectations of heteronormativity.

30. Chief among popular mammy/uncle figures was Uncle Tom, especially in "Tom Shows," which were supposedly inspired by *Uncle Tom's Cabin* but were closer to black-face minstrelsy than social protest. Stage versions emphasized Tom's devotion to Little Eva and other whites, not blacks. Likewise, mammy figures have traditionally fawned over their white charges while being harsh with their own children. See Harris's *Saints, Sinners, Saviors,* and Wallace-Sanders.

31. Nancy Fraser uses the term "subaltern *counter*publics," but I avoid all language suggesting that the playwrights were in reaction mode. Reading Fraser in conversation with Herbst is helpful because Herbst emphasizes that marginalized groups nurture each other and do not simply work against the forces that oppress them.

32. Michel Foucault engages these ideas in several works. See especially *Power/ Knowledge*.

33. Here, I use Herbst's language again because she so powerfully defines marginalized groups as those whose truths the mainstream works to *silence*.

34. Many use Du Bois's declaration about theater by, about, for, and near African Americans as the marker for the Little Negro Theatre Movement; it appears in a

1926 manifesto, ten years after the NAACP helped stage *Rachel*. Thus, the one-act revisions of Grimké's work precede Du Bois's definition of the movement and the recognized inauguration of it. Still, even if the plays of this study preceded Du Bois's declaration, amateur theater among African Americans was not completely unrelated to the rise in little theater activity among whites. For histories of mainstream examples, see Mackay; Chansky.

35. See McHenry, especially 34–37, 53–54, 89, and the introduction.

36. Also suggesting that plays were used this way in the 1920s, Marita Bonner subtitled some of her works, "A Play to Be Read."

Chapter 2. Redefining "Black Theater"

1. According to Claudia Tate and Gloria Hull, once Grimké began writing about lynching, she became preoccupied with the topic, especially when writing drama. There are several drafts of *Mara*, a play similar to *Rachel*, and "the complete version exists as a holograph of nearly 200 pages" (Tate 217). However, there is no typescript, suggesting that Grimké had not attempted to have it published or produced, so her devotion to drama was not dependent on whether her work would reach her ideal theater audience. Hull believes that the number of white women who actually saw *Rachel* staged fell short of Grimké's ideal (118–21). Therefore, the fact that she later worked tirelessly on *Mara* suggests that she found motivation beyond traditionally defined theatrical success. (Probable date of *Mara* manuscript discussed by Hull, 124).

2. "Representational agency" is Daphne Brooks's term. Also, Brooks's work is among the recent scholarship that identifies the insurgency of turn-of-the-century entertainers.

3. Minstrelsy offered a viable livelihood and provided physical, social, and economic mobility available to few African Americans at this time (Toll 196).

4. Cole and Johnson used their popularity and relative autonomy to portray blacks as more complete human beings so that even segregated Broadway venues accommodated material "about us." *The Shoo-Fly Regiment* represented a step forward because it was the first time blacks performed serious, tender love scenes before a white audience (Woll 23). At that time, no one expected whites to believe that blacks experienced true love, so romantic scenes were heavily burlesqued (Johnson, *Black Manhattan* 171). It matters, then, that Cole and Johnson refused to mask black love. The team also advanced black theater by considering war's impact on black marriage and family life, anticipating lynching plays like *Mine Eyes Have Seen* and *Aftermath*. *Shoo-Fly Regiment* also made history by spotlighting a black man who is not only educated but also brave and patriotic (Woll 23).

5. For more on the "exile of the Negro" from mainstream stages, see Woll; Riis; Loften Mitchell; and Johnson's *Black Manhattan*.

6. Even after Walton left the Lafayette, he featured the Players in his column, through 1923 (Thompson 21).

7. Here, Chansky is quoting Stansell.

8. Formed in 1915, the troupe's career as "Lafayette Players" began in 1916 and faded by 1932. Given the mainstream material that Bush encouraged, lynching plays represent an attempt to transform existing black theater. The black playwright emerges partly because she wants to see black actors performing material written by and for African Americans. (Also note: Will Marion Cook initiated a less successful and more musically oriented stock company in Harlem in 1913. See Thomas Riis, 164.)

9. African Americans face challenges when embracing aesthetic expression that is not deemed "authentically" black (Brooks 317).

10. Most blacks who became mainstream stars as serious actors received their first opportunities in these theaters. Charles Gilpin is a much-cited example. See Johnson, *Black Manhattan* and Thompson.

11. The actors associated with Bush did not believe themselves to be involved in "imitation" at all. They were working to challenge the notion that they would have to imitate whites to be excellent. The work of white actors had become the standard because of socially constructed barriers, not some ultimate truth.

12. Again, what made this "new" was that the material was not musical and/or comedic.

13. At one point, the team offered a prize for the best play about black life, but there is no evidence that this call was fruitful (Thompson 19). Also, the call seems to have come from Walton's column, not the Players. Walton did not want anything to interfere with the troupe's success and seems to have tried to pacify a critical public. The announcement placed the onus on readers who wanted to see black-authored plays by giving them an opportunity to originate scripts. The advertisement is in the January 6, 1916, issue of the *New York Age*.

14. The exile ended in 1917 when Torrence used black actors (instead of black-faced whites) in his *Three Plays for a Negro Theatre* at Broadway's Garrick Theatre.

15. Rachel's despair allies her with her biblical namesake: " . . . Rachel weeping *for* her children . . . would not be comforted because they are not" (Matthew 2:18).

16. I say that *Rachel* follows an Aristotelian conception of dramatic form to suggest that the play emphasizes action—an unmistakable beginning, middle, and end—and works to establish cause-and-effect patterns as it progresses. David Krasner would resist this characterization by emphasizing the play's alignment with Walter Benjamin's analysis of German tragic drama, *Trauerspiel*. Krasner argues, "Unlike tragedy, with its rational coherence and concise beginning, middle, and end, *Trauerspiel* questions our confidence in making sense of the world" (103). Yet the four-year lapse between Acts 1 and 2 helps the play to unfold in ways similar to a bildungsroman, allowing for a gradual unveiling of the many ways in which racism affects this sensitive girl. In this sense, cause-and-effect is very much at work. Still, Grimké revises Aristotelian form in that fault lies with society, not the individual. That is, Grimké does not depict Rachel's fragility and naiveté as hubris so much as a sign that society corrupts that which it should protect.

17. The plays that were not published in these periodicals did not see publication until drama scholars collected them. Johnson's *A Sunday Morning in the South* was published in 1974 in the first edition of *Black Theatre U. S. A.*, and *Safe* appeared in *Wines in the Wilderness* in 1990. However, when a play won a magazine prize, readers could contact the editors if they were interested in it, as the Krigwa Players of Washington, D.C., may have done in the case of *Blue Blood*, which they performed in 1927. (Letter from Willis Richardson to W. E. B. Dubois; Du Bois Papers, Schomburg Archives). Also, in 1928, *Blue Blood* received its first printing in Frank Shay's collection *Fifty More Contemporary One-Act Plays*.

18. Here, I underscore the cultural work accomplished when, as Melissa Harris-Lacewell asserts, blacks gather for everyday talk. See *Bibles, Barbershops, and B.E.T.*

19. In emphasizing the importance of direct address, I am influenced by cultural theorist Kelly Oliver. She argues that identity and subjectivity (as opposed to the subject position assigned by repression) develop through address-ability, the ability to address another and feel that you will be recognized. There can be no autonomous identity without this, so becoming an "I" is inherently relational, but her theory makes room for socially disempowered people to operate outside of their relationship to oppression and oppressors.

20. Black women initiated lynching drama and set forth its most consistent conventions; I therefore identify the genre's foundational scripts as those written by women before 1930. The conventions I examine here are based on analysis of Grimké's *Rachel* and the revisions offered by *Mine Eyes Have Seen* (1918), *Aftermath* (1919), *For Unborn Children* (1926), *A Sunday Morning in the South* (1925), *Blue Blood* (c. 1926), and *Safe* (1929). Black men began writing these plays later, and their work offers revisions that reflect their distinct relationship to lynching.

21. It is unlikely that the playwrights used domestic settings simply to deal with the logistical challenges of production. Focusing on the home was not just a way to avoid staging a lynching; there were plenty of ways to indicate the violence if necessary—an onstage noose, for example.

22. I include children in the community conception of citizenship, following Elsa Barkley Brown.

23. Historical analyses have often divided the domestic from the political, as is well summarized by Cathy Davidson and Jessamyn Hatcher, who challenge the assumption of "separate spheres." My approach to lynching drama takes for granted that the private and political are inextricably linked. I aim to operate with the same awareness that lynching playwrights had at the turn of the century.

24. The often-paternalistic attitude of uplift ideology can sometimes be gleaned in the conventions that characterize lynching drama. Kevin Gaines has traced this paternalism among middle-class blacks, and he argues that it was the bedrock of a moral economy in which behavior could trump financial standing. The poor could therefore redeem themselves by adhering to propriety. Even in the context that Gaines delineates, I would suggest that the plays step away from paternalism by offering modest characters and encouraging readers to embrace their words and actions

through embodied practice. Even the scripts that feature dialect do not signify in the same register as comedy and minstrelsy, so a more complex alignment is being encouraged among blacks of different classes.

25. Commentator in a 1902 issue of the mainstream periodical *The Independent*. (Quoted in Giddings, *When and Where* 82.) This statement helped spur the nationalization of the black women's club movement.

26. Black men also struggled for the franchise, given the emergence of Black Codes.

27. As whites claimed that "hard work" and "integrity" fostered American success, no mention was made of the slave labor, sharecropping, and other institutionalized oppression that made American prosperity possible.

28. Because the black whore and rapist myths relied on each other, these women's tendency to focus on black men should not be read as a willingness to prioritize men's oppression over women's. Ann duCille warns against "phallocentric" readings that are preoccupied with how black men are figured and show little regard for how accurately black women's lives are represented. See "Monster, She Wrote" in *Skin Trade*. Scholars who share duCille's concern may wonder if these 1920s women dramatists were phallocentric in their portrayal of lynching. This question becomes more pertinent when we consider Elsa Barkley Brown's work. Brown argues that black women of the 1890s and early 1900s attempted to "de-sexualize" themselves as a response to the overwhelming charge that they were whores. The historical fact of black women's sexual exploitation was willfully silenced as they presented themselves as personifications of sexual morality. As a result, black women's gender-specific struggles were not fully integrated into the race's overall political agenda. The stage was set by the early 1900s, Brown argues, for political activism to become male-centered. See "Negotiating and Transforming the Public Sphere."

In not mentioning female mob victims, lynching plays seem to exemplify the male-centeredness that Brown chronicles and that duCille warns literary critics to avoid. However, the playwrights' literary strategies arise from their interests at a specific moment in history, and our historical moment need not take precedence over theirs. We cannot assume that our hindsight is 20/20. The women were aware of female mob victims but chose to write about men. Their doing so does not necessarily indicate acquiescence to "phallocentricism." In fact, given the *interdependence* of the black whore and rapist myths, foregrounding men's victimization does not rob the dramas of their ability to put forth a genuine and *simultaneous* commentary on women's oppression.

29. African Americans have long identified with the plight of Jesus Christ. See JoAnne Terrell, especially 35–62, and Moses, *Black Messiahs and Uncle Toms* 75–85, and Moses, *The Wings of Ethiopia* 190–93.

30. The dramatists focused on black men, not because women were less important, but because they faced a historically specific cultural conversation. As Jonathan Markovitz makes clear, "[B]ecause lynching was justified by referencing myths of black *male* sexuality and criminality, antilynching activists were forced to devote the bulk of their resources toward combating these myths" (3). While Markovitz

believes that this focus made them "less able to confront racist representations of black women," I maintain that, when they contradicted the idea that black men were rapists, black women *simultaneously* addressed the notion that they were whores— because these myths relied on each other. Also, I urge scholars not to read the texts as if they disrupt lynching discourse by *simply* conforming to heteronormativity. Certainly, the plays document the fact that this nation has long created "hierarchies of property and propriety" based on heterosexual privilege (Berlant and Warner 548). The genre therefore reminds us that what was true in the 1990s was also true in the 1920s. However, scholars should not assume a simple binary of complicity/ resistance, especially given that the first two plays in the tradition were written by women who could not be labeled heterosexual: Angelina Weld Grimké and Alice Dunbar-Nelson. That is not to say, of course, that they could not be complicit in perpetuating heteronormative patterns, but it is important to resist jumping to that conclusion. These writers had other reasons for suggesting that domestic success requires male presence.

31. In *Mine Eyes,* the father was lynched in the South before the action begins and the mother died after settling North. In *Aftermath,* the mother and father both died before the action begins. In *A Sunday Morning,* the middle generation is never mentioned. Finally, in *For Unborn Children,* the middle generation is mentioned only to reveal that the mother was white, so that the grandmother's warning against interracial marriage is more credible.

32. Though these characters refuse to become mothers, the plays do not neces- sarily participate in Margaret Sanger's crusade to control birth rates among the poor. Lynching playwrights Mary Burrill and Angelina Weld Grimké supported Sanger's *Birth Control Review,* but these characters' actions cannot be interpreted as a wholesale acceptance of Sanger's cause. Daylanne English shows that African Americans embraced eugenics in that they wanted to create a stronger race through selective procreation, which is quite different from killing children who are already born. Given black eugenicists' hopes, Rachel and Liza are particularly disturbing because if they *had* become mothers, their children would presumably have advanced the race; their beloveds were honorable black men who offered excellent genes and positive moral influence. Understood in this context, Rachel's and Liza's situations demonstrate that "breeding" superior members of the race will *not* discourage white brutality. Living an honorable life does not protect existing men, and birth- ing and rearing increasingly admirable specimens will not halt the violence either. Therefore, the refusal to have children in these plays is less about eugenics than about depicting the long-term effects of mob violence—including insanity. Lynch- ing causes physical, spiritual, emotional, and psychological damage; because the mutilation exceeds the physical, it lasts long after the single act. For a discussion of how "African American writers and intellectuals were not necessarily entirely alienated . . . from now-discredited but then-normative [eugenicist] ideologies," see English, "Family Crisis."

33. For a discussion of black children in lynching drama, see Bernstein.

34. One way of representing alternative family configurations is to feature what Patricia Hill Collins calls "other mothers." Grimké's protagonist Rachel mothers neighborhood children, so the genre does not completely leave this phenomenon unrepresented; but for many, this does not challenge heteronormative messages. Thaddeus Russell argues that conservative politics have prevented representations of families that challenge heterosexist norms, so while I tend to disagree with Carolivia Herron's claim that Rachel's refusal to marry is related to the author's homosexuality, Russell's work makes that argument more compelling. Accepting Herron's reading might further challenge suggestions that this genre privileges conservative uplift strategies above all else.

35. Consult Frazier's and Moynihan's texts for fuller context, but Hortense Spillers offers a compelling discussion of how these sociologists inspired the nation's tendency to think of and speak of blacks as pathological.

36. As Wells explained in *A Red Record*, blacks were too valuable as slaves to be killed, so lynching African Americans came into vogue after freedom, and the rape excuse emerged belatedly, in the 1890s. Wells and Douglass therefore asked why black men were never accused of rape during the Civil War when white women and children were left in their charge (as southern white men went to fight to keep blacks enslaved).

37. As historian Kidada Williams has found, many women encouraged their partners to flee if violence were on the way, hoping that whites would be less ruthless if only women and children were at home.

38. I cannot raise all of the possible issues here, but I want to suggest that we have not fully accounted for the psychological impact of knowing that you can be lynched at any moment. For instance, how might such knowledge influence one's decision to marry? These plays suggest that black men's possible victimization led some *women* to hesitate before marrying and having children. Is it not possible that lynching would similarly affect black men?

CHAPTER 3. THE BLACK SOLDIER

1. Periodical evidence of the debate about *Rachel* includes Grimké's rationale for the play, originally published in the January 1920 issue of *Competitor* magazine, and a review in the March 19, 1917, edition of the *Washington Post*, which compliments the work but also claims that its content is dangerous if presented "indiscriminately" before audiences with "subnormal powers of differentiation and analysis." See Hull 120–24 for an account of responses, including those following the play's 1920 publication.

2. Periodicals overflowed with editorials, letters to the editor, cartoons, and other features of the black soldier. Besides issues of magazines such as *Crisis* and *Opportunity* and newspapers such as the Chicago *Defender*, recent studies offer synthesis. See Whalan; Williams, "Vanguards" and *Torchbearers*; Lentz-Smith.

3. On Dunbar-Nelson's war work, see Nikki Brown.

4. Hull 71. This assessment matches that of most critics, including Claire Tylee and Nikki Brown.

5. My earlier reading of this play falls into the trap of assuming that Chris has been converted. This book therefore offers a revision of the interpretation found in my contribution to *Post-Bellum, Pre-Harlem*.

6. The "bleak climate" may not have been the only reason for the mother's death; she was likely refused treatment at Northern hospitals. The text may therefore point to what Karla Holloway calls *black death* or "how *we* die."

7. Chris is alone among the characters, but not necessarily among readers and authors, including Dunbar-Nelson herself.

8. For the history of U.S. practices of memorializing soldiers, see Blight; Savage.

9. For more on race riots, see Rucker and Upton, eds.

10. Ida B. Wells prioritized defending the race's name while exposing the real reasons for lynching. Frederickson and Logan both illuminate the social climate in which she set this priority.

11. Williams, "Vanguards" 348.

12. Millie's wavering faith in prayer haunts the action when John leaves to avenge his father's murder. The mob and military affect black families similarly, so John is as vulnerable at home as overseas, and Millie will continue to have reason to doubt the power of prayer.

13. Because Lonnie helps illustrate how complicated black men's position is, in some ways Burrill's creation of him anticipates Richard Wright's "The Ethics of Living Jim Crow," which so brilliantly emphasizes the role of both choice and luck.

14. Periodicals frequently bore witness to black bravery as soldiers helped galvanize a spirit of armed self-defense. Actions inspired written accounts, and having written accounts inspired more action and more accounts.

15. In contrast, the dialect in *Mine Eyes Have Seen* is more reflective of the cultural differences introduced into the home by the presence of visitors within it.

16. While categorizing them as "general interest" magazines, Susan Harris Smith's study demonstrates that turn-of-the-century mainstream magazines had a very specific interest: maintaining the country's (white supremacist) status quo.

17. Federal authorities assumed that blacks were radical even when they were not and confused their ideological commitments even when clearly articulated. See Kornweibel, "Seeing Red."

18. Eastman transitioned into editing *The Liberator* shortly after *The Masses* became defunct. See Herbst 131–34, and Cantor.

19. *Liberator* editor Max Eastman wanted blacks to join forces with labor groups that did not necessarily prioritize race. In his September 1919 editorial about the riots, Eastman fails to suggest that because race is imbricated with class in the United States, perhaps the "general proletariat" needs to prioritize "the race-problem." Yet this is what many blacks urged. As Robin Kelley reminds us, W. E. B. Du Bois, as early as 1906, insisted that "the colored laborer" was "the key to socialism's success" (43). While not conceding that blacks need their own organizations, this issue of

The Liberator features the following advertisement: "The Race Riots Scientifically treated from the Negro Standpoint in the September Number of *The Messenger*" (49). With this, the magazine did not leave the race riots unaddressed but it avoided treating them at any length. The *Messenger* ad was an implicit acknowledgment that such race-specific issues were not the province of *The Liberator*.

Despite George Hutchinson's characterization of black scholars' approaches to such material, one need not be cynical about white motives to acknowledge that they did not always fully account for African American wellbeing. Furthermore, one need not "re-create the symbolic victimization" of black authors to acknowledge that leftist white critics and editors did not necessarily have black self-affirmation in mind when engaging them and their work. Sometimes, they were driven more by a desire to "enlighten" blacks about the limits of focusing on their unique experiences in the United States. (Hutchinson's declarations that scholars of the Harlem Renaissance have reified racial boundaries are plentiful. Above, I am quoting and paraphrasing mostly from 257–72.)

20. Herbst 19.

21. Wedding racial solidarity to class consciousness was central to groups like the African Blood Brotherhood, which published *The Crusader*. In the June 1920 issue, an unsigned commentary instructed, "Don't mind being called 'Bolsheviki' by the same people who called you 'nigger'" (qtd. in Kelley 44).

22. I am emphasizing that the readership for periodicals did not follow some easy racial line, which might allow *The Liberator*'s white readership to be assumed (and its black readership to be assumed insignificant). In this way, Hutchinson's point about the interracial nature of the New Negro Renaissance is well taken. Black authors valued magazines like *The Liberator* and wanted to see their work published in such venues. Thus, African Americans certainly read these periodicals. In addition to Hutchinson's discussions, I have found letters between *Liberator* editor Max Eastman and Angelina Weld Grimké. She was a charter subscriber who contributed significant sums beyond the subscription price (Moorland-Spingarn Archives).

23. As Anne Carroll reports, it is not clear who created *Crisis*'s layout.

24. On April 10, 1918 (the same day that *Strange Fruit* lists for the Wilmington showing), Dunbar-Nelson granted permission to Dunbar High School in Washington, D.C., to stage the play. See Hull 72, and Hatch and Hill 189–90.

25. See the introduction to the play in Perkins and Stephens, *Strange Fruit*.

CHAPTER 4. THE BLACK LAWYER

1. I say that these experiences influenced blacks' views of themselves, not just their citizenship, because mistreatment often convinced them that their character made them more deserving of citizenship than the whites who withheld it. This tendency has a long history, dating at least to 1829 in David Walker's *Appeal* (McHenry 29–30).

2. There are different versions of what transpired. White newspapers reported that Caldwell had insisted on sitting in a section reserved for whites, while others

said that Caldwell was simply refusing to let the conductor cheat him out of his fare. See Lentz-Smith, especially 169–205.

3. The right to protect one's person, property, and liberty has been the most basic right of Western citizenship since the late eighteenth century. See Wallerstein.

4. Such recognition does not override the fact that the NAACP had a policy of using white attorneys, as discussed later in this chapter. Still, it is worth noting that the hesitancy toward black attorneys began to fade after World War I, partly because seeing black soldiers lynched in their uniforms inspired a more militant racial pride.

5. See Williams; McNeil cited here; and McNeil's *Groundwork: Charles Hamilton Houston and the Struggle for Civil Rights.*

6. Houston became the first African American to serve on the Harvard Law Review.

7. Legal scholars agree that Houston was the architect of the assault against segregation in education; he charted a course that could and did lead to the Supreme Court. See McNeil 125–30; J. Clay Smith's *Emancipation;* Meier and Rudwick; and the Peter Gilbert documentary *With All Deliberate Speed* (Discovery Communications, Troy, Mich.: Anchor Bay, 2005).

8. See the biographical note that precedes her play in the 1926 issue of *Crisis* magazine and the encyclopedia entry, "Myrtle Smith Livingston," *African American National Biography,* 2nd ed, Henry Louis Gates, Jr. and Evelyn Brooks Higginbotham, eds. (New York: Oxford University Press, 2008, vol. 5. 281–82.)

9. One of those federal employees was her spouse, Lincoln Johnson.

10. The government routinely made decisions that flew in the face of equality. Segregation for federal employees under Woodrow Wilson's administration was just one prominent example that disturbed the many African Americans who had supported him, including Du Bois and Dunbar-Nelson. The capital city's tendency to embody the contradictions engendered by racism has a long history. See Masur; Clark-Lewis.

11. I take "aristocrats of color" from Gatewood's study. I emphasize that they lived up to—and exceeded—purported standards of citizenship in order to acknowledge that American citizenship, like that of the Western world more generally, has never been based on equality but on creating standards by which one group could gain the benefits of belonging to the liberal state by distinguishing itself from others. See Wallerstein. Also, Feimster demonstrates that white women used lynching to gain political access at the expense of blacks.

12. On the Dyer Bill, see Zangrando.

13. Lynching photographs proved to be uniquely modern and distinctly American commodities. On the role of lynching photography in the nation's march into modernity, see Goldsby; Hale; Shawn Michelle Smith.

14. Even when courts used a different Bible for swearing in blacks so that whites would not have to touch the same book that black hands had, equality was supposedly not truly disrupted by this practice. Witnesses were being accommodated separately but "equally." See Woodward.

15. Melissa Harris-Lacewell, "Subjects or Citizens."

16. Johnson wrote other plays and sketches about the failure of the Dyer Bill: *And Yet They Paused* and *A Bill to Be Passed*. See Stephens's anthology *The Plays of Georgia Douglas Johnson*.

17. Johnson's script notes that the melody for "Going Home" comes from Dvorak's World Symphony.

18. See Dray, Patterson, and the introduction to *Without Sanctuary* for examples of when mobs prolonged the "show" by being careful to torture victims without killing them too quickly. Also see Mary Church Terrell's 1904 account of the Sam Hose lynching, which took place on Sunday.

19. I borrow Ann duCille's emphasis on "coupling" rather than marriage, despite lynching drama's largely heteronormative and conservative orientation.

20. This threat should remind readers of the father whose death hovers over *Mine Eyes Have Seen*. Had his family not been burned out of their home and forced to relocate, that play too might have been set in a middle-class household.

21. Wells used "Sampson" to refer to black men whose behavior was similar to the biblical Samson. I am not sure whether this is a mistake or simply her way of signifying on (repeating with a difference, as Henry Louis Gates would have it) biblical passages.

22. LeRoy's receiving a note resonates with historical cases in which correspondence between a black man and white woman helped prove that the relationship was consensual. Wells offers such an example in *Southern Horrors*, published in 1892: "Frank Weems of Chattanooga, who was not lynched in May only because the prominent citizens became his body guard until the doors of the penitentiary closed on him, had letters in his pocket from the white woman in the case, making the appointment with him" (57). However, innocence-proving correspondence did not always work. See Dray.

23. This is why the boxing match between Jack Johnson and Jim Jeffries became so important. See Bederman. For a performance-centered analysis, see Krasner.

24. Wells also explains that the laws were never about preventing relationships between white men and black women; they simply allowed whites to kill black men while continuing to demand sexual access to black women (*Southern Horrors* 53).

25. Literature casting lynch victims as Christ figures is plentiful. Examples include W. E. B. Du Bois's "Jesus Christ in Georgia" (1911 short story); Countee Cullen's "Christ Crucified" (1922 poem) and "The Black Christ" (1929 poem); and Langston Hughes's "Christ in Alabama" (1931 poem).

26. While a student at Howard University, Livingston won third place in the drama category of the magazine's 1925 literary competition. When the piece appeared in the July 1926 issue, she was likely in Colorado pursuing a teaching degree.

27. I say that the play preserves "multiple" perspectives that would not have been welcomed in the mainstream because LeRoy is reading against the grain as much as his sister and grandmother are. He sees himself as a citizen who should be able to

choose his partner freely, and as Adriane Lentz-Smith argues, "To claim more for oneself than Jim Crow afforded was to commit a political act" (28).

28. Assertions that blacks were becoming more criminal as the rest of the nation progressed were abundant. For analysis that informed activists like Du Bois, see Smyth's "Negro Criminality."

29. Sometimes, especially before World War I, *Crisis* contributed to the tendency to doubt black lawyers' ability to win cases. When an African American attorney in Arkansas refused to associate himself with white colleagues, Du Bois accused him of having "taken his cause before the courts half-prepared" (August 1915 issue, qtd. in Meier and Rudwick 135).

30. For example, "even highly race-conscious men like Marcus Garvey and A. Philip Randolph occasionally employed prominent white lawyers to handle important legal work" (Meier and Rudwick 131).

31. This sort of professional reliance on whites likely helped inspire Du Bois and others to insist that black elites did not want to mingle socially and sexually with whites. See Ross, especially 160–61.

32. Opposition was both formal and informal, but the ABA changed its standards to exclude African Americans, Jews, and other groups at the turn of the century. See J. Clay Smith as well as Friedman.

33. Another example: "Armond W. Scott, a graduate of Shaw [University's] law school, was run out of Wilmington in the early part of the twentieth century for defending a black man accused of raping a white woman" (Smith, *Emancipation* 206).

34. Again, this resonates with David Walker's 1829 critique. See McHenry 26–35.

35. I again emphasize the difference between active and passive citizenship. Though blacks welcome the responsibility of active citizenship, it is withheld and they are denied passive citizenship as well. See Harris-Lacewell and Wasserstein.

CHAPTER 5. THE BLACK MOTHER/WIFE

1. The trauma of a "commonly occurring violence" is relevant even though, as Amy Wood argues, lynchings were relatively uncommon. Photography made the violence terrifying and ever present. Lynching photographs appeared in newspapers that entered black people's homes, for example, creating a sense of ubiquity that in turn produced the terror that Richard Wright so famously described: "Indeed, the white brutality that I had not seen was a more effective control of my behavior than that which I knew. The actual experience would have let me see the realistic outlines of what was really happening, but as long as it remained something terrible and yet remote, something whose horror and blood might descend upon me at any moment, I was compelled to give my entire imagination over to it" (*Black Boy*).

2. For more on how black women defined freedom and citizenship, see Hunter; Feimster.

3. My descriptions of the social landscape are often influenced by Rosen, who focuses on Reconstruction and post-Reconstruction. However, these issues remain resonant through the late 1920s, as I hope the body of the chapter makes clear. While writing in the 1920s, Johnson sets her plays in earlier decades, thereby addressing the trauma of the era that Rosen discusses. Also, the practices did not just disappear, as is clear from the home-centered violence that often characterizes race riots. Jim Crow, which reigned through at least the 1940s, hinged on terror—a terror fueled by blacks' awareness that their person and property could be violated and they had little or no recourse.

4. Examples of home-centered violence in other riots abound. The 1919 Washington, D.C., riot raged for five days, and the worst damage was in the black neighborhood, near Seventh Avenue and T Street. See Rucker and Upton.

5. To understand the inextricable link between public rights and private behavior, consider that citizenship was construed as manhood rights in this era. Full citizenship meant heading a household, which purportedly required not only authority over others but also self-discipline. Disqualifying black men in this era of "universal male emancipation" required whites to create legal systems that hinged on assertions that black men epitomized "sexual deviance and consequent social irresponsibility" (Ross 11). Mainstream rhetoric therefore insisted on "equating or analogizing the unreliable passions and uncountable impulses of men of African descent to the unaccountable mysteries of women as legitimately disenfranchised creatures" (Ross 11).

6. The black women whom Higginbotham studied were not alone in these strategies. Marlon Ross has found that Booker T. Washington also insisted on charting race progress via the household and the evidence that greeted one's senses there (70).

7. See Rice "White Islands," and Edmunds.

8. They may have been meeting regularly by September 1922 because Johnson writes at that time to Alain Locke, saying, "We (Mamie + I + all the rest) want to hear all about your trip some fine Saturday evening . . . at my house" (qtd. in McHenry 270). McHenry notes that Johnson explained that her "Saturday evening talks . . . continued through about ten years and came to life intermittently now and then to the present," but the interviewer did not make clear when this interview took place (McHenry 269, 378n34).

9. Declaration made by black clubwoman Victoria Earle Matthews as she addresses the First Congress of Colored Women in Boston in 1895.

10. Johnson's *A Sunday Morning in the South* was not published until 1974 in the first edition of *Black Theatre U. S. A.*, and *Safe* first appeared in print in 1990, in *Wines in the Wilderness*. *Blue Blood* received wider circulation much earlier. Its title appeared in the May 1926 issue of *Opportunity* magazine when it won recognition in its literary contest. Though it was not published, readers could contact the magazine if they were interested in it, as the Krigwa Players of Washington, D.C., may have done to perform it in 1927. However, given the Washington connection,

the group may simply have gotten the script from Johnson herself. *Blue Blood* was first printed in 1928 in Frank Shay's *Fifty More Contemporary One-Act Plays*.

11. I recognize the heteronormative orientation of this logic. The genre's investment in propriety lends to its tendency to favor the heteronormative nuclear family because many African Americans aligned themselves with the values espoused by the nation: that domestic success—as it was narrowly defined given U.S. inclinations toward Victorian standards of conduct—confirmed one's readiness for civic equality. While committed to representing accurately the assumptions bolstering the genre, I value critiques of African American acceptance of this rhetoric offered by Russell, and also Ferguson.

12. I am suggesting that the Captain may have raped Mrs. Bush if she had not consented and that she knew this and knew that she would have no recourse. The circumstances are different in *Incidents* because Jacobs decides to be with Mr. Sands to avoid being raped by a *different* white man, her master. Despite these differences, as well as the difference that slavery makes, there are important parallels.

13. May's predicament illustrates that the threat of racial violence sometimes kept black women from remaining single and building a life without a spouse.

14. However, the Sam Hose incident actually happened in 1899. See Dray, especially 3–16.

15. Amy Wood has found that the victim's name was Sam Holt. Many historians continue with the name more often used in newspapers of the time, Hose. Of course, getting the victim's names right was not always the media's priority; the sensationalism of their supposed crimes was more important. For my purposes, the fact that "Hose" was used in newspapers confirms that Johnson engages a broader conversation by using "Hosea" in this play. Many thanks to Anne Rice for her explanation of how scholars have come to have incorrect names for lynch victims. For more on how the media could be careless with facts, such as the victim's race, see Gonzales-Day.

16. For a review of newspaper descriptions of Sam Hose, see Dray 3–16.

17. As Marlon Ross says of the period from the 1890s through the 1930s, "Black men discover that to have won 'emancipation' is not to have won the gendered entitlements granted to white men upon reaching the age of twenty-one" (13).

18. This disturbing choice anticipates that made by Sethe in Toni Morrison's *Beloved,* published decades later.

19. Preventing blacks from claiming parental control would enable whites to benefit from the labor of African American children too.

20. *Crisis* magazine coverage suggests that the Dyer Bill–defeating filibuster of late 1922 remained a topic of discussion. In his opening editorial for the January 1923 issue, Du Bois promises that the legislature's failure has not ended the fight (106), and the magazine often highlights Congressman Dyer's efforts to increase support. In June 1923, the magazine reports that a debate between Atlanta and Howard Universities will be based on the topic, "Resolved: That the Republican party by its

attitude towards the Dyer Bill has forfeited the allegiance of the Negro voters of the United States" (73).

21. Johnson had offered Mrs. Temple as a black woman whose husband places her on a pedestal, and Pauline seems to have had a similar experience, but Johnson does not rid her of dialect. This suggests that these plays corroborate Deborah Gray White's contention that social standing had more to do with lifestyle and perceived morality than economic status. This is also in line with Evelyn Higginbotham's findings regarding the "politics of respectability" whereby the emphasis was placed on morals, not resources. Even an uneducated woman could claim the cultural capital associated with upstanding behavior, and Pauline seems to have done precisely that.

22. The undeniable links between public rights and personal reputation consistently placed blacks in a quandary. As they read their surroundings, many black clubwomen and other activists saw "no distinctions between respect and protection— one afforded the other. They found themselves denied protection because they were not perceived as respectable. But without respectability, they could hardly demand protection" (Feimster 116).

23. I am referring to the "rape/lynch scenario" that historian Crystal Feimster has identified. The black rapist myth—and the lynchings it excused—were designed to distract Americans from the historical fact of white men raping black women. Therefore, when we think of lynching, we should remember black women's rape, even though mainstream rhetoric centered on the rape of white women in order to veil the connections. Many others have noted the dominant discourse's investment in concealing the rape of black women: Wells, Hine, Gunning, Harris, and Elsa Barkley Brown.

24. However, black mobs were willing to lynch those who raped black women. See Feimster.

25. Notice that Pauline's line remains unclear: did the father die taking care of them, or has Jack simply been busy taking care of them? Either way, the genre has shown us that black men who support their families ignite white men's rage. Also note: as in so many other plays, we are never told how the father died, leaving open the possibility that he has been lynched.

26. At the turn of the century, the legislature was preoccupied with "white slavery." See Mark Connelly, *The Response to Prostitution in the Progressive Era* (Chapel Hill: University of North Carolina P, 1980). This concern did not at all extend to black women's vulnerability. Johnson's Washington, D.C., location is again significant; she witnessed the legislature's double standard. Furthermore, because prostitution was called "white slavery," it was important to highlight the fact that black women's sexual vulnerability in the 1920s was a very real extension of conditions under slavery.

27. As we will see in chapter 6, lynching plays written by men do not invest in this sort of modesty.

28. Wells's personal struggles with the gender politics of her day are well documented. See McMurry; Bay; Giddings.

29. However, a play written by a white woman during this time takes up the lynching of black women: Mary White Ovington's *The Awakening* (1923).

30. I recognized this "silence" because I am aware of Julie Buckner Armstrong's path-breaking work on the legacy of Mary Turner.

31. For a discussion of Grimké's literary treatments of Mary Turner, see Rice, "White Islands." Julie Armstrong's forthcoming book illuminates how profoundly Mary Turner's story touched writers other than Grimké and Toomer. Still, to the extent that she engages Toomer, she adds her voice to several others. For example, see Barbara Foley, "In the Land of Cotton: Economics and Violence in Jean Toomer's *Cane.*" *African American Review* 32.2 (Summer 1998): 181–98. Also see George Hutchinson, "Jean Toomer's Washington and the Politics of Class: From 'Blue Veins' to Seventh-Street Rebels." *Modern Fiction Studies* 42.2 (1995): 289–321.

32. White, "The Work of the Mob" 222.

33. One of the most well-known examples of a woman who was raped and then lynched is Laura Nelson, whose image has reentered circulation in *Without Sanctuary*. She stands out because she is hanging from a bridge and fully clothed in a modest, body-covering dress. Because pictures like that required consciously posing for the camera and preparing the scene for a good shot, her having been raped but also photographed in modest attire speaks volumes. For discussion of preparing for lynching photographs, see Shawn Michelle Smith and Goldsby. For details about women lynch victims, both black and white, see Feimster, who notes that some black women were lynched for resisting sexual assault.

34. For more on infanticide in slavery, see Angela Davis.

35. Caruth 7.

CHAPTER 6. THE PIMP AND COWARD

1. Two plays by black men emerged in 1925: Garland Anderson's *Appearances* and G. D. Lipscomb's *Frances*. The latter contributes to the tradition being traced in this study because it uses the black home as setting and targets black audiences through periodical culture. In contrast, *Appearances* is set in a hotel and is more concerned with suggesting that black men can overcome rape charges because transcending racism simply requires controlling one's destiny by adhering to Christian Science ideals.

2. Also, men were not as prolific as women while mob violence was most prevalent.

3. This is only one example of the vernacular tradition and call and response. Jazz and the blues also rely on exchanges of energy between, for instance, singer and audience, human voice and instrumentation. See Patricia Liggins Hill; Baker; Gates, *Signifying Monkey*.

4. As mentioned, the other drama written by a black man before 1930 is *Appearances* (1925) by Garland Anderson, but it does not address black homebuilding. Anderson wanted to reach an integrated audience, and he succeeded. He sent the script to Al Jolson, who helped him come to New York to pursue production. He

also gained attention from President Coolidge. The show opened at the Frolic Theatre on October 13, 1925, making it the first full-length black drama on Broadway (three acts, nonmusical) (Hatch and Shine 95–96). The show toured for two years, with stints in Los Angeles, Seattle, Chicago, and San Francisco. Then it opened again in New York at the Hudson Theater for twenty-four performances (Hatch and Shine 96).

Clearly, emphasizing the possibility that a black man's innocence could prevent lynching proved palatable to large audiences. Stories like this one made acknowledging historical examples with different outcomes seem less necessary. There is a parallel: the proliferation of narratives about slavery that emphasize the many good whites who bravely opposed the institution. If one uses the prominence of those narratives as a gauge, one wonders how slavery lasted so long and proved so profitable, given how routinely whites risked everything to benefit slaves.

5. As discussed in chapter 2, blacks recognized that whites often failed to embody patriarchal honor, but uplift ideology helped many to believe that their own willingness to do so confirmed that they were more suited to citizenship and leadership than whites. The plays discussed in this chapter feature characters who reject the notion that they should strive for ideals that the socially powerful ignore.

6. By suggesting that black women needed to be protected, Lipscomb operated in harmony with black women whose plays treat lynching as an attack on black households and on black men's right to shield black women. In this way, the genre corroborates what Sandra Gunning and others have suggested, that the home was often viewed as a corollary to the womb so that protecting one's home was the same as saving one's race from miscegenation.

7. Mitchell crafts Abrams's attitude to resonate with Booker T. Washington's philosophies, especially as articulated in his Atlanta Compromise speech. But, of course, property ownership has always mattered for determining citizenship. See Franklin; Hunter.

8. I am not suggesting that Charles Johnson, as editor of *Opportunity*, agreed with the cultural work that I argue was accomplished by featuring a coward in the community conversation. I would simply emphasize that Mitchell's work could find outlet in this magazine because Johnson prioritized creating artistic opportunity and connecting black writers to white editors and publishers. As Addell Austin makes clear, Johnson initiated his literary contests with a more ambitious agenda than Du Bois seems to have had for his magazine's competitions, and Johnson's goals would not allow him to prioritize propriety in the way that Du Bois was known to do when evaluating literature. See Austin.

9. To their credit, they place *happy* in quotation marks. Still, there is little discussion of the implications of applying this label to the play's action.

10. Stephens's analysis is much more nuanced than this quotation makes clear. She argues that *Son-Boy* operates in line with the "underground tradition" of black jokes about lynching that Mel Watkins traces in *On the Real: Laughing, Lying, and*

Signifying (New York: Simon, 1994). She explains, "According to Watkins, the existence of such jokes and stories 'underscores the irony in much black comedy' as well as 'a comic sense of some white southerners' barbarity'" (664). Stephens continues, "The technique is successful because Mitchell's ability to relieve a life-threatening situation with everyday domestic humor (the marital bickering between Dinah and Zeke) produces an ironic look at white 'Southern hospitality' from a black perspective" (664).

Though I do not altogether agree with Stephens's findings, humor is subjective, so to the extent that *Son-Boy* sparks laughter, it offers a powerful commentary on not only lynching but also minstrelsy's long reach, as I suggest later in my interpretation of this script.

11. For analysis of black-face crimes in the United States, see Fuoss; Lott.

12. The possibility remains that a black man was lynched before the white man who had blacked-up was rightly accused.

13. Additional lyrics of Dinah's song appear in the body of the play, but the beginning and end include only the refrain.

14. Mitchell directly identifies the family's cycle of poverty when Dinah says that Son-Boy will never be able to change his life if he continues doing the sort of work that he is doing (81). She wants him to escape the labor not only because it is back-breaking but also because the long hours and low wages leave no time for self-improvement.

15. As explained in chapter 2, many scripts are missing a mother and father and depict only grandmothers and grandchildren. Given the genre's tendencies, Zeke and Dinah represent a "middle generation" even without the depiction of grandparents and grandchildren. And, as I hope I make clear, Zeke and Dinah's survival is a generic revision, but one that makes the same statement about the mob's purposes.

16. Dinah even implies that she will kill Zeke. When Zeke says that she will have to leave the house over his dead body, Dinah gives him "a hard push," declaring that doing so will not be hard (87). Again, women's plays refrain from depicting physical violence; men's scripts do not.

17. As suggested in note 10, I do not altogether agree with Stephens's reading, but to the extent that the play might provoke laughter, especially when staged, it demonstrates the impossibility of escaping the legacy of minstrelsy. And, as I argued in chapter 2, the success of entertainers who made Broadway audiences laugh could shield them from some Jim Crow hardships, but it did not make them immune to racial violence, so American humor and hostility are indeed intertwined for African Americans.

18. Not only was the *Quill* published by a black literary society in Boston, but also its first two issues were not even offered for sale. The yearly publication's purpose was "chiefly to present original work of Saturday Evening Quill Club members to themselves" ("Statement of Purpose" qtd. in McHenry 294).

19. Sambo's name becomes ironic when we hear his life story. In similar fashion,

Dinah's militancy contradicts her name, which is so often used in the plantation tradition for mammy figures. More on names in note 21.

20. The "Men of the Month" column was added to *Crisis* in May 1911 and ran for more than a decade (English, "Family Crisis" 300). Over time, women were featured as well.

21. I believe that Son-Boy is the title character in order to call attention to the text's overall interest in naming, which is also indicated by the presence of "Snow-Ball," who easily melts under pressure, and "Sambo," whose behavior contradicts the associations of his name. By choosing names that seem more generic than specific, Mitchell gestures toward the biased labeling practices upon which lynching depended; his metonymic monikers point to the need to question their representational capacities. Specifically, *Son-Boy* spotlights the influence that race has on the meanings attached to even the most ordinary labels. "Son-Boy" evokes a double meaning because a son is not necessarily a boy, and a boy not necessarily a son. More than this, race complicates "Son-Boy" because being called "son" or "boy" by a member of the black community carries a different connotation than if a white man refers to a black nineteen-year-old in these ways. Thus, as Son-Boy walks through life with this name, its import oscillates from friendly and approving to condescending and dehumanizing. If all black men are someone's son and were once boys, this moniker rightly applies—but so does its fluctuating connotation. "Son" and "boy" are shown to be anything but universally endearing.

22. This calls to mind E. Franklin Frazier's famous declaration that black households led by black women epitomized the race's familial pathology. I speak of Frazier's work and Herbert Gutman's critique of it in chapter 2 while discussing lynching drama's foundational literary conventions.

23. I quote Shane Vogel to suggest that the plays of this chapter might be usefully read through the lens that he offers for understanding the "critique function" of literature by "Cabaret School" authors, such as Langston Hughes, Zora Neale Hurston, Claude McKay, and Wallace Thurman.

24. Actually, the focus on artistic freedom for *The Saturday Evening Quill* may have stemmed from the fact that this play appears in its first issue, one of the two that was not for sale. Even if it was only privacy that gave members the freedom to prioritize craft over propriety, then the literary society no doubt engaged a key question of the time: "How Shall the Negro Be Portrayed?" This question was so important that *Crisis* ran a symposium on the topic in 1926, which is reprinted in Gates and Jarrett.

25. Ross 1.

Conclusion: Documenting Black Performance

1. Hopkins was also a singer and actor. On connections between Hopkins's literary career and her understanding of the power of performance, see Brooks.

2. Hopkins's reference from "Prospectus of the New Romance of Colored Life, *Contending Forces*" in *Colored American Magazine* 1.4 (September 1900); and Lewis's quotation from *The Messenger*, October 1926, 302.

3. Today, we often see "kitchen sink" dramas as cliché, but there were high stakes to valuing depictions of blacks in their own homes at the turn of the century. I hope I have made the reasons clear, especially in chapter 2.

4. When I say that they needed to transform *theatricality* in the United States, I use the term deliberately and accurately. Historical specificity requires acknowledging that, in the United States, racism and racist violence have played active roles in shaping how audiences take meaning from the various elements of theatrical production, from a simple prop and blunt gesture to subtle postures and tones of voice. The ability of any of these aspects of theatricality to convey meaning to an audience member has been influenced by racism—a racism that has propelled, and been bolstered by, theatrical productions called lynchings.

5. Hatch, "Here Comes Everybody" 155.

6. Du Bois Papers, Schomburg. Letter dated May 18, 1927.

7. Du Bois never published an amended plea in *Crisis*, as Richardson apparently wanted.

8. Lewis's reputation is corroborated by Kornweibel, and by James Hatch, Sandra Richards, and Margaret Wilkerson in the roundtable discussion in Elam and Krasner.

9. Emphasis added. As he imagines how best to present the drama, family and black households figure prominently. Letter from Du Bois to Eulalie Spence, 1927. (Du Bois Papers, Schomburg).

10. As theater scholar Ethel Pitts Walker argues, "[Harlem Krigwa] was the first black theatre company to emphasize dramaturgy rather than performance" (348).

11. Here, I am influenced by Carla Peterson's *Doers of the Word* more than by J. L. Austin's speech act theory. I am suggesting too that simply having these scripts in periodicals encourages embodied practices among African Americans that affirm their sense of themselves as citizens. If nothing else, because one-acts are made up primarily of dialogue, reading them encourages similar dialogue among periodical readers.

12. Note the distinction: "Negro dramas" *written by whites* were quite successful. Also, theater created by blacks was lucrative if it was musical; the challenges arose for those invested in serious, nonmusical drama.

13. As Marlon Ross has found, promoters of the race routinely emphasized their "self-modernization," and their doing so was not simply about trying to impress whites: "It was, more accurately, a self-conscious ideological struggle to stage the reform of the race in order to achieve collective agency . . . in the face of a Jim Crow regime bent on reducing the race to a material and ideological condition of political dependency, economic servitude . . . and physically violated victimization" (23). Just as I emphasize white response to black achievement, Ross notes that society was intent on repressing blacks.

14. To similar effect, Harry Elam has made clear: "[A]t its inception, the American 'race question' is inherently theatrical. From the arrival of the first African slaves on American soil, the discourse on race, the definitions and meanings of blackness, have been intricately linked to issues of theater and performance. Definitions of race, like the processes of theater, fundamentally depend on the relationship between the seen and unseen, between visibly marked and unmarked, between the 'real' and the illusionary" (4).

15. See Hartman.

WORKS CITED

Archives

W. E. B. Du Bois Papers. Schomburg Center for Research in Black Culture. New York, New York.

Angelina Weld Grimké Papers. Moorland-Spingarn Research Center. Howard University. Washington, D.C.

May Miller Papers. Manuscripts, Archives, and Rare Books Library. Woodruff Library. Emory University. Atlanta, Georgia.

Primary

Burrill, Mary. *Aftermath*. 1919. In Perkins and Stephens, *Strange Fruit*, 82–91.

———. "To a Black Soldier Fallen in the War." *The Liberator* 1.10 (December 1918): 11.

Dunbar-Nelson, Alice. *Mine Eyes Have Seen*. *Crisis* (April 1918): 271–75.

Grimké, Angelina Weld. *Rachel*. 1916. In Perkins and Stephens, *Strange Fruit*, 27–78.

Johnson, Georgia D. *Blue Blood*. 1926. In Stephens, *Plays*, 63–73.

———. *Blue-Eyed Black Boy*. 1930. In Perkins and Stephens, *Strange Fruit*, 116–20.

———. *Safe*. 1929. In Perkins and Stephens, *Strange Fruit*, 110–15.

———. *A Sunday Morning in the South*. [black church] 1925. In Stephens, *Plays*, 139–53.

———. *A Sunday Morning in the South*. [white church] 1925. In Stephens, *Plays*, 129–38.

Lipscomb, G. D. *Frances*. *Opportunity* 3.29 (May 1925): 148–53.

Livingston, Myrtle. *For Unborn Children*. *Crisis* (July 1926): 122–25.

Mitchell, Joseph. *Son-Boy*. 1916. In Hatch and Hamalian, *Lost Plays*, 76–92.

Secondary

Allen, Carol. *Peculiar Passages: Black Women Playwrights, 1875 to 2000.* New York: Peter Lang, 2005.

Allen, James, John Lewis, Leon F. Litwack, and Hilton Als. *Without Sanctuary: Lynching Photography in America.* Santa Fe: Twin Palms, 2000.

Anderson, Lisa M. *Mammies No More: The Changing Image of Black Women on Stage and Screen.* Lanham, Md.: Rowman & Littlefield, 1997.

Apel, Dora. *Imagery of Lynching: Black Men, White Women, and the Mob.* New Brunswick, N.J.: Rutgers University Press, 2004.

Armstrong, Julie Buckner. *Mary Turner and the Memory of Lynching.* Athens: University of Georgia Press, 2011.

Austin, Addell. "The *Opportunity* and *Crisis* Literary Contests, 1924–1927." *CLA Journal* 32.2 (1988): 235–46.

Baker, Houston. *Blues, Ideology, and Afro-American Literature: A Vernacular Theory.* Chicago: University of Chicago Press, 1984.

Bakhtin, Mikhail. *The Dialogic Imagination: Four Essays.* Ed. Michael Holquist. Trans. Caryl Emerson and Michael Holquist. Austin: University of Texas Press, 1981.

Baldwin, James. "Everybody's Protest Novel." 1949. In *James Baldwin: Collected Essays,* edited by Toni Morrison, 11–18. New York: Library of America, 1998.

Bay, Mia. *To Tell the Truth Freely: The Life of Ida B. Wells.* New York: Hill and Wang, 2009.

Bederman, Gail. *Manliness and Civilization: A Cultural History of Gender and Race in the United States, 1880–1917.* Chicago: University of Chicago Press, 1995.

Berlant, Lauren, and Michael Warner. "Sex in Public." *Critical Inquiry* 24.2 (Winter 1998): 547–66.

Bernstein, Robin. "'Never Born': Angelina Weld Grimké's *Rachel* as Ironic Response to Topsy." *Journal of American Drama and Theatre* 19.2 (Spring 2007): 61–75.

Bial, Henry, ed. *The Performance Studies Reader.* 2nd ed. New York: Routledge, 2007.

Blight, David. *Race and Reunion: The Civil War in American Memory.* Cambridge: Harvard University Press, 2001.

Boal, Augusto. *Theatre of the Oppressed.* 1979. Trans. by Charles A. and Maria-Odilia McBride. New York: Theatre Communications Group, 1985.

Branch, William. *Black Thunder: An Anthology of Contemporary African American Drama.* New York: Penguin, 1992.

Brooks, Daphne. *Bodies in Dissent: Spectacular Performances of Race and Freedom, 1850–1910.* Durham, N.C.: Duke University Press, 2006.

Brown, Elsa Barkley. "Negotiating and Transforming the Public Sphere: African American Political Life in the Transition from Slavery to Freedom." *Public Culture* 7 (Fall 1994): 107–54.

Brown, Nikki. *Private Politics and Public Voices: Black Women's Activism from World War I to the New Deal*. Bloomington: Indiana University Press, 2006.

Brown-Guillory, Elizabeth. *Their Place on the Stage: Black Women Playwrights in America*. New York: Greenwood, 1988.

———. *Wines in the Wilderness: Plays by African American Women from the Harlem Renaissance to the Present*. New York: Greenwood, 1990.

Brundage, W. Fitzhugh. *Lynching in the New South: Georgia and Virginia, 1880–1930*. Urbana: University of Illinois Press, 1993.

Cantor, Milton. *Max Eastman*. New York: Twayne, 1970.

Carby, Hazel. *Reconstructing Womanhood: The Emergence of the Afro-American Woman Novelist*. New York: Oxford University Press, 1987.

Carroll, Anne. *Word, Image, and the New Negro: Representation and Identity in the Harlem Renaissance*. Indianapolis: Indiana University Press, 2007.

Caruth, Cathy. *Unclaimed Experience: Trauma, Narrative, and History*. Baltimore: Johns Hopkins University Press, 1996.

Castronovo, Russ. "Beauty along the Color Line: Lynching, Aesthetics, and *The Crisis*." *PMLA* 121.5 (October 2006): 1443–59.

———. *Beautiful Democracy: Aesthetics and Anarchy in a Global Era*. Chicago: University of Chicago Press, 2007.

Chansky, Dorothy. *Composing Ourselves: The Little Theatre Movement and the American Audience*. Carbondale: Southern Illinois University Press, 2004.

Clark-Lewis, Elizabeth, ed. *First Freed: Washington, D.C., in the Emancipation Era*. Washington, D.C.: Howard University Press, 2002.

Clinton, Catherine. "'With a Whip in His Hand': Rape, Memory, and African American Women." In *History and Memory in African American Culture*, edited by Genevieve Fabre and Robert O'Meally. New York: Oxford University Press, 1994.

Collins, Patricia Hill. *Black Feminist Thought: Knowledge, Consciousness, and the Politics of Empowerment*. 2nd ed. New York: Routledge, 2000.

Cook, Raymond Allen. *Fire from the Flint: The Amazing Careers of Thomas Dixon*. Winston-Salem: Blair, 1968.

Cooper, Anna Julia. *A Voice from the South*. 1892. Edited by Mary Helen Washington. New York: Oxford University Press, 1988.

Cutler, James. *Lynch-Law: An Investigation into the History of Lynching in the United States*. New York: Longmans, Green, 1905.

Davidson, Cathy, and Jessamyn Hatcher, eds. *No More Separate Spheres! A Next Wave American Studies Reader*. Durham, N.C.: Duke University Press, 2002.

Davis, Angela. *Women, Race, and Class*. 1981. New York: Vintage, 1983.

Davis, Tracy C., and Thomas Postlewait, eds. *Theatricality*. New York: Cambridge University Press, 2003.

Dray, Phillip. *"At the Hands of Persons Unknown": The Lynching of Black America*. New York: Random House, 2002.

Du Bois, W. E. B. "The Black Soldier." *Crisis* (June 1918): 60.

———. "Close Ranks." *Crisis* (July 1918): 111.

———. "Criteria of Negro Art." *Crisis* (October 1926): 290–97.

———. "Krigwa Players Little Negro Theatre: The Story of a Little Theatre Movement." *Crisis* (July 1926): 134–36.

———. "Paying for Plays." *Crisis* (November 1926): 7–8.

———. "The Perpetual Dilemma." *Crisis* (April 1917): 270–71.

———. *The Souls of Black Folk [1903]: Authoritative Text, Contexts, Criticism.* Edited by Henry Louis Gates and Terri Hume. Norton, 1999.

———. "Thirteen." *Crisis* (January 1918): 114.

———. "The Strivings of Negro People." *Atlantic Monthly* 80.478 (August 1897): 194–98.

duCille, Ann. *Skin Trade.* Cambridge: Harvard University Press, 1996.

———. *Coupling Convention: Sex, Text, and Tradition in Black Women's Fiction.* New York: Oxford University Press, 1993.

Edmunds, Susan. "The Race Question and the 'Question of Home.'" *American Literature* 75.1 (2003): 141–68.

Elam, Harry. "The Device of Race: An Introduction." In Elam and David Krasner, *Critical Reader,* 3–16.

Elam, Harry, and David Krasner, eds. *African American Performance and Theater History: A Critical Reader.* New York: Oxford University Press, 2001.

Ellis, Mark. "'Closing Ranks' and 'Seeking Honors': W. E. B. Du Bois in World War I." *Journal of American History* 79.1 (June 1992): 96–124.

English, Daylanne. *Unnatural Selections: Eugenics in American Modernism and the Harlem Renaissance.* Chapel Hill: University of North Carolina Press, 2004.

———. "W. E. B. Du Bois's Family Crisis." *American Literature* 72.2 (June 2000): 291–319.

Ernest, John. *Chaotic Justice: Rethinking African American Literary History.* Chapel Hill: University of North Carolina Press, 2009.

Feimster, Crystal. *Southern Horrors: Women and the Politics of Rape and Lynching.* Cambridge: Harvard University Press, 2009.

Ferguson, Roderick. *Aberrations in Black: Toward a Queer of Color Critique.* Minneapolis: University of Minnesota Press, 2004.

Finkelman, Paul. "Not Only the Judges' Robes Were Black: African American Lawyers as Social Engineers." *Stanford Law Review* 47.1 (1994): 161–209.

Fischer-Lichte, Erika. *The Semiotics of Theater.* Trans. by Jeremy Gaines and Doris L. Jones. Indianapolis: Indiana University Press, 1992.

Flexner, Eleanor, and Ellen Fitzpatrick. *Century of Struggle: The Woman's Rights Movement in the United States.* Cambridge: Belknap/Harvard University Press, 1975.

Foreman, P. Gabrielle. *Activist Sentiments: Reading Black Women in the Nineteenth Century.* Urbana: University of Illinois Press, 2009.

Foucault, Michel. *History of Sexuality, Volume I: An Introduction.* New York: Vintage, 1990.

———. *Power/Knowledge: Selected Interviews and Other Writings, 1972–1977.* Edited by Colin Gordon. New York: Pantheon, 1976.

Franklin, John Hope, and Alfred Moss. *From Slavery to Freedom: A History of African Americans.* 8th ed. New York: Knopf, 2000.

Fraser, Nancy. "Rethinking the Public Sphere: A Contribution to the Critique of Actually Existing Democracy." In *Habermas and the Public Sphere,* edited by Craig Calhoun, 109–42. Cambridge: MIT Press, 1992.

Frazier, E. Franklin. *The Negro Family in the United States.* 1939. Chicago: University of Chicago Press, 1966.

Frederickson, George. *The Black Image in the White Mind: The Debate on Afro-American Character and Destiny, 1817–1914.* 1971. Middleton, Conn.: Wesleyan University Press, 1987.

Friedman, Lawrence. *A History of the American Law.* 3rd ed. New York: Simon & Schuster, 2005.

Fuoss, Kirk. "Lynching Performances, Theatres of Violence." *Text and Performance Quarterly* 19.1 (1999): 1–37.

Gaines, Kevin. *Uplifting the Race: Black Leadership, Politics, and Culture in the Twentieth Century.* Chapel Hill: University of North Carolina Press, 1996.

Gates, Henry Louis. "The Trope of a New Negro and the Reconstruction of the Image of the Black." *Representations* 24 (Fall 1998): 129–51.

———. *The Signifying Monkey: A Theory of Afro-American Literary Criticism.* New York: Oxford University Press, 1988.

Gates, Henry Louis, and Gene Jarrett, eds. *The New Negro: Readings on Race, Representation, and African American Culture, 1892–1938.* Princeton: Princeton University Press, 2007.

Gatewood, Willard. *Aristocrats of Color: The Black Elite, 1880–1920.* Bloomington: Indiana University Press, 1990.

Giddings, Paula. *Ida: A Sword among Lions; Ida B. Wells and the Campaign against Lynching.* New York: Amistad, 2008.

———. *When and Where I Enter: The Impact of Black Women on Race and Sex in America.* New York: Morrow, 1984.

Goings, Kenneth. *Mammy and Uncle Mose: Black Collectibles and American Stereotyping.* Indianapolis: Indiana University Press, 1994.

Goldsby, Jacqueline. *A Spectacular Secret: Lynching in American Life and Literature.* Chicago: University of Chicago Press, 2006.

Gonzales-Day, Ken. *Lynching in the West, 1850–1935.* Durham, N.C.: Duke University Press, 2006.

Gray, Christine R. *Willis Richardson, Forgotten Pioneer of African-American Drama.* Westport, Conn.: Greenwood, 1999.

Gregory, Montgomery. "Chronology of Negro Theatre." In *Plays of Negro Life: A Sourcebook of Native American Drama,* 409–23. Westport, Conn.: Negro Universities Press, 1927.

Grimké, Angelina Weld. "'Rachel': The Play of the Month; Reason and Synopsis by the Author." 1920. In Hatch and Hamalian, *Lost Plays*, 424–26.

Gunning, Sandra. *Race, Rape, and Lynching: The Red Record of American Literature, 1890–1912*. New York: Oxford University Press, 1996.

Gutman, Herbert. *The Black Family in Slavery and Freedom, 1750 -1925*. New York: Pantheon, 1976.

Hale, Grace. *Making Whiteness: The Culture of Segregation in the South, 1890–1940*. New York: Vintage, 1998.

Hall, Jacquelyn Dowd. "'The Mind that Burns in Each Body': Women, Rape, and Racial Violence." In *Powers of Desire: The Politics of Sexuality*, edited by Ann Snitow, Christine Stansell, and Sharon Thompson, 328–49. New York: Monthly Review Press, 1983.

Hall, Stuart. *Representation: Cultural Representations and Signifying Practices*. London: Sage, 1997.

———. "What Is This 'Black' in Black Popular Culture?" In *Stuart Hall: Critical Dialogues in Cultural Studies*, edited by David Morley and Kuan-Hsing Chen, 465–75. New York: Routledge, 1996.

Harper, Frances. *Iola Leroy, or Shadows Uplifted*. 1893. Boston: Beacon Press, 1987.

Harris, Trudier. *Exorcising Blackness: Historical and Literary Lynching and Burning Rituals*. Bloomington: Indiana University Press, 1984.

———. *Saints, Sinners, Saviors: Strong Black Women in African American Literature*. New York: Palgrave, 2001.

Harris-Lacewell, Melissa. *Barbershops, Bibles, and BET: Everyday Talk and Black Political Thought*. Princeton, N.J.: Princeton University Press, 2004.

———. "Subjects or Citizens: Feeling Black in Post-Katrina America." W. E. B. Du Bois Center Lecture Series, Harvard University, March 31, 2009. Located at http://dubois.fas.harvard.edu/video/melissa-harris-lacewell-w-e-b-du-bois-lecture-series-melissa-harris-lacewell-1. Last accessed November 2, 2010.

Hartman, Saidiya. *Scenes of Subjection: Terror, Slavery, and Self-Making in Nineteenth-Century America*. New York: Oxford University Press, 1997.

Hatch, James. "Here Comes Everybody: Scholarship and Black Theatre History." In *Interpreting the Theatrical Past: Essays in the Historiography of Performance*, edited by Thomas Postlewait and Bruce McConachie, 148–65. Iowa City: University of Iowa Press, 1989.

Hatch, James, and Leo Hamalian, eds. *Lost Plays of the Harlem Renaissance*. Detroit: Wayne State University Press, 1996.

Hatch, James, and Errol Hill. *A History of African American Theatre*. New York: Cambridge University Press, 2003.

Hatch, James, and Ted Shine, eds. *Black Theatre, U.S.A.: Plays by African Americans; The Early Period, 1847–1938*. Revised and Expanded. New York: Free Press, 1996.

Hay, Samuel. *African American Theatre: An Historical and Critical Analysis*. New York: Cambridge University Press, 1994.

Herbst, Susan. *Politics at the Margin: Historical Studies of Public Expression outside the Mainstream.* Cambridge: Cambridge University Press, 1994.

Herron, Carolivia. Introduction. *Selected Works of Angelina Weld Grimké.* New York: Oxford University Press, 1991.

Higginbotham, Evelyn. *Righteous Discontent: The Women's Movement in the Black Baptist Church, 1880–1920.* Cambridge: Harvard University Press, 1993.

Hill, Patrica Liggins, ed. *Call and Response: The Riverside Anthology of the African American Literary Tradition.* Boston: Houghton Mifflin, 1998.

Hine, Darlene Clark. "Rape and the Inner Lives of Black Women in the Middle West: Preliminary Thoughts on the Culture of Dissemblance." 1988. In *Words of Fire: An Anthology of African-American Feminist Thought,* edited by Beverly Guy-Sheftall, 380–88. New York: New Press, 1995.

Hodes, Martha. *White Women, Black Men: Illicit Sex in the Nineteenth-Century South.* New Haven: Yale University Press, 1997.

Holloway, Karla. *Passed On: African American Mourning Stories; A Memorial.* Durham, N.C.: Duke University Press, 2002.

hooks, bell. "Performance Practice as a Site of Opposition." In *Let's Get it On: The Politics of Black Performance,* edited by Catherine Ugwu, 210–21. Seattle: Bay Press, 1995.

Hopkins, Pauline. *Contending Forces: A Romance Illustrative of Negro Life North and South.* 1900. New York: Oxford University Press, 1988.

Horton, James O., and Lois E. Horton. "Violence, Protest, and Identity: Black Manhood in Antebellum America." In *Free People of Color: Inside the African American Community,* edited by James Oliver Horton, 80–97. Washington D.C.: Smithsonian Press, 1993.

Houston, Charles Hamilton. "The Need for Negro Lawyers." *Journal of Negro Education* 4.1 (January 1935): 49–52.

Hughes, Langston. "The Negro Artist and the Racial Mountain." 1925. In *The Norton Anthology of African American Literature,* 2nd ed., edited by Henry Louis Gates and Nellie McKay, 1311–14. New York: Norton, 2004.

Hull, Gloria T. *Color, Sex, and Poetry: Three Women Writers of the Harlem Renaissance.* Bloomington: Indiana University Press, 1987.

Hunter, Tera. *To 'Joy My Freedom: Southern Black Women's Lives and Labors after the Civil War.* Cambridge: Harvard University Press, 1997.

Hutchinson, George. *The Harlem Renaissance in Black and White.* Cambridge: Harvard University Press, 1995.

Jacobs, Harriet. *Incidents in the Life of a Slave Girl (1861): A Norton Critical Edition.* Edited by Nellie McKay and Frances Smith Foster. New York: Norton, 2001.

Johnson, James Weldon. *Along This Way.* 1933. New York: Penguin, 1990.

———. *Black Manhattan.* 1930. Introd. Sondra Kathryn Wilson. New York: Da Capo, 1991.

Kelley, Robin D. G. *Freedom Dreams: The Black Radical Imagination.* New York: Beacon, 2002.

Knowles, Ric. *Reading the Material Theatre*. Cambridge: Cambridge University Press, 2004.

Kornweibel, Theodore. *"Seeing Red": Federal Campaigns against Black Militancy, 1919–1925*. Bloomington: Indiana University Press, 1998.

———. "Theophilus Lewis and Theater of the Harlem Renaissance." In *The Harlem Renaissance Remembered*, edited by Arna Bontemps, 171–89. New York: Dodd, Mead, 1972.

Krasner, David. *A Beautiful Pageant: African American Theatre, Drama, and Performance in the Harlem Renaissance, 1910–1927*. New York: Palgrave Macmillan, 2002.

Lentz-Smith, Adriane. *Freedom Struggles: African Americans and World War I*. Cambridge: Harvard University Press, 2009.

Lerner, Gerda. *Black Women in White America: A Documentary History*. 1972. New York: Vintage, 1992.

Lewis, David Levering. *W. E. B. Du Bois—Biography of a Race, 1868–1919* .New York: Henry Holt, 1993.

———. *When Harlem Was in Vogue*. New York: Knopf, 1981.

Litwack, Leon. *Trouble in Mind: Black Southerners in the Age of Jim Crow*. New York: Knopf, 1998.

Locke, Alain. "Introduction." 1927. In Locke and Gregory, *Source-Book*, i–vi.

———. *The Negro in Art: A Pictorial Record of the Negro Artist and of the Negro Theme in Art*. 1940. New York: Hacker Art Books, 1968.

———. "Steps toward the Negro Theatre." 1922. In Hatch and Hamalian, *Lost Plays*, 440–45.

Locke, Alain, and Montgomery Gregory, eds. *Plays of Negro Life: A Source-Book of Native American Drama*. Westport, Conn.: Negro Universities Press, 1970.

Logan, Rayford. *The Betrayal of the Negro*. 1965. New York: Da Capo, 1997.

Lott, Eric. *Love and Theft: Blackface Minstrelsy and the American Working Class*. New York: Oxford University Press, 1993.

Mackay, Constance D'Arcy. *The Little Theatre in the United States*. New York: Henry Holt, 1917.

Madison, Soyini, and Judith Hamera, eds. *The Sage Handbook of Performance Studies*. Thousand Oaks, Calif.: Sage, 2006.

Margolick, David. *Strange Fruit: The Biography of a Song*. New York: Ecco, 2001.

Markovitz, Jonathan. *Legacies of Lynching: Racial Violence and Memory*. Minneapolis: University of Minnesota Press, 2004.

Masur, Kate. *An Example for All the Land: Emancipation and the Struggle over Equality in Washington, D.C.* Chapel Hill: University of North Carolina Press, 2010.

Matthews, Victoria Earle. "The Value of Race Literature." 1895. In *With Pen and Voice: A Critical Anthology of Nineteenth-Century African-American Women*, edited by Shirley Wilson Logan, 126–48. Carbondale: Southern Illinois University Press, 1995.

McCaskill, Barbara, and Caroline Gebhard, eds. *Post-Bellum, Pre-Harlem: African American Literature and Culture, 1887–1919.* New York: New York University Press, 2006.

McHenry, Elizabeth. *Forgotten Readers: Recovering the Lost History of African American Literary Societies.* Durham, N.C.: Duke University Press, 2002.

McMillen, Neil R. *Dark Journey: Black Mississippians in the Age of Jim Crow.* Urbana: University of Illinois Press, 1989.

McMurry, Linda O. *To Keep the Waters Troubled: The Life of Ida B. Wells.* New York: Oxford University Press, 1998.

McNeil, Genna Rae. "Charles Hamilton Houston." *Black Law Journal* 3.2 (1974): 123–31.

Meier, August, and Elliott Rudwick. "Attorneys Black and White: A Case Study of Race Relations within the NAACP." In *Along the Color Line: Explorations in the Black Experience* (1976), edited by August Meier and Elliott Rudwick, 128–73. Urbana: University of Illinois Press, 2002.

Mitchell, Koritha. "(Anti-)Lynching Plays: Angelina Weld Grimké, Alice Dunbar-Nelson, and the Evolution of Black Drama." In McCaskill and Gebhard, *Post-Bellum,* 210–30.

Mitchell, Loften [no relation]. *Black Drama: The Story of the American Negro in the Theatre.* New York: Hawthorn, 1967.

Morrison, Toni. *Playing in the Dark: Whiteness and the Literary Imagination.* New York: Vintage, 1992.

Moses, Wilson Jeremiah. *Black Messiahs and Uncle Toms: Social and Literary Manipulations of a Religious Myth.* Rev. ed. University Park: Pennsylvania State University Press, 1993.

———. *The Wings of Ethiopia: Studies in African-American Life and Letters.* Ames: Iowa State University Press, 1990.

[Moynihan, Daniel P.] United States Department of Labor Office of Policy Planning and Research. *The Negro Family: The Case for National Action.* Washington, D.C.: Department of Labor, 1965.

Oliver, Kelly. "Witnessing and Testimony." *Parallax* 10.1 (Winter 2004): 78–87.

Patterson, Orlando. *Rituals of Blood: Consequences of Slavery in Two American Centuries.* Washington, D.C.: Civitas/CounterPoint, 1998.

Perkins, Kathy. *Black Women Playwrights: An Anthology of Plays.* New York: Routledge, 1998.

Perkins, Kathy A., and Judith L. Stephens, eds. *Strange Fruit: Plays on Lynching by American Women.* Bloomington: Indiana University Press, 1998.

Peterson, Carla. *"Doers of the Word": African-American Women Speakers and Writers in the North (1830–1880).* New York: Oxford University Press, 1995.

Postlewait, Thomas. "The Hieroglyphic Stage: American Theatre and Society, Post–Civil War to 1945." In *The Cambridge History of American Theatre,* vol. 2., edited by Don B. Wilmeth and Christopher Bigsby, 107–95. New York: Cambridge University Press, 1998.

Reid-Pharr, Robert. *Conjugal Union: The Body, the House, and the Black American.* New York: Oxford University Press, 1999.

Rice, Anne P. *Witnessing Lynching: American Writers Respond.* New Brunswick, N.J.: Rutgers University Press, 2003.

———. "White Islands of Safety and Engulfing Blackness: Remapping Segregation in Angelina Weld Grimké's 'Blackness' and 'Goldie.'" *African American Review* 42.1 (2008): 75–90.

Richardson, Willis. "The Hope of a Negro Drama." In *Lost Plays of the Harlem Renaissance 1920–1940*, edited by James Hatch and Leo Hamalian, 437–39. Detroit: Wayne State University Press, 1996.

Riis, Thomas. *Just before Jazz: Black Musical Theater in New York, 1890–1915.* Washington D.C.: Smithsonian Institution Press, 1989.

Roach, Joseph. *Cities of the Dead: Circum-Atlantic Performance.* New York: Columbia University Press, 1996.

Rosen, Hannah. *Terror in the Heart of Freedom: Citizenship, Sexual Violence, and the Meaning of Race in the Postemancipation South.* Chapel Hill: University of North Carolina Press, 2009.

Ross, Marlon. *Manning the Race: Reforming Black Men in the Jim Crow Era.* New York: New York University Press, 2004.

Royster, Jacqueline Jones. "Introduction: Equity and Justice for All." In *Southern Horrors and Other Writings: The Anti-Lynching Campaign of Ida B. Wells, 1892–1900*, edited by Jacqueline Jones Royster, 1–46. New York: Bedford, 1997.

Rucker, Walter, and James Upton, eds. *Encyclopedia of American Race Riots.* New York: Greenwood, 2007.

Russell, Thaddeus. "The Color of Discipline: Civil Rights and Black Sexuality." *American Quarterly* 60.1 (March 2008): 101–28.

Sanders, Leslie Catherine. *The Development of Black Theater in America: From Shadows to Selves.* Baton Rouge: Louisiana State University Press, 1988.

Savage, Kirk. *Standing Soldiers, Kneeling Slaves: Race, War, and Monument in Nineteenth-Century America.* Princeton, N.J.: Princeton University Press, 1997.

Smith, J. Clay. *Emancipation: The Making of the Black Lawyer, 1844 -1944.* Philadelphia: University of Pennsylvania Press, 1993.

Smith, Shawn Michelle. *Photography on the Color Line: W. E. B. DuBois, Race, and Visual Culture.* Durham, N.C.: Duke University Press, 2004.

Smith, Susan Harris. *Plays in American Periodicals, 1890—1918.* New York: Palgrave Macmillan, 2007.

Smyth, John Henry. "Negro Criminality." In *Twentieth Century Negro Literature; Or, a Cyclopedia of Thought on the Vital Topics Relating to the American Negro*, edited by D. W. Culp, 434–41. Naperville, Ill.: J. L. Nichols and Company,1902. Available at http://aabd.chadwyck.com/toc/htxview?template=basic.htx&content=title071. htx; accessed January 28, 2011.

Spillers, Hortense. "Mama's Baby, Papa's Maybe: An American Grammar Book."

1987. In *Black, White, and in Color: Essays on American Literature and Culture*, 203–29. Chicago: University of Chicago Press, 2003.

Stansell, Christine. *American Moderns: Bohemian New York and the Creation of a New Century.* New York: Metropolitan Books, 2000.

Stephens, Judith L. "Lynching Dramas and Women: History and Critical Context." In Perkins and Stephens, *Strange Fruit*, 3–14.

———, ed. *The Plays of Georgia Douglas Johnson: From the "New Negro" Renaissance to the Civil Rights Movement.* Champaign: University of Illinois Press, 2005.

———. "Racial Violence and Representation: Performance Strategies in Lynching Dramas of the 1920s." *African American Review* 33.4 (1999): 655–71.

Stewart, Jacqueline. "Negroes Laughing at Themselves? Black Spectatorship and the Performance of Urban Modernity." *Critical Inquiry* 29 (Summer 2003): 650–77.

Tate, Claudia. *Domestic Allegories of Political Desire: The Black Heroine's Text at the Turn of the Century.* New York: Oxford University Press, 1992.

Taylor, Diana. *The Archive and the Repertoire: Performing Cultural Memory in the Americas.* Durham, N.C.: Duke University Press, 2003.

Terrell, JoAnne. *Power in the Blood? The Cross in the African American Experience.* Maryknoll, N.Y.: Orbis, 1998.

Terrell, Mary Church. "Lynching from a Negro's Point of View." *North American Review* 178 (June 1904): 853–68.

Thompson, M. F. "The Lafayette Players, 1917–1932." In *The Theater of Black Americans, Volume II—The Presenters: Companies of Players; The Participators: Audiences and Critics. A Collection of Critical Essays,* Edited by Errol Hill, 13–32. Englewood Cliffs, N.J.: Prentice-Hall, 1980.

Toll, Robert. *Blacking Up: The Minstrel Show in Nineteenth Century America.* New York: Oxford University Press, 1974.

Tolnay, Stewart E., and E. M. Beck. *A Festival of Violence: An Analysis of Southern Lynchings, 1882–1930.* Urbana: University of Illinois Press, 1995.

Tylee, Claire. "Womanist Propaganda, African-American Great War Experience, and Cultural Strategies of the Harlem Renaissance: Plays by Alice Dunbar-Nelson and Mary P. Burrill." *Women's Studies International Forum* 20.1 (1997): 153–63.

Vogel, Shane. *The Scene of Harlem Cabaret: Race, Sexuality, Performance.* Chicago: University of Chicago Press, 2009.

Waldrep, Christopher. "Word and Deed: The Language of Lynching, 1820–1953." In *Lethal Imagination: Violence and Brutality in American History,* edited by Michael Bellesiles, 229–60. New York: New York University Press, 1999.

Walker, Ethel Pitts. "Krigwa, a Theatre By, For, and About Black People." *Theatre Journal* 40.3 (October 1988): 347–56.

Wall, Cheryl. *Women of the Harlem Renaissance.* Bloomington: Indiana University Press, 1995.

Wallace-Sanders, Kimberly. *Mammy: A Century of Race, Gender, and Southern Memory.* Ann Arbor: University of Michigan Press, 2008.

Wallerstein, Immanuel. "Citizens All? Citizens Some! The Making of the Citizen." *Comparative Studies in Society and History* 45.4 (October 2003): 650–79.

Walton, Lester. "Music and the Stage." Column in *New York Age*,1908–23. Became "Dramatics and Athletics" in 1915. In-text citations by date.

Wells, Ida B. *Crusade for Justice: The Autobiography of Ida B. Wells*.1930. Edited by Alfreda Duster. Chicago: University of Chicago Press, 1972.

———. *A Red Record*. 1895. In Royster, *Southern Horrors*, 73–157.

———. *Southern Horrors: Lynch Law in All Its Phases*. 1892. In Royster, *Southern Horrors*, 49–72.

Welter, Barbara. "The Cult of True Womanhood: 1820–1860."*American Quarterly* 18.2 (Summer 1966): 151–74.

Whalan, Mark. *The Great War and the Culture of the New Negro*. Gainesville: University Press of Florida, 2008.

White, Deborah Gray. *Too Heavy a Load: Black Women in Defense of Themselves, 1894–1994*. New York: Norton, 1999.

White, Walter. *Rope and Faggot: A Biography of Judge Lynch*. 1927. New York: Arno, 1969.

———. "The Work of the Mob." *Crisis* (September 1923): 221–23.

Wiegman, Robyn. *American Anatomies: Theorizing Race and Gender*. Durham, N.C.: Duke University Press, 1995.

Williams, Chad. *Torchbearers of Democracy: African American Soldiers in the World War I Era*. Chapel Hill: University of North Carolina Press, 2010.

———. "Vanguards of the New Negro: African American Veterans and Post–World War I Racial Militancy." *Journal of African American History* 92.3 (2007): 347–70.

Wilmeth, Don B. "Introduction." *Staging the Nation: Plays from the American Theater, 1787–1909*. Edited by Don B. Wilmeth. Boston: Bedford, 1998.

Woll, Allen. *Black Musical Theatre: From Coontown to Dreamgirls*. Baton Rouge: Louisiana State University Press, 1989.

Wood, Amy. *Lynching and Spectacle: Witnessing Racial Violence in America, 1890–1940*. Chapel Hill: University of North Carolina Press, 2009.

Woodward, C. Vann. *The Strange Career of Jim Crow*. 2nd rev. ed. New York: Oxford University Press, 1966.

Young, Harvey. "The Black Body as Souvenir in American Lynching." *Theatre Journal* 57 (2005): 639–57.

Zangrando, Robert. *The NAACP Campaign Against Lynching, 1909–1950*. Philadelphia: Temple University Press, 1980.

INDEX

affection, among African Americans, 27, 34, 37–38, 61, 129, 179

African Americans. *See* black men; black women

Aftermath (Burrill), 2, 18, 81–84, 147; analysis of, 97–114; and conventions of lynching drama, 71, 211n4, 213n20, 215n31; publication and production history of, 58, 113–14

alternative public sphere (also, alternative public space; alternative discursive space), 38–39, 81–84, 95, 127, 177; created by whites, 104–7; Johnson's literary salon as, 150–51

amateur performance, 16, 53, 109, 204n17, 211n34; criticized by Du Bois, 195–99; and documentation of theater history, 195–98; as preferred mode for lynching drama, 12–15, 27, 36–42, 60–61, 188; as racially affirming, 69, 77, 104, 112–13, 150

antilynching legislation, 4, 9, 151, 166; apology in lieu of, 4, 6, 202n6. *See also* Dyer Bill

Apel, Dora, 6, 203n11

archive and repertoire, 23, 52, 97, 103, 122, 207n3; always interact, 24, 28, 64; lynching plays as access point to, 84, 108, 143, 191; periodicals as access point to, 122; representative figures as access point to, 97, 103, 143, 187–88

attorneys, 87, 115–22, 147; black compared to white, 219n4, 221n29, 221n30;

blacks' real-life experiences as, 143–46; and lynching drama, 15, 18–19, 122–43, 151, 176–77

Baker, Houston, 31, 225n3

Bakhtin, Mikhail, 126

Baldwin, James, 201n4

Bederman, Gail, 66–69, 128, 138, 220n23

black audiences, 43, 103–4; and amateur performance, 15, 40–42, 198, 209n25, 225n1; new theater demands of, 45, 49–53; and periodicals, 31–34, 208n18

black body: dignified representations of, 29–30, 118–19; as evidence of mob's brutality, 3–7, 64, 73, 76, 194; expressive capacity of, 90, 91, 93, 98; and manhood, 68, 141, 227n16; in modest dress, 225n33; negative interpretations of, 24, 29–30, 36–39, 54; as part of mob's ritual, 24, 32, 209n21, 210n28; as property, 207n4; in racially affirming performance, 13, 37–38, 40, 61, 133, 194, 197; respect for, 8–9, 31; as target of violence, 2, 94, 161, 207n6, 220n22

black homes, 2–3, 217n15, 221n1, 226n6; blacks' knowledge of, 33–34, 70, 127, 134; and conventions of lynching drama, 61–64, 71–76, 213n21, 225n1, 229n3; as focus of lynching plays, 2, 26–28, 41–42, 139–43, 152–72; lynching plays portray devastation of, 9, 54–56, 87–89, 175–78, 190–91; mainstream assumptions about, 38; as performance space for

KORITHA MICHELL is an associate professor of English at The Ohio State University.

THE NEW BLACK STUDIES SERIES

The University of Illinois Press
is a founding member of the
Association of American University Presses.

1325 South Oak Street
Champaign, IL 61820-6903
www.press.uillinois.edu